"The Rocks Are Ringing"

Bannock — Paiute Indian War
Oregon 1878

The inside front cover is from the cover of Harper's Weekly as published in New York on Saturday, August 17, 1878. The scene was drawn from a sketch made in the field, depicting the Battle of Birch Creek in Oregon, on July 8, 1878. The back cover photograph of "Grandpa" Hubert Egan was taken on March 28, 2001, courtesy Patricia Egan, and Nancy L. Egan (Qua-see-ah). All other front and back cover photos are courtesy of Greg Hodgen and Larry Purchase.

The origin of the title "The Rocks Are Ringing," is a
Northern Paiute Dreamer Song, translated by James Mooney, and reads:

> *There is dust from the whirlwind,*
> *The whirlwind on the mountain,*
> ***The rocks are ringing,***
> *They are ringing in the mountains.*

"This song was explained to refer to the roaring of a storm among the rocks in the mountains." It refers to the coming storm that will wash all whites and disbelieving Indians from the earth, leaving only Dreamers and their reincarnated descendents. ("The Ghost Dance," by James Mooney.)

Native Americans were more in tune with Mother Nature than we generally are today, living out our glass, steel and asphalt lives in the cities and suburbs. An electrical phenomenon of nature is that just before lightning strikes a rock outcrop formation, the cracks in the rock exhibit a ringing sound, something like that from a loud group of crickets. The positive charge is building up on the ground, getting ready to electrically join the negative charge coming down from the storm cloud. It is something I experienced in a storm near the summit of the Grand Teton, Wyoming on July 29, 1991. (Larry Purchase.)

CONTENTS

Prelude

"Near here...."

Several years ago, my close friend Larry Purchase called me to ask me to brush away the cobwebs of time and try to recall our families' Sunday travels to Battle Mountain State Park, so named for the engagement between the U.S. Army and bands of Bannock and Paiute Indians on July 8, 1878. There we joined with friends and families in preparing summer morning breakfasts beneath the tall pine trees near the summit of the Blue Mountains in Eastern Oregon. I can still smell the aroma of lingering pinewood smoke interspersed with coffee, flapjacks, and bacon.

I remembered playing cowboys and Indians with Larry and the other children once our mothers had finally excused us from the table, allowing us to climb down from the rough hewn pine seats we sat on at the large wooden park tables.

Somewhere along the way, my parents told me that a very real Indian battle had been fought here at one time with the U.S. Cavalry. Once that sunk in to my small developing brain, I drifted away from the other children and began to really explore the campground, searching for arrowheads or perhaps a revolver or Army carbine dropped by a combatant in that long ago battle. One question loomed: Where did the battle occur?

Standing just off the narrow lanes of Highway 395 was a large log-framed state historical marker describing the battle. I couldn't read it then, but I remember begging my grandmother to follow me to the sign and read it. I'm sure she got tired, re-reading the words to me over the years, but it made history come alive for me and has remained so to this day. The first two words describing the battle on that dark pine marker were carved deeply into the wood and painted in silver paint and said simply "Near here...."

I had always pondered just where "Near here" was.

I paused on the telephone for a second, before Larry popped the question. "Do you want to find where 'Near here' is?" I think it took a split second before I answered, "Yes!"

After a journey of nearly eight years of researching, interviews, letters, library visitations, and field explorations, we have found where "Near here" is. It is over two miles to the northeast of the State Park, hidden within the foothills of the Blue

Mountains. Typically, however, the most important thing gleaned from the research was not the brief words on the vague historical marker, but the story of how the battle happened to be, and why it happened here in the remote mountains of Umatilla County.

In 1877, Rutherford B. Hayes, who followed Ulysses S. Grant's two terms in office, inherited a country suffering from depression and governmental corruption within the Department of the Interior. The War Department had tried unsuccessfully to bring Native Americans within its own supervision and control, having experienced firsthand the deplorable conditions brought about by inept Indian Agents struggling under the distant supervision of the Secretary of the Interior and the United States Congress. Army commanders in Washington and in far-flung outposts and forts on the Western frontier knew Indian issues intimately and knew if treated fairly and honestly, most Indians would at least try to fit the uncomfortable mold expected of them. Many Indian Agents, assigned to reservations had failed miserably in most respects. By 1878, following the bloody protracted Sioux War in which Sitting Bull and his followers escaped northward into Saskatchewan, under the strained supervision of the Royal Canadian Mounted Police at Fort Walsh, Canada, the Indian issue seemed for the moment unresolvable and distanced. There were more immediate issues needing attention in Washington.

Today, if one looks closely at the series of events that involved American Indians across the Western frontier from June of 1876 through June of 1878, one finds that a clandestine cult movement was methodically struggling to hatch itself against the unseeing eyes of Washington. Only isolated frontier citizens and the small, undermanned Army felt the first deep tremors.

The series of events began with one of the largest confederations of Indians in recent history on the Little Big Horn River in southern Montana, resulting in the disastrous death and defeat of Lieutenant Colonel George A. Custer, and elements of the Seventh Cavalry Regiment. The next year, 1877, saw the bloody outbreak and march of Chief Joseph and his small band of non-treaty Nez Perce as they tried unsuccessfully marching to Canada to join Sitting Bull, who by then was still licking his wounds at Fort Walsh. The Army stopped the majority of the Nez Perce, but many escaped into Canada to join Sitting Bull.

The following year, 1878, bands of nearly two thousand Bannock, Northern Paiute, and other Northwest Indians, fanatically ablaze with the Dreamer or Ghost Dance religion, broke from their reservations in Idaho and Oregon. They murdered and plundered their way northeastward on a bloody exodus, toward Saskatchewan and safety.

It wasn't until after the tragic Battle of Wounded Knee at Pine Ridge Agency, South Dakota, in December 1890, that the government finally decided that perhaps it would be in its best interest to send a representative to study the so-called "Ghost Dance" religion that had caused so much death and destruction. They sent James Mooney under the auspices of the Bureau of Ethnology to conduct research on the phenomena that had supposedly caused so much bloodshed and discontent. Mooney traveled directly to the Cheyenne Tribe and began his research in earnest. What was to be a few weeks project ended up extending for three years, taking him across the continent, as he visited and studied those Indians discreetly practicing the "Dreamer" faith. His studies showed a surprising correlation between the Dreamers within Sitting Bull's Sioux, Joseph's Nez Perce Dreamers, and the Bannock-Paiute Dreamers involved in the outbreak of 1878.

Certainly the Dreamer Prophet Smohalla, on the Columbia River Plateau, held power over many Indians and was directly or indirectly responsible for creating and fueling unrest among those suffering the most from an incompetent governmental bureaucracy. Was there a conspiracy amongst some tribes of the northwestern United States to reunite in Canada and attack southward across the border into the United States? Written government and public correspondence supports the theory.

This book is a personal day-by-day factual account of the travels and actions of the participants in the Bannock-Paiute Indian War of 1878. It opens with the first engagement with the U.S. Army at Silver Creek, Oregon, and closes with the assassination of Chief Egan and his family at the hands of Umatilla and Cayuse Indian Dreamer acolytes in the Blue Mountains of Eastern Oregon. Simply, it is the tragic story of a group of dispirited and alienated Native Americans caught up in a fiery racial cult attempting to find the world which they had lost, against all odds. Standing in their way was a small undermanned army, led by an unpopular, spiritual, and compassionate general. This is their story.

Acknowledgements

The authors wish to thank the following historians, authors, archivists, technicians, relatives of the participants within this history, and the everyday people whose passion for unwritten and researched history inflames them, without whose assistance and encouragement this project would not have come to pass. Our apologies to those we have failed to mention here.

Pamela Severe, Pendleton Underground Tours, Inc.
Nancy L. Egan and Family, Duck Valley Paiute Indian Agency, Idaho.
Jim and Elia Sheperd, Burns, Oregon.
Harvey Spears, Riley, Oregon.
Dick Hotchkiss, Riley, Oregon.
Wayne and Mary Ann Low, Pilot Rock, Oregon.
Walter J. Gary, Fort Walla Walla, Washington.
Ann Clark and Betty Elliott, archivists, Oliver Museum, Canyon City, Oregon.
Reiba Carter-Smith, Long Creek, Oregon.
Roberta Conner, director, Tamastslikt Cultural Institute, Pendleton, Oregon.
Malissa Minthorn and Martha Franklin, Tamastslikt Cultural Institute, Pendleton, Oregon.
Dr. Robert H. Ruby and John A. Brown, authors.
Jean Shaw and Virginia Roberts, archivists, Umatilla County Library, Pendleton, Oregon.
Julie Reese, director and Elnor Alkio, Umatilla County Historical Society, Pendleton, Oregon.
Steve Corey, past president, Oregon Historical Society, Portland, Oregon.
Sieglinde Smith and Steven Hallberg, Oregon Historical Society, Portland, Oregon.
Regina Davis, National Archives and Records Administration, Washington, D.C.
Joyce Justice, National Archives and Records Administration, Seattle, Washington.
Patrick Temple and Dean Clark, Pendleton, Oregon.
Gus Norwood, past director, Clark County Historical Museum, Vancouver, Washington.
Ruth Little, word processing assistant, Portland, Oregon.
Leroy Sanchez, geographical information specialist, Portland Oregon.
Jan Keiski, computer trouble shooter, Portland Oregon.
Warren Aney, Oregon National Guard historian and author.
Kathleen Myers and Family, Vancouver, Washington.

Finally, but not least in importance, we wish to thank Bunny Heiner for her relentless and unselfish time spent in editing this project. To our many friends and relatives, especially Judy Shultz, who aided and supported us during this undertaking, we thank you.

To our wives, Doris and Wenonah, a debt of gratitude is owed for believing in us and for allowing us the many hours away when we were needed at home. Without you this project would have been impossible.

To the long departed ghosts who drifted out of the fog and mists of time to greet us during the creation of this work, we humbly thank you for allowing us to share your story. The authors pray that we have done you justice.

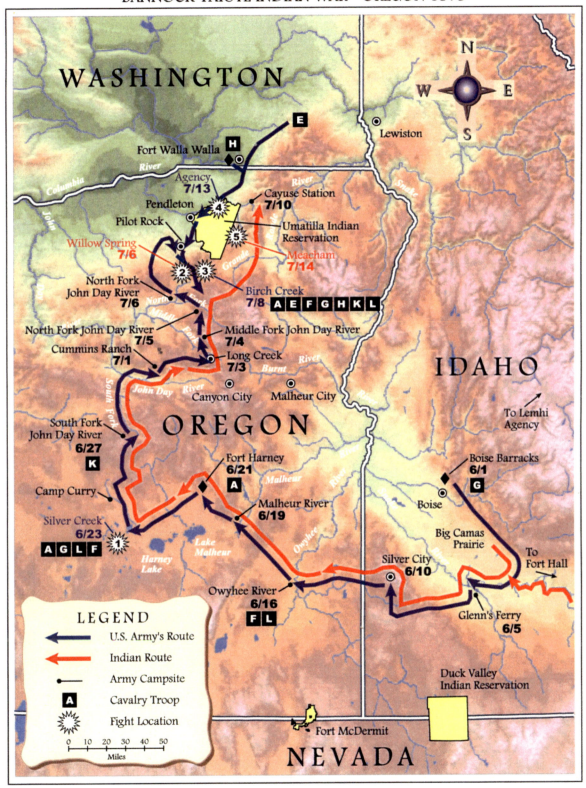

Scene of the Bannock War, 1878; showing locations of Bernard's fights.
(Based on contemporary maps.)

Washington, June 11.
Telegram From Donelson, Indian Agent at Fort Hall Reservation, Idaho.

"Could not keep the roaming Bannocks here while the amount of supplies was scarcely enough to feed the Indians engaged in farming. See your dispatches of April 3rd and 9th."

The Portland Oregonian. June 13, 1878.

"Did the government tell you to come here and drive us off this reservation? Did the Big Father say, go and kill us all off, so you can have our land? Is the government mightier than our Spirit-Father, or is he our Spirit-Father? Oh, what have we done that he is to take all from us that he has given us? His white children have come and have taken all our mountains, and all our valleys, and all our rivers; and now, because he has given us this little place without asking him for it, he sends you here to tell us to go away."

Paiute Chief Egan, to Malheur Indian Agent W.V. Rinehart.

"One stage driver killed and stage burned on the road from Boise to Winnemucca and two more stages over due and not heard from."

The (Pendleton) East Oregonian, June 15, 1878.

Chapter 1

Contact

Heat waves vibrated the images in his field glasses as his eyes strained to capture the details in the distance before him. Through the rippling heat waves in the binoculars, movement churned before him on the rocky ridge. Visions of scurrying human forms on the multicolored lava ridge in the distance disclosed flashes of bright colors. "It's them!" whispered the middle-aged cavalry captain to himself as he shot upright in his Army saddle. The mysterious forms in the distance had discovered the captain's presence as well, violating their secluded encampment.

It was 9 a.m., Sunday, the 23rd of June, 1878, in the remote Southern Oregon Desert. The field glasses were quickly dropped, thudding against the captain's breast as he turned to his Adjutant and immediately ordered Officers Call. His eyes were already beginning to sting from an unusual sweat in the cool morning air. Quickly preparing his brain for action, Captain Reuben Bernard, commanding a battalion of four companies of the First Regiment, U.S. Cavalry, and twenty civilian Idaho volunteers, readied himself for combat. His heart began to pound beneath his dark-blue Army blouse, its gold buttons flashing in the bright morning sunlight. In the distance, hidden from view by the lava ridge and thick stands of willow trees and high sagebrush lining Silver Creek, stood a village of four hundred lodges containing nearly two thousand Indians.

Inside the canvas-covered lodge, there still remained musty-smoke smells and cool air from the night before. The lodge's darkness was suddenly shattered by a burst of sunlight, as the front flap was abruptly thrown back, allowing warm air and sunlight into its interior. A silhouetted form appeared in the teepee's entranceway, partially blocking the sunlight from its occupants. "Soldiers! Blue coats! They are here; they are preparing to attack us. The men are already running to the rocks! The bluecoats will take time to get ready as before!" blurted the form.

From inside his lodge, Egan (Ezich'que-gah - The Blanket Wearer), the leader of four bands of Northern Paiute, could tell from the gravely voice coming from the short man standing at his doorway, that it was Oits (Left Handed). His shrill voice had always irritated Egan for some unexplained reason, as did the man himself. The short form instantly disappeared from the entranceway, allowing sunlight to again burst into the lodge's interior. It was getting hotter. The sounds outside his lodge told Egan that the alarm had been sounded. Running feet, barking dogs, and the shrill calls of women calling for their children could be heard. Even before Oits had interrupted his morning, his bronzed arm was instinctively reaching through the half-darkness, his strong hand resting on the cold hardened steel of the Winchester carbine where it lay invisible in the darkness. Egan knew the carbine's every line and curve, just as he knew his wife, Evening Star, lying quietly beside him even now, but instantly much closer than before. He felt her slim body tense, her small fingers gripping him, not from her fear of her own safety, but that of their two teenaged daughters, who were rustling from beneath their blankets.

In an instant Egan was at the doorway, buckling on his belt, which contained a large knife, traded for long ago at the Malheur Agency Store. The knife rested snugly inside an elk hide sheath, which was ornamented by multicolored glass beads of blue, green, white, red, and black. His wife had made the sheath for him a year after their marriage. He treasured it. On the right side of Egan's belt, resting inside its worn and battered holster, was a model 1873 Colt Single Action Army Revolver. Its long barrel was seven and a half inches long, and fired the large .45 caliber cartridge, the same as was used by the Army, now preparing to kill him, three-quarters of a mile away.

The revolver had been given to him by the Bannock Chief, Buffalo Horn, when they'd recently visited together at Fort Hall, Idaho Territory. Buffalo Horn had told Egan that he'd taken the revolver from "a woman-hearted bluecoat soldier, who would not be needing it any longer!" as he'd thrown his head back in gruesome laughter. It had made even Egan shudder. Now, Buffalo Horn's bones lay rotting in the sun, and he was no longer laughing.

Egan turned briefly, looking inside his lodge. Evening Star's eyes met his instantly, as did those of his two daughters. The girls had stopped their frantic but organized efforts preparing for the coming attack.

Then he was gone, running with the others, wading through Silver Creek, climbing to the rock ridge where fighting positions had been prepared. He led his large buckskin warhorse, which wore his prized red blanket beneath its saddle. Some called Egan "Pony Blanket" or "Blanket Wearer" because of it. Egan, a Umatilla, was born a Cayuse in northeastern Oregon, and had been raised from childhood as a member of the Paiute. Together, he and Oits the Paiute Dreamer Prophet, and War Jack, who was leading bands from Fort Hall, Idaho, were commanding two thousand Bannock, Paiute, and other

4

smaller bands of Umatilla, Cayuse, and Shoshoni Indians. The warriors totaled seven hundred and fifty armed and ready men.

As Egan checked his carbine and revolver, he remembered how the new white agency chief, W.V. Rinehart, had not helped them as Agent Parrish had. Parrish had been fair and kind to the Northern Paiute during his tenure at the Malheur. He had created work for the Indians, and paid them. He had made sure that their allotments were issued as agreed upon. The Agency had been showing signs of improvement, and pride was beginning to return to the Indians. But then suddenly Parrish and his wife were gone, replaced with Rinehart, who had come to them from Canyon City just north of their reservation boundary. Rinehart had the white ranchers and politics behind him, and maneuvered slyly in allowing the encroachment of whites onto the reservation as set aside for the Indians by treaty. Where Parrish had been friendly and productive, Rinehart was the opposite. He had no tolerance for the Paiute children who ran and played among the buildings at the Agency. He once struck a small boy for laughing at him. That incident drove a wedge between him and the Indians from that day forward. Under Rinehart, jobs were few and the Indians were required to purchase supplies from his Agency store, the same supplies allocated to them by treaty. Food and supply allotments were short or none at all. The agency chief's heart was not good for them.

Egan's mind traveled back in time as he remembered how he'd tried to settle down to the white man's way, building a small house on the reservation and forsaking the Old Way. He had also sold his most prized possession to his white neighbor. The large buckskin horse. He remembered how he would close his eyes and imagine each war scar on the animal, imbedded in his mind. When he rode the animal, they were as one, as it should be.

As the low, guttural chanting sounds from the warriors on both sides began to reach his ears, he recalled the rhythmic chanting from the members of the "New Dance" that had become so powerful recently. More and more of the people had begun traveling far distances to listen to Smohalla, the great Dreamer Prophet, who lived on the Columbia River to the north. Oits had become a leader in the cult, welcoming anyone who wanted to converse with his dead relatives. Together, Smohalla and Oits had spread the cult's mystic power to thousands of Indians in the Northwest. Outlawed by Indian Agents, the meetings were held in secret. The high pitched chanting of Oits brought in new believers every day, wanting to hear of the coming "Messiah" and of the "New World" he promised. Out on the prairie at night, feet shuffled, toe-heel, toe-heel, in a slowly revolving circle, as participants dropped into clouds of dust, exhausted, yet able to tell of conversations with the dead. Egan had at first watched from the distance with suspicion, then shrugged it off. Now however, he half believed in its message of hope, even if it did teach that all "non-

Believers," Indian and white alike, would be thrown from the earth in a great flood. It was against his traditional beliefs. For now, where else could he look for hope for his people?

Egan remembered the day when he'd walked to his white neighbor's farm. Finding the house empty, he had carefully placed thirty silver dollars neatly along a crack in the floor of the farmhouse. It was a payback to his friend for something he'd sold, and now realized he shouldn't have. Leaving the unoccupied farmhouse, he strode to the corral and opened its gate carefully, entering its confines. Standing stonelike before him was a large buckskin horse. The splendid animal's dark wet eyes bored into Egan's like rods of lightening, searching and scanning his every thought and nerve for a clue to his intentions. The horse stared menacingly at the corral's intruder. Egan began a soft low song, the palms of his hands open for the noble animal to see. Slowly, ever so slowly, he half stepped toward the motionless animal, stopping only when the horse's head would twitch backwards or the animal would paw at the hardpacked earth of the corral. The horse sensed the breath of Egan through his wide twitching nostrils, searching for the reasoning of the man approaching him. Egan gently eased the rawhide lariat over the buckskin's head, requesting permission to again rule the animal. A warm whinny from the buckskin horse re-cemented the old bond.

Returning to his small farmhouse, he'd packed up his family and meager belongings and returned to the Old Way, uncertain of anything anymore. Evening Star took one last look at the small interior of the framed house. Her eyes studied the walls covered with the pages of yellow-stained newspaper which had been brought to her along with the good coffee by the kind neighbor's wife. The white man's talking papers kept out the drafts during the cold winters. She was just beginning to understand some of the strange markings on the paper, which formed words in the white man's paper language. When the white woman would come to see her, she would bring coffee and newspapers to share with her. She would then show Evening Star how the strange markings on the papers formed words. Over time, the two had formed a strange friendship known only to women sharing the same struggles on the frontier. Evening Star looked at the small, worn cast iron wood stove that Egan had purchased, and remembered the fine meals she and her daughters had prepared for her husband and workhands that occasionally stopped by. She remembered how the little stove had burned cherry red in their small house as it consumed dried sagebrush and juniper limbs. The wood burned super hot, keeping her family warm against the bitter Malheur winters. She would miss this life. But she and her daughters had to follow her husband. Their three chickens had been butchered and fried and were wrapped in paper for their next meal. With moist eyes and warm memories of a life that was not to be, she slowly turned away and walked to the wagon. Soon the tattered, overburdened buckboard with its lonely passengers groaned and crunched its way southward down the dusty, narrow sagebrush-lined road vanishing in the dusty haze.

6

Looking eastward from his lava rock firing position, Egan strained his eyes to make out the small group of dark blue forms a mile away in the distance. The only thing separating them was the flat sagebrush and grass-covered ground that gently flowed upward to meet their rocky position. A meadowlark chirped and burst into song in the now warming air. No one noticed.

Captain Bernard had dismounted and stood looking into the faces of the officers before him, who were anxiously awaiting instructions. He quickly eyed each one individually before speaking. His cold dark eyes immediately demanded full attention. "Rube, how many?"

Idaho volunteer scout Orlando "Rube" Robbins' eyes left Bernard's quickly, flickering momentarily towards the distant rocks across the landscape. Dust drifted slowly upward from the rocky ridge as well as from both sides, gently spreading outward and upward. Robbins' medium frame was stocky, and perhaps not suited for long distance marching on horseback, yet he was the leader of the volunteers. Covering his head was a worn, wide-brimmed hat, placed just above his bushy eyebrows and whiskered, reddened face. He and his volunteers had been following this band of Indians from Idaho, after the outbreak of the Bannocks there. He was the leader of nearly twenty Idaho volunteers, including a few cowboys from the local "P" Ranch. He'd been keeping a close eye on the cowboys. He fingered his double-barreled ten-gauge shotgun, suddenly realizing that he was very thirsty.

"Cap'n," Robbins cleared his throat. "Respectfully speakin, we ain't had a chance in hell to count em right as hard as we been pushin, and no red man within five hunderd miles even standin up to breathe a word bout this bunch. Too much Power! They say. But takin a look at the smoke and dust that camp is makin...," he paused to spit a dark stream of tobacco, sending it plopping into the dust. Wiping his mouth with a buckskin sleeve, his eyes blazed momentarily, then returned to their normal blue. "Cap'n," he growled, "I'd have to say fifteen hunderd to two thousand souls, maybe more, maybe less. The size of that trail we been followin is wider'un a city street on Sunday. Maybe over seven hunderd shooters not includin women, but you know they're meaner than the bucks when they gotta be!"

"Unfortunately, I have to agree, Rube," said Bernard, looking at the growing line of dust ahead of him. He paused for a moment, taking in through his binoculars every small piece of the ominous preparations of death lying before him. He stood ramrod straight, as only twenty-three years of fighting from a cavalry saddle could hammer into a man. He wasn't a West Point graduate like so many other officers he served with. He was a "Mustang."

He'd enlisted in 1855 as a private in the First U.S. Dragoons and had slugged his way up through the ranks to his present rank of captain. His forty-five years were beginning to show, with a slight sandy color beginning to form in his hair, his beard remaining coal black. His dark brown eyes were bright now, silhouetted by a burned and reddened forehead and nose. It had been a grueling and hard five hundred mile campaign so far, filled with the images of burned ranch houses and homesteads, some containing the charred remains of their owners and the pungent-sweet smell of burned human flesh. Those responsible for the deaths and destruction were as brutal and fiendish as any he'd ever seen. And now he'd caught up with them. His fingers had stopped their slight trembling as they always did before an action, not from fear but the rush of adrenaline. He was now in every way in his element.

"Gentlemen!" The dusty blue clad officers stiffened as he turned to them. A high pitched keening could be heard in the distance, drifting toward them. There was more dust rising from the ridge. Nervous, inexperienced eyes of second lieutenants began to pinpoint and dart back and forth, while experienced eyes held steady amongst them. Hearts began to pound and palms were beginning to perspire. "We are going to mount a pistol charge as foragers against that lava outcropped ridge and its flanks. I want a pistol charge with six-yard intervals between troopers. I need to know what the hell we've got out there! A frontal attack on their works should show you what we're up against. Should you rout them so much the better, but don't outdistance yourselves from me. If they don't break, fall back as skirmishers, dismounted! Do not let your men fire their carbines while mounted! They'll only waste ammunition. Get them dismounted quickly! And fall back as skirmishers. Bring back your wounded. I needn't say more on that. Captain Whipple, what is the ammunition count per trooper?"

"One hundred rounds including saddlebag, Sir," answered Whipple.

"That should be adequate for this work," responded Bernard. "Start unpacking the ammunition from the pack train immediately, we may need it quick!"

Whipple turned to First Lieutenant Charles Cresson standing at his side, throwing a quick glance, half-grinning beneath his dark walrus mustache. Cresson snapped a salute, "Yessir," as he turned and jogged to the awaiting pack train and Company L, kicking up dust and barking orders as he disappeared over the ridge.

Bernard quickly returned his attention to the group standing before him. The keening sound resembled singing now and the "k-Thump, k-Thump" of drums was non-stop. New beads of sweat formed on foreheads, and eyes darted quicker now among some of the men. "Gentlemen, the order of battle." Fists and jaws flexed amongst the officers. "Lieutenant

Bomus will lead the advance, with F Company. Remember the fight at White Bird last year, Lieutenant." Bomus' face and neck burned with the hot-blooded memory of the humiliation the company had suffered at the hands of the Nez Perce warriors one year ago, in Western Idaho.

Good, but undisciplined, poorly trained troopers had been shot down like panicking running dogs. This time however, it would be different. Important lessons had been learned from the disaster. Bomus' mouth felt as though it were stuffed with cotton. He nodded curtly to Bernard, tapping his white leather gauntlet against his leg. For a second, he thought he could hear the West Point Marching Band, as he'd marched in the Long Gray Line for the last time upon the Great Plain. It was the fifteenth of June, eight short years ago. He could feel the first lieutenant shoulder straps through his blue wool blouse. "Odd, I've never felt them before," he reflected to himself.

Bernard turned his attention to a straight-backed, suntanned officer. "Frank, you will lead G Company, in the second rank." First Lieutenant Frank K. Ward nodded quickly, both men's eyes locking. They'd been together for some time now. A knowing look was all it took. His blonde hair shimmered a little in the small, occasional breeze, warmer now. Sweat glistened beneath his light brown, trimmed mustache. The lieutenant's deep blue eyes shone.

Bernard then addressed a tall, well-muscled, dark-complexioned captain standing silently with the group of officers. "Captain McGregor, you will form the rear rank behind Lieutenant Ward's G Company and also assist in closing any empty ranks before you." Thomas McGregor's jaw was set tight, his lean frame standing as straight as it did in the saddle. His body still resembled the athlete he'd been during his secondary school days. His reddish hair and complexion matched his thick accent. He was every inch a cavalryman, which was why Bernard had assigned A Company as the rear rank. His company was the power base behind the other ranks. No one would pass through A Company's rank in the charge, red or white. Now, he resembled a foot racer on his mark. Unflinching, ready! "Guide to the right and maintain your lines with at least a one hundred and fifty yard interval between ranks," Bernard continued. "Don't let them bunch up, they make worse targets that way. When you charge, keep your eyes open to the front and flanks of the enemy's works. Keep the pace of your charge slow enough to maintain a clear view of that ridge and its flanks to your front. Time is not as important now as knowing who and what you are attacking in those works to your front. We have been discovered and we no longer have the element of surprise."

A medium-built captain, wearing green colored shoulder straps designating a medical officer, looked anxiously at Bernard, who now focused on him. "Surgeon FitzGerald will set up the medical aid station here for our wounded. Do you need any assistance, John?" Assistant Surgeon Captain John FitzGerald's eyes snapped to the increasing activity on the far ridge before them, quickly returning to Bernard's stare. The Civil War veteran had served as Assistant Surgeon of the 70th Indiana Infantry and in the same capacity at West Point. FitzGerald was indeed prepared for action and the bloodletting that he knew was about to come.

"No, Sir, my assistants are prepared and I believe our medical supplies are adequate for moderate casualties," answered FitzGerald.

"Moderate?" FitzGerald thought to himself, this could end up being a bloodbath and he wasn't prepared for that. He thought of his wife, Emily, and their two small children, Bess and Bertie, back at Fort Lapwai. He was glad that they didn't know the danger that he was facing at the moment. Yet he too felt caught up in the excitement.

Bernard nodded. "Any questions, Gentlemen?"

"Sir?" Bernard's eyes snapped to the slender man standing to the side. He wore a dark, dust powdered Army campaign hat. A threadbare red and blue checkered shirt was tucked into tan trousers, held up by a worn pair of suspenders. His eyes were narrowed and lined by the sun and wind, and keen as a hawk.

"Scout Myers?" Bernard looked into the eyes of William Myers impatiently. Myers was an enrolled Scout for the Army, and assigned to the Battalion. Bernard trusted him. He wasn't as foot-loose as the Volunteers were and was dependable. He could track well and knew Indians, especially these. He was from Atlanta in Idaho Territory and knew many of the Indians now waiting for him across the field. He knew some of them personally.

"Request permission to join the charge, Sir," said Myers, knowing full well that he was not required to, according to his Army contract.

"Very well, you will join Lieutenant Ward and Company G," acknowledged Bernard, approving the anticipated request. Ward nodded his approval. Bernard continued looking at Robbins. "Scout Robbins and his men will ride as flankers." Robbins spat again, gazing into the distance.

Bernard took in a short breath. "Gentlemen, I will remain at this position. This is Headquarters and the rally point for the Battalion. I will remain in support with L Company here. If there are no further questions?" Silence. Singing and drums sounded from the far ridge. "Return to your companies and prepare for an immediate advance, and good luck."

In a flurry of hand salutes, the blue clad officers jogged down the ridge to the awaiting double column of cavalrymen and scouts. They'd been enjoying a much-needed rest, but they now knew all too well that something big was about to happen. Troopers immediately arose from seated and reclined positions of faked leisure, as they heard the yet indiscernible orders being shouted by officers and sergeants at the front of the battalion. Their turn was coming. "Shit runs downhill!" muttered a trooper as he raised himself stiffly from the sandy ground, adjusting his ammunition belt. His eyes were glued upon the officers now scampering down the ridge towards him.

"And here it comes!" blurted another, as the entire column up and down the line of approximately two hundred horses and men sprang to life, as if struck by a lightening bolt. It gave everyone a feeling of sudden, chilling excitement. Bomus, in the saddle now, wheeled his mount around and cantered to his awaiting Company F and its thirty troopers, themselves up and standing to their mounts.

Even the horses felt the mounting excitement, their dark ears up and motionless to the front. The sounds of neighing and nickering horses resounded along the column, their eyes dark and wet, unable to control their growing nervousness. Bomus' executive officer, Jacob G. Galbraith, had already issued the order of battle to the company sergeants and corporals, who in turn were barking orders to tighten cinch straps on saddles. Near side stirrups were grasped and laid back over the black McClellan saddles, exposing the leather cinch straps. Right knees were pushed into the sides of horses' bellies, pushing in the relaxed muscles, allowing an extra inch or so of slack. The cinch slack was then quickly taken up, tightening the saddles to the horses. Stirrups were then dropped to the animals' sides.

Along the column, troopers were still wearing their dusty, dark blue Army blouses with brass eagle buttons. Within seconds, most were quickly removed and hastily rolled and tied to the rear of the black saddles with straps. It was going to get hot very quickly, thought the veterans amongst them. Most wore the black wool felt campaign hat with its three and one-half inch wide brim, issue of 1876. Others wore straw hats purchased at the post sutler's store at inflated prices, while yet others wore the regulation blue forage cap with its black varnished leather bill. The forage cap was usually worn only during duty hours within the garrison or fort. Uniform regulations were slackened on campaigns. Nearly all wore sky blue woolen trousers, reinforced in the seat by an additional layer of fabric sewn on by company saddlers. Some wore their trousers tucked-in and others over the tall knee-high black cavalry boots. A few "bootees," or high-topped leather laced shoes, were seen, some with spurs. Most of the troopers wore gray or white woolen or muslin pullover shirts, with and without pockets, beneath sweat stained suspenders. A few of the men wore brightly colored shirts purchased or lovingly made by sweethearts at home.

Certain troopers wore black leather belts with white canvas secured cartridges, centered with an octagonal solid brass "U.S." buckle with a spread-eagle design. Some showed the familiar oval "U.S." instead. Attached to the belt's right front was a black leather pouch, containing rounds of .45 Colt pistol ammunition cushioned by a raw woolen insert. Resting on the troopers' right hips were black leather cavalry holsters, containing a dark-blued walnut handled Colt's Army Revolver, model 1873. It weighed two and one-half pounds. It had a seven and one-half inch barrel, and it could hold six cartridges in its cylinder. These troopers carried their revolvers with one empty chamber for safety purposes. More than one cavalryman walked with a limp caused from a fallen saddle stirrup striking the revolver's hammer, firing a bullet downward, grazing or entering his leg. It could be, and had been, fatal. The pistol fired a .45 caliber soft-lead semi-pointed bullet, weighing 250 grains. It was propelled by a load of 30 grains of black powder, which sent the bullet toward its target at 950 feet per second. It struck the target with 450 foot pounds of energy at one hundred yards.

Various knives in more various leather scabbards could be seen. Some scabbards were plain, others were brightly beaded. Most were purchased; others were "battlefield pickups." All troopers wore slung over their left shoulders a two and one-half inch wide black leather carbine sling. Attached to the sling was a metal swivel snap attachment, which in turn snapped through a steel ring located on the left side of the carbine. The carbines rested in a small leather "boot" at each trooper's right side, held by the sling and snap. Most of the troopers had already assumed their positions, standing at the left-front side of their horses' heads, right hands grasping the black leather reins just short of the animals' lower jaws, their noisy chatter ceasing quickly as they prepared for the anticipated orders to come. Everyone was sweating. Only fifteen minutes had passed since they'd stopped and orders to dismount and rest had been given. No bugles had been sounded as their officers had cantered to the front, following a verbal call. The sergeants and corporals had come back through them, yelling, "Take dat damned pipe outa yer mouth, Sweeny, and titen dat damned looze cinch! Trooper! titen yer coat straps! By God! You'll lose yer coat und shelter by God! Smit! pick up der carbine, it can't do you no good dere! By the gods! Where did I get these lovely darling, cannon fodders anyway? Take me back to Kilkenney, away from these fort nite, iron bred sons of Erin! They'll keel me certain! By the gods!"

So it went, non-commissioned officers (corporals and sergeants) quickly moving up and down the ranks of their companies, sharp eyes missing nothing as they harshly corrected young privates about missing or overlooked details that could get themselves or others killed. Bernard spoke to his chief musician (bugler) standing to his left and rear. Without moving the field glasses from his eyes and the field before him, he ordered, "Bugler, sound Mount, and Guidons Out!" The patiently waiting trumpeter turned, brought the glistening brass bugle to his mouth, pressing it to his lips. The clear, high pitched sound broke the concentration of the cavalry column below. As "Prepare to Mount" was sounded, a low rumble reverberated throughout the column as one hundred and seventy-nine left-footed cavalry boots entered saddle stirrups and froze. "Mount," the next note played, as cavalrymen and scouts threw their right legs over the rumps of their mounts, right toes finding the offside stirrups. The Battalion settled into its black McClellan saddles, movement quickly ceasing along the two columns as the troopers' Springfield Carbines were swung around and their shiny dark blue barrels were pushed into the saddles' leather carbine sockets. The Model 1873 carbines resting in their leather sockets fired a .45 caliber soft lead bullet, propelled by 55 grains of black powder. The bullet weighed 405 grains. The single shot carbine could accurately fire at ranges of over three hundred yards, and traveled at 1,100 feet per second, striking its target with 930 foot pounds of energy. It could be fired and reloaded 12-13 times per minute by a practiced trooper.

A second bugle split the air, sounding "Guidons Out." As one, each of the four companies' guidon bearers, at the head of each company, quickly slid the canvas flag covers from the flagstaffs. The bright red over white flags bristled forth, unfurling their colors in the morning air as the breeze picked them up gently from their staffs. The cavalrymen straightened in their saddles as the colors were presented. Only the sounds of an occasional horse's whinny and responses from elsewhere in the column could be heard. A meadowlark chirped its own call and fluttered nervously to another gray-green sagebrush, watching these large mysterious intruders before her.

First Lieutenant Peter Bomus looked toward the rocky ridge before him, then into the eyes of Captain Bernard. Bernard revolved in his saddle, looking towards the column, then returned to Bomus. Bomus' spurs gently nudged the sides of his large chestnut gelding, causing the horse and rider to canter smoothly towards Bernard. Reining in to a dusty stop before Bernard, Bomus raised his right hand in salute. "Request permission to order the advance, Sir!"

"Granted!" snapped Bernard, returning his salute. For a moment they spoke with eyes only, then Bomus spun the big gelding to the left and galloped to the right front of the column. As Bomus' eyes moved along the length of the battalion, practically every eye was on him, including those of the civilian volunteers under Robbins. Bomus could feel the increasing urgency of the power awaking before him. He looked at his young executive officer, Second Lieutenant Jacob G. Galbraith. He could still smell the gunsmoke at Whitebird from last year. He was ready.

Bomus raised slowly in the stirrups, facing the column to his left. His trumpeter sat to his left rear, ready. "Ba-tal-yon!" he shouted. "Com-pan-EE!" responded from the throats of company commanders throughout the column. "For-ward, march!" Bomus' right arm raised slowly then dropped as he and his trumpeter wheeled to the right, moving to the front of the column as the trumpeter finished the call. Immediately, the column of cavalry pushed forward, dust greeting nearly seven hundred iron-shod hoofs, drifting upward and outward from the battalion. Robbin's volunteers split apart into two groups, one directly to the right, the other to the left, spreading out to the left flank of the column. The pack train and L Company veered off to the right, heading towards the top of the lava ridge where Bernard and his trumpeter stood staring across the field before them. Dust billowed upwards from the far ridge in the distance. Captain Stephen G. Whipple, commanding L Company, was mentally forming the defensive positions to be hastily prepared for the pack train and its men. As he neared the position, he could see that there wasn't much to work with. There were no breast works or trees, but there was a slight elevation above the field to its front, facing northward. Surgeon FitzGerald and his two medical assistants were hurriedly unpacking chests containing medicine and bandages. Sunlight flashed as it reflected off the shiny steel bone saw and other surgical instruments as they were removed and placed at the ready.

The column had now reached the rocky ridge and had passed by Bernard as it dropped quickly onto the sagebrush and grass covered field below. Its iron-shod horses raised a noisy clatter as they passed over the red lava rocks, raising red dust as it mingled with boiling clouds of white powdered alkali, covering everything. It filled the mouths and noses of troopers and their mounts and stung eyes that were already smarting from burning sweat, painting fine black smudges around the eyes of all. Bernard looked through his field glasses. He could hear the F Company trumpeter sound "Left Front Into Line." The two columns of the battalion began to automatically veer to the left, splitting into three lines as each company's turn came. At Bomus' command, the trumpeter sounded "Halt," bringing the three lines to a stop, facing the enemy.

The choking dust boiled upward and through the ranks, drifting slowly to the east. Horses and men coughed within the ranks. Robbins' volunteers rode up into line on either side of the formation, their dust settling on the already dust-choked troopers. Low curses were heard from within the Army ranks. The pungent fresh-sweet smell of crushed sagebrush and grass rose upwards, mingling with the acrid smells of horse sweat and leather.

Oits watched through narrowed eyes as the dust cloud across the flat drifted away to the east, exposing a line of dark horses and cavalrymen extending across the flat to the front of his position. They included mixed colored horses and men in two groups on either side of the Army's formation. "White man scouts!" he snickered, shaking his head slowly. "Brave women!" He was kneeling on one knee, supporting himself with his brand new Winchester, Model 1873. The recently arrived Bannock war party had given it to him. It had been taken from a captured stagecoach, which had contained two cases of the treasured repeating weapons. Ammunition had also been found. The carbine felt good in his hand. It was power.

Of short stature, Oits wore no shirt. He wore a pair of old, fringed buckskin leggings, dark and greasy from perspiration and animal fat wiped from hands at the completion of many meals. He wore beaded moccasins. His braided hair was long, in Dreamer fashion, shining from liberal applications of rendered bear and deer tallow. His hair was never cut short as some reservation Indians were, which the "Hair mouth" white agent would not approve of. He was the Dreamer Prophet of the Northern Paiute. The only local teacher of the doctrine, he'd finally found a time and a place to exert his teachings upon the poor unfortunates on the reservation who would listen. He recited songs and prayers learned from the Paiute sub-chief, Ta'vibo (White Man), father of Wovoka, living in Mason Valley, Nevada. He'd also listened, and learned well, from the very powerful Wanapam Dreamer-Washat Prophet, Smohalla, who resided at White Bluffs in southeast Washington Territory on the Columbia River.

Smohalla had constantly visited the Bannocks and Paiutes in recent months, traveling unsuspected by the white agents and soldiers under the guise of peaceful visitation. Instead, he'd been secretly teaching the doctrine of the Dreamer faith. He'd taught Oits how to seek out the spiritually weak members of the tribes, and those unwilling to change to the whiteman's way. Now, Oits was a prophet-teacher himself. After the new agent chief Rinehart had come to the Malheur Agency and refused them food and clothing from their allotments, the people became hungrier and even more disillusioned. They began to feel their growling bellies and moods grew colder toward all whites in general. And how could they eat the unused, now rusting steel lumber saws and unopened cans of government paint? They had no houses. Immediately, Oits and his few but close followers had set out to recruit new members to the "Faith." As desperation and worse hunger set in, more of the people came to the secret teachings until the Dreamer followers now numbered into the hundreds.

Oits had prophesized to the newly initiated members of the cult the approaching deaths of all whites and of Treaty and Traditional Indian non-believers. They would fall from the earth when the Messiah came, bringing a new world without their presence. He himself *may have had some doubts about it in the beginning, but now that so many of the people danced and listened to him, how could this be wrong? He'd never been a standout in his own tribe, but now he had the "Power!" The thought brought goose pimples along his naked spine. He <u>was</u> somebody and now he would lead the people north, through the homelands of the Cayuse, Umatilla, and Yakima tribes. They'd been drifting in for days now, riding from the north.*

Oits didn't trust Egan. He'd never liked him. Oits was jealous of Egan's political status within the Northern Paiute. After all, he wasn't a direct member of the tribe, only a purchased Cayuse captive sold to the Paiute from the Shoshoni many years ago. He wasn't one of them, but few dared say so. Egan had voted against the outbreak, however Oits needed Egan's followers and their rifles. He would watch Egan closely. He hoped that the Sioux Dreamer Prophet Sitting Bull, now living in exile in Canada after escaping from the U.S. Army following the defeat of Custer on the Little Bighorn River in 1876, would receive them as agreed. The Nez Perce Chief Joseph and his small band of Dreamers had failed in the attempt a year ago. He would succeed. Canada and "Old Uncle Bull" didn't seem so far away now, as he watched the scene unfolding before him. Oits wondered if the stupid blue coats before him knew how outnumbered they were.

A gentle breeze moved the black tipped white eagle feather tied in his dark hair. Reaching down, Oits grasped a handful of sandy soil in his left hand. He stood up slowly, amongst the chanting and singing warriors. He tossed the handful of earth high into the air. The airborne dust was carried off to the east, as earth and pebbles dropped amongst the warriors with a "swish!" "EeeeeYaaaa!" screamed Oits across the flat toward his enemy, his mouth drawn back, exposing a grotesque, yellow-toothed grin surrounded by black and yellow warpaint. The singing stopped. Immediately, over seven hundred Bannock and Paiute warriors disappeared from sight. Some lay behind piled lava rocks, others behind sagebrush, parted just enough to allow a good sight picture for their rifles. Others lay in hollowed-out fighting positions.

The warriors wore a mixture of military and civilian white man's trousers, shirts, shoes, boots, and hats. These had ornaments of beads and feathers. Traditional buckskin leggings were seen, no shirts, beaded moccasins, and eagle and hawk feathers worn in their hair at different angles. All wore colored paint upon their faces; those without shirts proudly displayed their painted bodies. The primary colors were red, yellow, blue, green, and as many tints as they could manufacture. The purpose of the paint was not only to strike fear into enemies, but also to protect their skin from the elements. It was "Medicine." The various hues were made from the precious clay mixtures traded from other tribes. They were painstakingly made by mixing water or tallow with the powdered pigments and applied slowly and deliberately. A piece of broken mirror or shiny metal aided in the task.

16

The warriors' warhorses was treated in the same fashion. The warriors were armed with Winchester and Henry repeating carbines and rifles, mostly in 44-40 caliber, propelled by 40 grains of black powder. The 200-grain bullet traveled 1,125 feet per second, and struck with 568 pounds of energy. While not having the accurate range of the cavalry's carbine, they had the decided advantage of firepower, in that they contained 11-15 cartridges that could be fired without reloading, The Springfield rifle and carbine had to be reloaded after each shot.

Two years past, repeating rifles and carbines had been used against the 7th Cavalry Regiment with disastrous results, against troopers on the Little Big Horn River in Montana. Many warriors carried various makes of old percussion shotguns, some with the barrels sawed off and shortened, in several gauges. These were well liked because they only required percussion caps and powder to fire them. Just about anything could be fired from them: lead rifle and pistol balls, chunks of chopped lead, nails, bolts, rocks. At close range, they had no equal. Some stolen .50 caliber Army issued U.S. Spencer carbines were carried, as well as shortened smooth bore trade rifles. Ominously, recently issued Springfield 45-70 rifles and carbines were seen, taken from dead Army soldiers. Arrow quivers bristled with mostly metal arrowheads. They would be used as back-up weapons. Arrowheads of bright, shiny obsidian lay inside some quivers, as nearby Glass Mountain, the traditional mecca for arrowhead makers, sat but a few miles from their present location. Most of the warriors carried knives inside homemade scabbards. Some carried Army holsters made of black leather. They contained various types of handguns. Colts and Remingtons were in the majority.

Where once singing and shouting warriors were seen, only a few could now be identified.

The hundreds of women and children had been moved away from the village to the north as a group, seen in the distance. They were flanked and protected by a small number of young and very old men, poorly armed and mounted on horseback. Evening Star and her two daughters stood within the large circle of women, children, and the elderly. She could feel the young hands of her two daughters, grasping hers. She knew they were frightened. She unthinkingly glanced downward at her faded calico print dress, the print barely visible from so many washings. Her mind traveled back in time as she remembered when Egan had bought it for her with his meager earnings from the Agency store. It had been her first store bought dress. Today, she was as proud of it as she had been on that special day so long ago, tattered as it was. She wondered how it might be, living without Egan. She thought how it would be, trying to explain his death to her daughters, as she looked into their dark, wide, innocent eyes so full of questions. It would be easier on their older son, Honey. She caught herself. It had been hard trying to stand by quietly as her husband wrestled within his heart, searching for the right path to take them. In the old days it had been easy, but now with no game to hunt and the new Agency chief working against them, there was no way out.

Her mind again returned to the past, remembering General O.O. Howard when he'd come to the Agency to visit them. His powerful but soothing voice had at first frightened her, as she stood watching and listening beside Egan. She remembered the general's kind weary smile, as he'd shaken Egan's hand. It was a smile of firmness, yet with a certain compassion for the People. "I wish he was our agent," she'd secretly thought as he'd introduced himself and his daughter, Grace, to her and Egan. The two women were the same age. Howard had seemed so much like her own now dead brother, Shenka. She remembered the day she'd seen Egan for the first time. It had been many summers ago. Egan had visited her brother Shenkah's lodge, riding the large buckskin warhorse. As he'd dismounted and approached her brother, she had quickly maneuvered from the inside the lodge, hoping to pass unnoticed. But it wasn't to be. Their eyes met for a second only. She remembered the deep warm butterfly in her belly, awaking for the first time. She hadn't understood it. Frightened, she quickly disappeared around the side of the lodge. Evening Star had resented the feeling at first. Later, when her brother Chief Shenkah had quietly scolded her for being discourteous to their visitor, she'd blushed and lowered her eyes. Something had changed within her body and it distressed her.

In the fall when the leaves had turned to brilliant reds and oranges, Egan had asked Shenkah for permission to court her. Her brother had given permission and they were introduced. The strange butterfly in Evening Star's stomach again fluttered to life as she realized it had grown stronger since she had first met Egan and it embarrassed her, but not as much as before. Later that afternoon they had walked together through a grassy meadow away from the village. The soft swishing sounds of their moccasins was the only sound as they walked slowly across the tall green carpet of meadow grass. Egan cleared his throat, looking away from her.

"I am not of the Paiute People. I am a Umatila. I was taken from my people, the Cayuse, when I was very young. They say the Shoshoni came as we picked berries. They traded us to the Paiute People. It was very hard at first. There were times I did not think I would live. I have grown strong among the Paiute People and have fought beside them." His head turned from the distance where he'd been gazing, towards her. Their eyes met and locked. Egan slowly and methodically reached for her warm, soft hands. As the two figures stood looking into each other's eyes, hands clasped, the vast wilderness surrounded them like a comforting blanket. In the distance a mourning dove sang its low and mournful "hooo-hooo." The gentle tightening of her daughters' hands brought Evening Star back to the present. Her thin, strong fingers gently squeezed the smaller, softer hands of her daughters. "I pray for your safe return, my husband, and my son," she whispered. Unsure

18

now, which god she meant the prayer for. It didn't matter, it was already too late, she thought, as her teeth bit her trembling lower lip.

Within the lava rock positions Bannock and Paiute warriors checked their weapons. Bannock Joe knelt on one knee. He wore polished black boots, set off by a pair of rarely seen spurs. They were of Mexican make, polished silver with large rowels. He wore a bright colored red and white paisley shirt, with a brown vest over it. Black canvas pants were tucked into the tops of the high-up boots. Joe was proud of his abilities to work and trade on both sides of the Indian and white line. It had been profitable to him. His clothes were his most prized possessions, next to his guns and horses. His black hair was cut short like the white man, parted in the center and topped off by a black felt hat, tilted forward across his brow. A leather hat thong lay along each side of his face. The hat had a single eagle feather tied in its hatband. His broad face was painted with black diagonal stripes.

Surger, one of the few men still standing, was the proud brother-in-law of the Prophet Oits. He stood tall and was of stocky build. His naked upper body was dotted with one-inch white spots. His face wore lightening bolts on each cheek, one bright yellow, the other red. A six-inch wide band of black paint covered his upper face, to his forehead. He wore greasy buckskin leggings and beaded moccasins on his feet. His black shiny hair flowed over his shoulders. From his bloodstained cavalry cap, worn at an angle, hung two feathers, twisting slowly in the desert air. One eagle, the other red-tail hawk. His eyes squinted beneath the bill of the captured Army cap. They were black and sharp. He re-checked his loaded Henry rifle. The quiver full of arrows slung across his back felt comforting.

Beads lay prone, behind a small pile of red lava rock. The barrel of his stolen Army 50 caliber Sharps carbine pointed across the field towards the enemy. He was of medium build, weighing less than 175 pounds. He wore elk tanned buckskin leggings and jacket. Both had long, one-inch wide strips of multicolored beads sewn upon them. His moccasins were also heavily ornamented with beadwork, much more than most of the others. His face was divided at the nose by red and black paint.

Umapine, a Cayuse from the north, wore long fringed buckskins pants and a war-shirt. He lay prone with the others, his Army Springfield carbine also pointing across the field. In his right hand he held three long copper 45-70 cartridges, squeezed tightly between his fingers. He was ready to reload the single shot carbine quickly, a trick he'd learned from the blue coats as he'd watched them at rifle practice at Fort Walla Walla. He'd learned much about the whites, enough to know how to manipulate them as he wished. Right now all he wanted to do was shoot them and take their horses. He would sell them later to the

Yakima Indians when they reached Washington Territory. He licked his dry lips; his eyes were framed in a painted red mask. His mouth tasted like brass. "Come on!" he thought, as he looked across the field to his front. There were no birds fluttering around as there had been moments before. They seemed to sense what was coming. Umapine focused his eyes across the field before him. He could see the soldiers forming up in the distance. Clearer now.

F Company Saddler Private Joseph Schultz looked at the backs of lieutenants Bomus and Galbraith from his position in the front rank. He knew that only seconds remained before the order would be given to the Trumpeter, located to the left and rear of the two officers. Schultz gripped his mount's reins tighter. His mouth and throat were dry. His hands were clammy and he could feel a drop of sweat trickle down the center of his spine beneath his shirt. To his left was his "bunky" or "buddy," Company Blacksmith William Marriott. Like most, they had been through the Angel Island Recruit Depot in San Francisco. They'd made the long steamship journey together, steaming northward along the Pacific Coast, seeing the great Pacific Ocean for the first time. They'd also gotten seasick for the first time. They'd laughed and pointed jokingly at other seasick soldiers once they'd gotten their own "sea legs."

The grand mysteries of the great Pacific were unveiled daily, as they watched schools of gray whales shoot high misting geysers upward from their spouts and then sounding near them, disappearing into the mysterious depths of the ocean's darkness. The giant creatures seemed to enjoy the company of the large vessel as it steamed northward. Awestruck, the soldiers lined the ship's rails, watching the scenes unfold before them. Finally, the steamship arrived at the mouth of the Columbia River. After crossing the river's stormy and dangerous bar, the steamship plied upriver, soon slipping into the moorage at Fort Canby on the Washington shore of the river. Quickly, mail and supplies were off loaded. Soldiers disembarked, while others boarded the ship for the trip upriver to Fort Vancouver. Its business concluded, the steamship soon blew its shrill whistle. The ship's gigantic paddle wheels began to churn the river into froth, making way upriver. Two young Cavalrymen leaned on the ship's rail, wordless. They had never imagined a river so wide or powerful.

Every passenger was at the rails as the large ship dropped its anchor, splashing into the depths of the Columbia's cold dark water at the dock that rested at the foot of the hill below Vancouver Barracks. Word had already arrived of the ship's coming. Wagons and teams were waiting. The ship's whistle shrieked, alerting the world that she had arrived at its destination. A booming salute from the Fort's ceremonial cannon acknowledged the ship's arrival. A spring wagon and its military escort stood by to receive officers and dignitaries with their ladies or families.

While at Vancouver Barracks, the two soldiers pulled monotonous stable and kitchen details while awaiting their orders. They had worked in the great consolidated mess hall, peeling mountains of potatoes and onions, crying over the large piles before them. The few passes that they'd been lucky enough to get allowed them to go into the city of Vancouver at night after they'd finished their duties. They saw more saloons and fistfights than they'd ever thought possible, and had stared wide-eyed at the saloon "gals" trying to pry their meager Army wages from them, as well as from the other soldiers and customers. He and Marriott had grieved when they discovered that they had no more than 60¢ between them. They walked the town, taking in the sights and smells of a frontier Army town at its wonderful worst. They loved it! After having three drinks apiece, they were broke. They hiked back to the barracks, chatting quietly about home, non-existent girlfriends, and their next payday and the thirteen dollars a month (less the Soldier's Home deduction) they would spend.

Soon the two soldiers' orders arrived, assigning them to the First Regiment U.S. Cavalry at Fort Lapwai, Idaho Territory. After another two steamboat rides upriver, through the cavernous wide and powerful Columbia River, they found themselves at Fort Walla Walla, Washington Territory. Two weeks later they arrived and were assigned to F Company at the remote and barren Fort Lapwai, Idaho Territory. At Fort Lapwai they'd seen their first real Indians. Lean, narrowed-eyed, and suspicious, they watched the recruits as they climbed off the blue Army wagon. The Agency Indians resembled hungry wolves sniffing for an easy meal, as the two men eyed them back nervously. The Nez Perce war wouldn't come for two more years. They found their company's ranks much smaller than necessary, desertions having taken their toll. At night, they envied the "war stories" of surviving veterans who spoke in low tones of past Indian skirmishes, as they lay on their Snead and Company wrought-iron bunks after "lights out" had been called and the barracks were darkened. They listened to the large Army cast-iron #2 wood stoves hiss and pop, casting flickering beams of red and orange from their small glass door slits, forming dancing beams of light and shadows against the large wooden beams overhead in the darkness. Outside the icy wind moaned above them, whistling through the rusting stovepipe's guy-wires which secured them to the barracks rooftop. "Maybe next year," they'd hoped, as they snuggled beneath their gray Army woolen blankets and drifted off to sleep. They dreamt of gallant deeds on battlefields far away, as all young soldiers do.

They had both worked hard in the coming years, listening carefully to instructions and volunteering when possible. They had fought the Nez Perce bands of the Dreamer, Chief Joseph, in 1877. It had been a grueling and punishing experience for both men but they had both survived and lived to tell "war stories" themselves. They had seen the "Elephant."

Now, both men's heads looked straight ahead at attention in the F Company line. It was 1878, and staring back at them unseen on the lava ridge before them were nearly eight hundred Bannock and Paiute Warriors. In the second rank behind the two troopers, G Company's Lieutenant Frank Ward was positioned at the right end of the line. Behind Ward, to his left, was the Guidon Bearer.

At the opposite end of the rank's line was Scout Myers. Strange thoughts raced through the scout's head, as if he'd been forced to remember everything and everyone he'd ever loved in his lifetime. Pictures of loved ones dashed through his mind, leaving him with a dark melancholy in his gut. His pulse quickened as he struggled to push down the odd panic welling up inside him. He felt as if he had to recall these things now, before all conscious thoughts abruptly stopped. All his life Myers had never done anything halfway, always seeing his duties through to the last. Images of his wife and family flashed in his mind. "Calm down," he told himself. His hands trembled as he gripped the reins tightly.

Three troopers to Myers' right was Private Christian Hanson. Hanson wondered what the enemy across the field would look like up close. He remembered the grisly bodies they'd buried on their way to this place. "I wonder how bad does it hurt to get shot?" he thought to himself.

Behind him in the third rank was Corporal Peter Grantzinger of Company A. He'd checked his men carefully, but so many of them were inexperienced troopers! He kept a constant eye on them now, in case any one of them tried to bolt to the rear in panic. If one ran, others would follow. He wouldn't forget the wide unseeing, panicked eyes of troopers in other engagements.

To the far right of the line, Second Lieutenant Frank Edwards studied the backs of the troopers in the two ranks before him. "How many of them won't be here tonight?" he thought to himself. His horse was chomping at its bit. They were ready.

On the ridge behind them, Captain Bernard turned to Captain Whipple. "Captain, once all the packs are on the ground, open the ammunition boxes first, and see to it quickly. Have it ready to issue! When it's ready, start the men building up a circular rock breastwork with these rocks around us. This whole thing could end up right in the middle of our laps if it goes bad. Do you understand, Captain?"

"Yes, Sir!" responded Whipple. Sergeants and corporals began barking orders in earnest. Troopers jumped quicker to their work now. They felt the urgency in the orders.

Scarcely ten minutes had passed since the command had gone onto the field. On the flat below the ridge, Lieutenant Bomus turned his mount, facing his battalion. Drawing in a large breath, he shouted "Ba-tal-yon!" Red and white Guidons were raised to full height at the end of each rank. "Com-pan-ee!" resounded from each company commander. "Draw-Pistol!" Immediately, the low rustle of leather holster flaps being opened, and the withdrawal of one hundred and seventy-nine Colt revolvers, came from the ranks of troopers and officers to his front. Robbins' volunteers withdrew rifles and carbines from brown leather saddle scabbards. Scout Myers rested the butt of his Winchester carbine on his right thigh. The troopers' revolvers were held at the "High Port" position in their right hands, muzzles skyward. "Ba-tal-yon, Dress-Right!" Commanders and NCO's directed larger ranks into smaller ones, until the ranks were evenly numbered. Troopers' heads faced to the right, as they adjusted their position in line with the Guidon Bearer at the end of their rank. "Ready-Front!" shouted Bomus. All heads snapped to the front.

Lieutenant Bomus wheeled his dark gelding around, facing to the front. He raised his right arm horizontally to the front, moving it rapidly left to right. "Bugler, sound "Foragers-March!" The bugle was snapped to the Trumpeter's lips. The call was sounded, breaking the stillness. The three lines surged forward at a walk. Troopers extended outward so that six yards separated the mounts, stirrup to stirrup. Each company commander, Bomus, Ward, and McGregor, cantered to the front center of his company's line. The ranks were now separated one hundred and fifty yards apart. Some of the Army mounts were difficult to control, as they anticipated the coming charge. Their blood was up. The older horses settled down quickly; most carried scars from other battles.

Once the battalion had settled down and its ranks had formed straight, Bomus raised his right arm, pumping it up and down twice. The battalion quickened its pace slightly, closing the distance between the troops and the ridge ahead of them in the distance. Tight rein grips were required to hold the powerful, glistening cavalry horses in line. On the ridge to their rear, Bernard's field glasses were glued to his eyes, as his three companies began to raise the all-too-familiar dust in their wake. The last rank in the battalion, Captain McGregor's A Company, was now the only one that Bernard could see clearly, due to the powdery fog engulfing the battalion as it rode towards God knew what. Soon A Company too would disappear, melting into the gray-red cloud as it pushed onward, emitting a low powerful rumble as it crossed the grassy field that separated it from the enemy. To their front, the warriors on the lava ridge were preparing to defend it to the death. Bernard could barely make out the red over white Guidon flags snapping in the increasing velocity of the charge. "It won't be long now," he thought, his eyes boring into the field glasses.

Egan slowly crawled backwards, seeing the dark lines of dust rapidly approaching the ridge. He slipped down the embankment, scraping his knees and elbows on the sharp red lava rocks. To his right, fifty yards away, Oits stood, eyeing him suspiciously. His hands tightened on his carbine as he swung it toward Egan's back. If Egan were choosing to surrender to the Army, he would kill him. The thought troubled him as he began to sweat.

Suddenly, something caught Oits' attention. As he jerked his head to the right, he saw a tall warrior standing not ten feet away, loosely pointing the barrel of his rifle at his belly. It was Honey (Ezich'que), Egan's son. The dark narrowed eyes of the twenty-nine year-old man bored into Oits', unblinking, silent. His tall frame loomed over the small prophet. The two stood glaring at each other like two snakes, ready to strike.

Honey and his father could have been twins. His ink black hair fell from beneath his hat into two braids, which rested upon the broad shoulders of his white man's black suitcoat. He wore dust coated black gabardine trousers with a brightly colored shirt tucked into them. Dark suspenders held them and a wide belt containing cartridges and a Colt revolver. Honey was an athlete and a warrior. Egan had seen to that. Egan's teachings had softened his dislike toward the white man's ways, yet his father had also instilled in him a caution in regards to all white man teachings, as well as to the teachings of the new prophets coming into their lives. His own wife, Hattie, now into her twenty-fourth summer, had also tempered him toward the white man's ways, as she cared for their six-month-old son, Herbert (Qua-see-ah). She wanted a better life for their son. Honey was a man to deal with, and Oits feared him almost as much as he feared Egan.

Oits quickly turned the barrel of his carbine outward toward the Army in the distance. Honey, seeing that his father's back was safe, turned toward his other enemy.

Egan grasped the reins of the large buckskin, noticing the cherished red wool blanket on the horse's back. The big-chested horse sensed danger was near. The horse's eyes showed wide and white. With a quick springing motion, Egan swung his strong frame upon the horse's back, his left hand in the horse's mane, reins in his right. He dug his heels into the powerful buckskin's sides as they galloped around the ridge to the left, spewing small rocks behind them. He knew from experience that the soldier chiefs found the white volunteers hard to control. They would head for the village, where there was property and fewer bullets to dodge. He would meet them! Oits slowly shifted his re-assured gaze back to the dark line of dust approaching him in the distance. He began a low chant that raised in his chest with every heartbeat. Singers began to sing louder with each strain of the medicine song....

"I am here! I came into this world to die! My body is only to hold a spirit life! Should my blood be sprinkled, I want no wounds from behind! Death should come in front of me!"

Several warriors rose to kneeling positions, while a few stood. Most lay motionless along the ridge. All were aiming their weapons toward the Army troops across the field. The singing increased into a loud wailing crescendo. Closer!

Bomus, wanting to reserve the battalion's strength, was waiting until the very last moment before ordering the charge. He quickly scanned the ridge just yards ahead of him, calculating the precise moment to order the charge. He'd brought the battalion up to a fast canter now. More figures could be seen on the ridge ahead. "This could be easier than I thought," he reasoned to himself. The thought was quickly forgotten as he sped closer toward the deadly ridge in the distance. He kicked his brain into gear, trying to remember what his West Point training had hammered into him. "Surprise-Velocity-Shock." The loud rumbling of the thundering battalion following closely behind overwhelmed him. It reminded him of riding ahead of a speeding railroad engine. Raw thundering energy! Bomus' Trumpeter rode to his left and rear, a horse length separating them. The F Company Guidon bearer was on his right. He felt exhilarated! Privates Marriott and Schultz were grinning now, having shaken off the tension. They'd made it! The feeling ran like electricity through the troopers and their restrained mounts.

In the third rank behind A Company, Corporal Grantzinger, a file closer, was constantly looking to his left and right, correcting troopers with shouts. "Williams! Muzzle up! Jones! Guide right, Dammit!" In front of the A Company line, Captain McGregor smiled inwardly as he listened to his corporals and sergeants chewing and barking at the new, inexperienced recruits within the ranks. McGregor had the best. He knew the voices of each sergeant and corporal behind the shouted commands, and the troopers in the Company knew it. Closer!

Bomus' vision began to tunnel to the center of the ridge. He snapped his head to the left, shouting to his Trumpeter. "Bugler-Gallop!" The shrill notes rang in and out of his left ear, as the Trumpeter rotated the bugle left and right. Repeated calls from the companies to his rear assured him of their presence. Immediately, as one, the battalion sprang forward accelerating, as reins were loosened. The red-over-white Guidons snapped in the wind as the battalion traveled three hundred and fifty-two yards a minute, twelve miles an hour. Heads bent into the wind, horses whinnied. Closer!

In the thunder and roar of the galloping battalion, Bomus turned again to his Trumpeter; this time only the motion of his mouth and wide eyes ordered the charge, his shout enveloped in the thunder around them. The bugle went to the Trumpeter's mouth, sounding the charge. As the company trumpeters responded, the entire battalion jumped unexpectedly with an instant reflex, as if struck by a lightening bolt. The cavalry mounts knew in their very blood and instinct what that sound meant. A shrill

25

"Eeeeeeeee-Haaaaaaaaa!" erupted from within the ranks of the troopers as they charged four hundred and sixty-nine feet a minute, sixteen miles an hour, into hell itself! Bomus lowered the muzzle of his revolver, pointing it at the distant figures crouched and kneeling on the ridge before him. Immediately, the troopers to his rear repeated the same motion.

"Fire!" screamed Bomus, as his revolver jumped in his hand with a bright yellow flash, the large puff of gray-white smoke flying past his head. Gunfire ripped across the charging rank to his rear, sending leaden missiles toward the ridge in front of them, kicking up dusty plumes of earth and rocks below, into and over the ridge. No gunfire returned from it. "Splang!" an Army bullet struck the lava rock below Oits and whirred into the distance. Others zipped passed him and he instinctively ducked his head. He slowly raised his carbine, taking aim into the charging blue mass before him. The carbine bucked against his shoulder. He didn't feel or hear it as he fired, levering another cartridge into its chamber. Taking aim, he fired again.

Privates Schultz and Marriott were thumbing and firing their revolvers in the first rank. They screamed and fired with the rest of the charging battalion.

Umapine the Umatilla took careful aim into the charging troopers. He carefully squeezed the trigger.... "Thud-Smack!" Marriott and his horse disappeared from the rank beside Schultz, leaving only an empty space where they had been riding. "Bill! My God!" thought Schultz. He felt small bits of a warm, sticky substance on the right side of his face.

Bomus sucked in air with a gasp, as the entire front of the ridge exploded in one long line of fire and smoke. Something tugged at his hat and also at his left shoulder. Thinking that he'd been hit, he glanced at his shoulder. The yellow First Lieutenant's shoulder strap was flapping in the wind, clipped by a bullet. "Damn!" Bomus thought. Instantly, as planned, Bomus ordered a "Battalion-Right" to his Trumpeter, jarring his mount as he began a right wheel turn. Company F followed, reining in for the short turn. G Company was coming down, firing behind them.

Trooper Schultz's face had lost its smile. As the wind dried the animal and human blood on his pale face, he spurred his mount to the right, trying to maintain his position in the tightly swinging rank. His mount suddenly dropped from beneath him as if into a giant unseen pit, slamming horse and rider as they fell. The wounded animal, hit in the hindquarters, dragged its paralyzed hind legs, spinning crazily in circles. Schultz hit the saddle hard, knocking his breath away. His mount's front legs struggled in vain, pawing to raise them both, to no avail. Schultz was lost in a world of dust and bedlam as bullets cracked and zipped through the dust-clouded air around him. Quickly, he pulled his boots from the struggling mount's stirrups and swung from the saddle to the ground. The movement caused the horse to scream hideously from fear and pain. "Smack!" another bullet struck the wounded animal beneath its jaw, entering the neck. Instantly, a spout of bright crimson exited the wound, hastening the demise of the animal. Schultz dropped close to the large animal for protection; the animal was down now, eyes glazing over.

Suddenly, a line of mounted, screaming shadows burst from the clouds of dust, galloping past him. It was G Company wheeling through. None of the shadows stopped for him. He raised his carbine, loading it with trembling fingers. He'd lost his revolver. The air was alive with leaden hornets seeking him out. More shadows galloped past him, Company F. Afraid his own men would shoot him, he scrambled behind his dying mount, now sounding the end of its death rattle. He tasted sour bile mixed with dirt choking him. He vomited into the grass at his feet.

At the north end of the ridge, Egan watched as Robbins' volunteers flanked the ridge, entering the now empty village, shouting and firing into vacant lodges. Those tipped over by the volunteers began to burn from the dying morning fires within. Egan swung aboard his large buckskin in one fluid motion and galloped towards the volunteers. Boss and others from Egan's band followed. Rube Robbins' jerked his head down instinctively as a bullet missed it by inches. It had come from Egan's charging band of warriors to his rear. Robbins quickly looked over to the ridge where the Army should have been by now. It wasn't. The scouts were now cut off from the Army and any support. More bullets were zipping at them from the ridge. Robbins could hear bullets popping as they struck the canvas lodge coverings around him.

"Let's go!" screamed Robbins to his men, who were already galloping back towards him. He quickly wheeled his horse around and started back on a straight run directly into the charging Paiute warriors. "Only one way out, straight through em, boys!" Robbins screamed. Egan and Robbins saw one another at the same time as they charged each other at a full gallop, neither man giving way to the other. As they closed, Egan slid to the off side of the buckskin, aiming his carbine as best he could from beneath the running horse. He saw Robbins clearly for an instant, just feet away, and pulled the trigger as Robbins sped past him. He wheeled the horse around to pursue Robbins for another shot. Robbins had unexpectedly turned and was taking careful aim at Egan. Egan jerked the buckskin sharply to the right but it was too late. Robbins' carbine jumped. Suddenly, Egan felt as if an invisible giant had severed his left arm, sending a shock wave throughout his left side. His arm hung useless, dangling like a wet string. Robbins' carbine cracked again, as he wheeled and galloped over the end of the ridge with the other volunteers. The invisible giant wasn't through with Egan. This time he smashed the air from his chest, throwing him from the large warhorse onto the rocks and sagebrush below. He landed with a heavy grunt, seeing blue sky and white fluffy clouds above. No pain yet. It wasn't long in coming.

Egan's chest was burning and smeared with crimson colored froth, oozing from the bullet's entrance wound in his right breast. He tried to raise himself but an immediate choking seizure sent him backward with a painful grunt. Soon hands were on him, gently lifting him onto his red blanket and carrying him to safety. The warriors quickly carried him from the battlefield to the creek below. Evening Star looked with disbelief, as she watched the warriors carry the familiar red blanket and its bloody contents from the ridge. Her hand went to her mouth with a gasp as her eyes welled with tears. "Egan!" she screamed, as she ran to him. She unconsciously jerked her hands away, forgetting her two daughters. She'd never run so hard in her life. Her heart pounded in her chest. She stumbled and fell, scratching and bruising herself, then regained her feet in a flash. She felt nothing. She could hear her daughters screaming for her as they sprinted to catch up with her. She splashed into the cold water of the creek and scratched and clawed her way up the opposite bank. She stumbled up the small ridge to where the red blanket lay guarded by two Paiute warriors firing their rifles over the top of the ridge. Flopping to her knees in a hail of wet droplets beside the blanket, she pulled the blanket back gently, afraid of what she would see. It was Egan, unconscious but alive. She raised her tear-stained face to the gunsmoke-clouded sky and whispered, "Thank you, Father."

Evening Star immediately set to work helping the two warriors carry Egan down to the bank of the creek, where she began to treat his wounds. Honey's wife, Hattie, was running toward Evening Star, following the two sisters. Quickly, Egan's daughters arrived and began helping their mother. Soon other women arrived to assist the frantic women. The two warriors, who had guarded Egan unemotionally, jogged to the lava ridge above. Bullets buzzed and snapped through the air. Egan returned to semi-consciousness. He could hear the raging battle sounds, but they seemed very far away. His eyes began to see light, then blurred objects moving frantically above him like shadows. Suddenly, his eyes focused as someone wiped blood from his eyes. He saw her. It was Evening Star. His body wouldn't move for him. He was paralyzed. He tried to speak, but couldn't. Through his fog-framed vision, he saw her dark wet eyes and the smile that he so worshipped. From far away, at the end of a long tunnel, he heard her scream, "Egan!" Then darkness took him away again. The terrified eyes of his daughters watched the scene unfolding before them as the world around them roared with gunfire and death.

As the choking world of dust and gunsmoke drifted across the field, Private Schultz slowly raised himself to both knees, attempting to get his bearings. To his right he could see the lava ridge, perhaps seventy-five yards away from where he lay. Through the haze, he could see and hear the deadly occupants of the ridge. A quick shiver slithered down his sweat-soaked spine. He was alone! The warriors hadn't seen him yet; they seemed preoccupied with several of their numbers, perhaps wounded or dead. Schultz's eyes scanned to his left, the air was clearer there. Then he saw him. Marriott! Approximately one hundred and fifty yards away, leaning against his dead mount, carbine resting over the animal's rib cage. "He was alive!" Just like himself. Would they have stories to tell in the days to come! Schultz quickly sized up the situation. He'd have to get to Marriott in one attempt, or not at all. Together they'd stand some chance against the warriors should they counterattack. He hoped the battalion was forming for a second charge. They'd be found sooner that way. The flies were already buzzing around his dead mount. It had been only minutes, yet it seemed as if he'd been in this nightmare forever. He re-checked his carbine, pushed his black campaign hat down hard on his head, patted his canteen, and took in three large breaths of air...GO!

The warriors on the ridge had already seen him and began firing. "Bill!" Schultz screamed, as he zigzagged towards Marriott at full speed. He could hear gunfire and bullets flying past his head, over the sound of his pounding heart and lungs. He could also hear someone else running and struggling for air closely behind him. He didn't dare look back. Through blurring vision he saw a puff of smoke burst from Marriott's position. "ZzziP!" a bullet snapped inches from his head as it passed him. "Thud!" The deep grunt behind him said more than words. The running behind him suddenly stopped. Bill was alive! As he approached Marriott and the dead horse, Schultz's legs felt like rubber. He wheezed and choked for air as he flopped against the dead horse beside Marriott, who lay watching him. Bill looked pale and sick, his face shiny with perspiration. He smiled weakly at Schultz. "Damned if you didn't come back for me," said Marriott.

"Back hell, I came close to being scalped within an arm's reach a minute ago!" wheezed Schultz, his chest heaving.

"You got any water, Joe?" asked Marriott weakly, as he slowly pulled the right side of his blue coat away, exposing a slick red widening circle of blood, oozing from a hole in his gray Army shirt below the belt line.

"Goddamn, Bill!" whispered Schultz as he fumbled for his canteen, his eyes locked on Marriott's grisly wound. He gently passed the canteen over to his bunky with trembling hands.

"Can I help...?" asked Schultz quietly. Marriott's hand held Schultz back, shaking his head. He choked on the water from the canteen, gasping, nearly dropping it from his shaking hands.

"How the hell did you manage that shot, Bill?" questioned Schultz quietly, "You saved my life." He looked across the field where a small group of warriors were carrying a dead warrior back onto the ridge from where Marriott had shot him. Marriott smiled as he gazed weakly.

"The battalion will be here in a minute to pick us up, I sure hope they see us," said Schultz, raising himself over the carcass of the dead horse.

"Keep your damned head down, Joe!" gasped Marriott. "They got some shooters over there on that ridge. They hit my poor mount three times from there so far …. Sides, you and I are going back to Vancouver Barracks, Joe … an time we'll have jingle in our pockets…. It'll be a time won't it, Joe?" Marriott said weakly, pink spittle dribbled downward from the corner of his mouth.

Schultz didn't hear, he was preoccupied with looking for the battalion. His head bobbed up and down like a ground squirrel's.

Seeing the battalion forming in the distance, Schultz turned around, raising to his knees. Jerking off his campaign hat, he began waving it crazily in circles at the battalion. "It won't be long now, B...."

"Thud! - POW!" came from the distant ridge as a well-aimed bullet snapped across the flat, striking him dead center… Like a tossed rag doll, Schultz dropped backward onto his buttocks at Marriott's feet, a surprised expression crossing his face. He toppled, slowly collapsing to the earth, his head coming to rest against the dead horse's belly. Wide unseeing eyes stared into the bright sky above as if he were asking a question. Marriott gazed at his dead friend; tears welled into his gunsmoke-stung eyes as he tried to choke down a sob. The fire in his belly had subsided momentarily and he felt chilled now, as the crimson circle continued to spread across the gray Army shirt.

"Battalion! Forward at the trot! March!" shouted Lieutenant Bomus from the front of the newly formed three ranks of the battalion. The Trumpeter brought the bugle to his lips. The high pitched music merged with the rumbling horses and equipment as the ranks again pushed forward, much closer to the ridge this time. Revolvers had been reloaded and were again held at the high-port position. Word had been quickly passed to watch for wounded men on the field. "Battalion! Gallop!" shouted Bomus, the Trumpeter responding. Again, the battalion jumped forward at the gallop, riders loosening reins. "Charrrge!" screamed Bomus, barely audible over the thundering horses. Reins were dropped loose as spurs jabbed the flanks of mounts. The bugler spat out the rapid call as the entire battalion burst forward.

"Eeeee-Haaaa!" shot from troopers' throats, heads bent into the rushing wind. On the ridge to the rear, Bernard watched intently as the battalion went in again. His fingertips were white as they gripped the field glasses viewing the spectacle being played before him. "God, I wish I could be with them," he said to himself. "Take the Ridge! Take it!" he hissed as he watched the battalion split apart at its center as if sliced by a knife, opening then closing as each rank maneuvered around the dead horse and the two troopers. Bernard let out a sigh of relief as the battalion again disappeared into a billowing cloud of dust.

As the battalion approached the lava ridge, a wall of smoke and fire erupted along its entire length as warriors fired and reloaded weapons. The withering gunfire was undisciplined, as most shots failed to strike their targets. Bomus, suddenly seeing a large group of warriors forming a line to his right, shot his arm straight upward, reining in his mount. "Bugler! Sound Dismount as Foragers, Fight on Foot!" The three trumpeters sounded the calls, attempting to slow down the three ranks now pulling back hard on the reins. Confusion reigned as cursing troopers fought to control their mounts. Most reined to a stop while others bolted through the ranks, stopped only with the aid of file closers and horse handlers. Dust enveloped everything except the screams of wounded Army horses. On the right flank of the dismounting cavalrymen, Bannock warriors Paddy Cap and Big John, who were leading nearly one hundred warriors, saw that their trap had failed. They began running back to the ridge, stopping to fire occasionally at the troopers through the brownish red haze, now mingled with gunsmoke.

Bomus dismounted and shouted to his Trumpeter. "Stay close!" His sweat-soaked head snapped left and right as he shouted orders to sergeants and company commanders. Horse handlers were tugging and struggling with the extra mounts, leading them to the rear of the forming companies. "Whoa, you sons a bitches!" they yelled at the wild-eyed nearly hysterical animals.

Amazingly, amidst the confusion and clamor of battle a skirmish line formed, bristling with carbines. Orders were shouted. "LOAD!" Instantly the rattling sounds of carbine receivers being raised and long copper cartridges being pushed into chambers and closed with a metallic "Clack!" reverberated along the line of soldiers. "READY!" The clicking of hammers being rolled back to full cock rippled across the line facing the smoking ridge. Red-over-white Guidons fluttered in the warm breeze at the right end of each company. Suddenly, a strange silence reigned over the deadly field as both enemies struggled to gain their breath. On both sides, hearts pounded and bodies sweat. Instantaneously the Indian's ridge erupted with gunfire, sending bullets whizzing and snapping through the Army's line, again miraculously having little affect. "Fire!" shouted Bomus. The Army carbines roared, throwing death into the ridge. "RE-LOAD!"

Seeing that he was greatly outnumbered and faced repeating rifles, Bomus' mind flashed back to the disaster at Whitebird. Images of panicking troopers cut down like sheep flashed across his sweat-stung eyes. "NO, IT WON'T HAPPEN HERE!" he shouted to himself, his startled bugler looked at him with a puzzled expression. "Bugler! To The Rear as Foragers!" Bomus bellowed, ordering a rapid withdrawal which would widen the distance between them and the Indians, allowing his longer-ranged carbines advantage over the shorter-ranged repeaters now firing at him. The alternative was to remain where he was and be shot to pieces and over-run. Quickly, the battalion began its agonizing return, withdrawing across the field.

A Bannock warrior firing from the rocks on the south side of the ridge saw someone familiar in the skirmish line withdrawing before him. The white man was wearing a bright red and blue checkered shirt and tan pants. He wore a tattered black Army campaign hat. The man seemed to be more at ease on the field than the soldiers, as he fired and levered his Winchester. "Army Scout!" thought the warrior, as he took careful aim at the man just like Buffalo Horn had taught him to do. He slowly squeezed the trigger. The rifle bucked against his shoulder with a "Crack!" The scout's head jerked backward, hat spinning into the sagebrush. Myers collapsed to his knees, slumping into the brush. He was instantly thrown into darkness and silence. Several troopers, seeing him fall, bravely attempted to reach him where he lay in the brush, but were driven back by gunfire directed toward them. Myers was left for dead.

A youthful Paiute warrior struggled, forcefully trying to extract a stuck cartridge case from his .44 rimfire Henry Rifle. He frantically tried to pry the wrong-sized cartridge out of the chamber. No good! Without thinking he sprang to his feet to gain better leverage. A bullet struck him in the lower jaw, carrying away teeth and bone. He dropped to his knees stunned, still clutching the rifle. Instantly another bullet struck him in the right side, spinning him around and onto the blue-green sagebrush and red lava rocks. The sickening wet-slap sound of lead striking flesh followed by deep grunting carried along the lava ridge. With a shout, warriors sprang from the rocks to where Myers had gone down, rough hands grabbing arms and hair as they dragged their prey back to the ridge. They knew something that the soldiers didn't.

Chief Bearskin had been fighting intensely alongside the rest of the warriors. He had seen his bullets strike horses and soldiers. Yet, he wasn't satisfied. The scent of blood and gunsmoke acted like a narcotic to his senses; he needed more. With a roar he suddenly burst from the lava ridge.

"Watch it!" shouted non-coms over the gunfire as they saw the warrior running toward their line as if possessed by Satan himself. It was all they could do to control the young privates, without a Dreamer charging them as well.

Bearskin levered cartridges in and out of his rifle as he sped across the flat. His eyes fixed upon a lanky sergeant shouting commands to the soldiers in the Army line. The soldier with stripes was a leader and would fight bravely, his scalp on the charging Indian's belt would give him a great honor. Bearskin made a direct run at his target. Sergeant George H. Richmond of McGregor's A Troop had taken control of the right flank of the battalion and was finally managing the troopers in a rear guard action. He was satisfied with their performance so far, in spite of the bad situation they were in. Bearskin levered and fired his rifle until it was empty, then, throwing it away and screaming, he drew a small caliber revolver from his waistband. His feet seemed to glide on air as he neared the sergeant. His death song wailed even over the din of gunfire. Wide-eyed troopers watched in horror as the charging warrior closed with their sergeant. They instinctively drew away from the warrior's suicide attack. Richmond saw the charging warrior and fired the last two shots from his Army revolver, missing him. It was too late.

Bearskin struck Richmond full force, throwing both men away from the line of soldiers in a deathgrip, crashing into sagebrush and grass. The troopers resumed their firing and rear guard action, distracted from the two struggling men. Richmond ended up beneath Bearskin. Once they had stopped rolling he could see the black muzzle of the short barreled .44 Remington coming close to his right eye as he struggled to force Bearskin's hand away from his head. The warrior was very strong and pumped with adrenaline. But so was he. Bearskin's trembling thumb began to slowly draw the hammer back on the Remington. Richmond stared helplessly as he watched the cylinder turn, aligning its deadly lead bullet with the barrel. It would kill him. Richmond could smell the bear and deer tallow and the foul breath of his adversary just inches from his face. With every ounce of strength he had in him, Richmond suddenly kicked upwards between Bearskin's legs, striking him in the groin with his boot. The Indian grunted, struggling to pull the trigger of the revolver. It wasn't enough. Richmond gathered all of his strength and again kicked upward, striking Bearskin between the legs. This time it worked. The large Indian grunted and began to gag. Richmond immediately rolled from beneath the large warrior and on hands and knees began searching frantically for the revolver. His eyes caught the metallic glint of the gun lying in the brush. Quickly snatching it up, he cocked and fired, sending a bullet into the forehead of Bearskin as he reached for Richmond again. A bright spout of blood erupted from the small hole as the heaving warrior stared transfixed at his killer. Richmond fired again, the small revolver jumping, sending another bullet into the Indian's head. Bearskin's eyes rolled back as he slumped dead into the grass. Richmond kneeled on all fours, heaving, trying to gather his senses in the bloody grass as he struggled for air. As the sound of firing finally reached his senses, he picked up his Army revolver and loaded it with shaking fingers. "Hell of a way to make a livin!" he gasped, stumbling back to the retreating line of soldiers. They hadn't missed him.

Private Christian Hanson of F Company fumbled into his black leather cartridge pouch on his right side for another carbine cartridge. His carbine was hot in his left hand. Black smudges of gunpowder streaked his hands and face, mingling with sweat. His nose reeked of sulfur every time he drew a breath. As he inserted another long, black-snouted cartridge into the carbine's chamber, a bullet struck his left shoulder, knocking him backward with a half-turn and forcing him to drop his carbine. He blinked his eyes. Instinctively, he grasped his shoulder. Bright blood quickly spread into his gray sweat-stained shirt. "Funny! It don't hurt much," he thought, as he noticed his thumb and forefinger still held the long cartridge. Hanson reached down for his carbine, picked it up, and stumbled backwards, to catch up with the reversing line. The skirmish line crackled with gunfire and smoke, at times obscuring the view of the ridge.

"Maintain your intervals!" shouted Corporal Grantzinger of Company A, McGregor's seasoned Support Company. Grantzinger coolly and calmly passed back and forth along the line of troopers, yelling encouragement and instructions.

Dazed and going into shock from the loss of blood and still clutching his carbine, Hanson stumbled blindly backwards, colliding with Grantzinger. Thump! "Dammit!" the corporal snapped, nearly tripping from the unexpected impact with the stunned trooper. "What th…?" blurted Grantzinger, taking a quick look at the blood-soaked trooper. The corporal reached out and gently grasped Hanson's good arm, guided him around facing to the rear. He jabbed his finger toward the reversing horse handlers, "Go! Get a mount and go to the ridge, now!" Grantzinger yelled into Hanson's ear. The young, wide, shock-filled eyes looked left and right, then back into the corporal's steel eyes. He nodded, then staggered back toward the horse handlers, bullets whistled around him unnoticed. "Keep your intervals!" shouted Grantzinger to the line of men. "Don't… Ugh!" he bent over, as if kicked in the groin by a mule. His knees bent as he stumbled backwards, his face wore a look of disbelief as he brought a bloody hand away from his mid-section. His legs turned to jelly as he fell backward over small sagebrush, landing with a deathly thud. He was soon gone, his young lifeblood soaked into the desert sand. Rough hands grasped his collar, as troopers pulled the limp body through the grass and sagebrush.

Horses screamed behind the line. The warriors, seeing the increasing difficulty in hitting man-sized targets, slowed their firing, saving their precious ammunition. Bannock Joe ran to Oits, who was standing upright, full of the Dreamer Power. Oits and the warriors had stopped the U.S. Army. Not once, but twice. "Oits! Shoot for their horses. They are better targets than the soldiers are! Without them, they cannot follow us!" shouted Joe, his barrel chest heaving with excitement.

Oits' yellowed teeth shown through the painted death-like grin. He slapped Bannock Joe's bright paisley-print shirtsleeve, yelling... "Shoot for their horses!"

Suddenly, the firing increased along the lava ridge. Instead of bullets striking the reversing skirmish line of troopers at their front, they were now flying over the trooper's heads, into the groups of horse-handlers behind the line. "Slap!" bullets began to strike the already frantic mounts being led to the rear with difficulty. Some jerked their reins completely clear of the struggling handlers' grips, screaming and kicking at but not able to reach the growing bloody wounds in their bellies, backs, and withers. Mounts wild-eyed with pain galloped crazily throughout the retreating soldiers, some charging back through the skirmish line of troopers amidst firing yelling and confusion. "Watch yer rear! Heads up!" and "Gawd-dammit!" shouted the troopers, as pain-crazed animals galloped through the line towards the lava ridge beyond, reins steaming backwards in the wind, sweatstraps and stirrups flying up and down. Several mounts ran with their McClellan saddles slid beneath their bellies. G Company suffered four mounts killed within three minutes. A Company lost four, all screaming, pumping their essential blood away. Within five minutes, five additional mounts were hit, wounded, but managing to stay with their handlers. Officers' shots dropped the horses that galloped through the line towards the warriors' position. No trooper dared to shoot an Army mount without orders. At least the Indians wouldn't get them to use against them later. The horses carried valuable gear and ammunition.

The skirmish line approached Private Marriott and the body of Schultz, lying behind the dead mount. As the troopers gently lifted Marriott, he screamed. Startled, they nearly dropped him. "Let's go, boys," Marriott hissed through clenched teeth. Schultz's body was dragged back with them.

Captain Bernard dropped his field glasses, looking toward Captain Whipple. "Captain, send two men down to bring in that wounded trooper!"

"Yessir!" snapped Whipple. "Sergeant?"

"Consider it done, Sir!" spoke a tall lean sergeant. "O'Leary, Forster!" Two privates stopped stacking rocks and stood up. "I want yea both to go down on the field and relieve the troopers carrying that wounded man. Bring him back here at once!"

"Yes, Sergeant!" snapped both troopers as they began to trot off the ridge.

"By the love of Mary! Take yer damned carbines wit yea!" shouted the sergeant after them. The two troopers stopped, turned, and trotted back up the ridge, one nearly falling as he stumbled. Grabbing their carbines, they snapped their sling snaps onto their saddle bar rings and were off again. The sergeant shook his head slowly. Both troopers jogged towards the smoking noisy line in front of them. Once they saw the two nearly exhausted troopers struggling on either side of Marriott, they made a beeline towards them.

"We got him," said Forster to the two fatigued troopers as he quickly took one side of Marriott. The relieved troopers staggered back into the firing line. Marriott had to be half-dragged, only just conscious. His sky-blue pants were soaked with dark blood. "Hang on chum, yer gonna be all right now," puffed Forster, as they struggled along.

"SMACK!" Forster's left leg was thrown forward suddenly, collapsing beneath him as he fell. The three troopers dropped to the ground with a crash, cursing and grunting.

"What happened!" O'Leary shouted at Forster, as he gently rolled Marriott onto his back. Marriott emitted a deep groan, eyes half-lidded.

"Gawd, I'm hit in the leg!" blurted Forster, busy tying off his upper left thigh with his belt, blood flowed freely from a ragged hole in his sky-blue trousers. "Damn! That had to be from a gawd-damn buffalo rifle to have done this! Shit!" Finally he stemmed the flow of bright red blood. In the distance, two troopers were jogging towards them. Marriott groaned again. The two troopers arrived, one helped Forster to his one good leg, and the other helped O'Leary with Marriott. The five troopers headed out, trying to stay behind the quickly retreating skirmish line as it withdrew to comparative safety, to the low lying ridge held by the reserve company.

Army revolvers silenced screams from wounded horses, as young troopers bit lips and squeezed triggers. Some were teary eyed, caused by something other than acrid gunsmoke and stinging sweat. It had to be done. By now, the Army-held ridge consisted of a small stack of unpacked supplies. A large circular defense work had been built from red lava rocks covering the hill. It wasn't much, but it would protect the wounded. All pack animals and mounts were closely picketed together, under close guard on the reverse side of the ridge. The horse handlers were the first ones to reach the hill, still struggling with adrenaline pumped mounts. They immediately went to the line, setting to work picketing the horses.

"Get those damn saddle bags and gear off those mounts and bring em up here!" yelled a sergeant, knowing that the bags contained precious ammunition and rations. They would need it, no sense giving it to the Paiutes if the horses stampeded..

Soon the skirmish line was climbing the ridge carrying the wounded and dead. The grimy sweat-soaked troopers weren't talking much; few could hear with ringing ears. They'd just faced death and had escaped its clutches. Surgeon FitzGerald's assistants yelled and directed where the wounded men were to be placed inside the rock corral. FitzGerald removed his blue coat and quickly rolled up the sleeves of his white shirt and began assessing the three wounded men's injuries.

"Sir?" sounded behind him. Four sweat-soaked cavalrymen, struggling for breath, were carrying the pale, bloodied bodies of Grantzinger and Schultz. FitzGerald checked their glazed, upturned eyes and waved the troopers to where the dead were to be placed.

"Cover them," FitzGerald uttered quietly, then turned to the pain-racked troopers lying before him. It was time to go to work.

Bernard instructed the First Sergeant to immediately begin forming a perimeter around the top of the ridge and to start building rock defenses. The First Sergeant snapped a salute to Bernard and began bellowing orders to sergeants and corporals. Bernard ordered officer's call; its sharp call sounded across the ridge. The sun was getting hotter, no longer were the white puffy clouds drifting across the sky above them. Bernard worriedly glassed the smoke-and-dust-clouded field and ridge before him. There was much movement on the ridge. The field was littered with at least ten dead Army horses. The troopers had removed the saddlebags, canteens, and a few saddles. Pushed by a gentle breeze, a brown-gray haze crept slowly northward across the field, resembling a theater curtain opening to reveal its stage. Bernard turned to the sweat-stained grimy officers standing behind him. Lieutenant Bomus obediently looked into the eyes of his commander. Bernard's eyes softened momentarily as he spoke. "Well done. Report!" He searched for any signs of emotion from his staff. He needed answers quickly.

Bomus cleared his throat. His dry throat was hoarse as he responded to the question. "One dead, Sir, Saddler Schultz. Blacksmith Marriott is seriously wounded. He doesn't look good. Two mounts killed, Sir." Rube Robbins slapped his hat against his left arm, raising a small dust cloud, seemingly preoccupied with his own problems.

"Sir," reported Lieutenant Ward of G Company. "I've lost four mounts killed and Scout Meyers is missing and presumed dead." Bernard's lip twitched beneath his mustache, his eyes again softening.

Captain McGregor cleared his throat, eyes meeting Bernard's. "Sir."

"Captain?" questioned Bernard, aware of the captain's uneasiness, sensing a desire to be relieved of something.

"A Company lost four mounts killed, Sir. Five mounts were wounded, but still are serviceable. Sir," he paused. "A Company lost Corporal Grantzinger on the field." The two officers' eyes locked for a moment. It was a moment shared by only a few and then in only special circumstances such as combat. McGregor had broken through the strict rules of fraternizing with enlisted men, when it came to Grantzinger. He'd guided the young man through several enlistments, preparing him for sergeant's stripes. A natural leader, Grantzinger had made his mistakes in the past but had earned his way back into the ranks and the favor of McGregor. Now he was dead. McGregor and the company would miss him in the months to come, especially during morning stable call when the first pink rays of dawn broke at Fort Hall. He remembered hearing the corporal's youthful Irish brogue as he spoke quietly to his two assigned mounts in the lantern light of the stable. At times he sang an ancient Irish ballad softly as he forked fresh hay into the stalls in the frosty early morning air. A natural cavalryman, Grantzinger had been proud of his two large dark coated Morgans. To him, the cavalry and the two mounts had been the closest things to a family he'd known. But now he was gone.

Bernard cleared his voice and spoke. "Very well, see to your companies and wounded. Place the wounded into the rock corral. The dead I want placed on the north side of the ridge, downwind. I don't want the mounts spooked any more than necessary. Gather all canteens and place a trooper in charge of them. Inventory your ammunition..."

"Zip!" a stray bullet whined overhead; all instantly ducked their heads.

Bernard grinned at everyone's reaction, including his own. "Draw more ammunition from the packs as needed. The Indians may counter attack at moment. Rube? How are you and your people fixed?"

Robbins' hat was back on his head now. He leaned forward, caught himself and turned, spitting onto the ground. He stared at Bernard. "We figured you'd take the ridge as planned, Captain," he said, wiping his mouth with a sleeve. "Our asses were hangin out in the wind for awhile, in that village behind the ridge. Nobody was home. We got outta it by the skin of our scalps. Killed General Howard's Injun friend Egan, though!" He spat, again wiping on his sleeve. Bernard stiffened. He glared at Robbins, unblinking. Robbins continued. "I shot his ass off that damned big buckskin of his. Tried to catch it, but there was too damned much lead flyin to rope him. Lucky my boys and me got out at all. I got two wounded."

"Put your men on the flanks of our position," ordered Bernard.

"Yes, Sir!" mumbled Robbins as he walked to his volunteers, shaking his head slowly.

"Sir, it will be dark soon, should we start our cooking fires now?" blurted a wide-eyed, smoke-smudged second lieutenant.

Bernard pulled the chain of his pocket watch, snapping open the watch cover. "Well, Sir, we started this party at nine a.m., and by my watch it's nine forty-five a.m. We've got a ways to go before supper, mister." A chuckle resonated among the officers. "Dismissed!" Salutes, then the officers quickly returned to their companies.

"Lieutenant Bomus and Captain McGregor, please remain," ordered Bernard. The two hadn't moved. Bomus waited for the reprimand he expected, since he hadn't taken the ridge as planned. McGregor stood straight, looking deeply into Bernard's eyes for a sign. "Gentlemen, what do I have in front of me out there? Lieutenant?" addressing Bomus.

Bomus reached inside himself for strength, his red-rimmed eyes burned. "Sir, it can't be seen from here, but behind that ridge is a drop in elevation of thirty to fifty feet. The village is huge, probably consisting of three to five hundred lodges. Robbins reports that it was empty when he entered it. They had apparently moved the women and children off in the distance, expecting a charge through the camp. They were ready for us. He wasn't in it long and very nearly got cut off." Bomus' eyes lowered, then raised again to Bernard's. "The warriors held their fire until the last minute, even after my company had volley fired into them. They displayed very unusual fire discipline. They seem well coordinated; however, thank goodness, they didn't display good marksmanship. I'd guess we faced over six hundred combatants in the first charge. On the second charge, nearly one hundred additional warriors came from out of nowhere, probably from behind the lower ground on my right flank. I didn't want to chance going into a certain crossfire situation, so I halted the charge and fought as skirmishers rearward across the field. Another fifty or so warriors appeared about that time from the obverse of the ridge. The men did quite well, Sir, considering what we ran up against."

"Captain McGregor?" asked Bernard.

"I agree with Peter, Sir. The battalion struck a well-defended position, against superior numbers. Considering all of that, I believe we got out in good shape, Sir." His eyes darted

39

to the gray Army blankets covering the corpses lying in a row to his right. His eyes snapped back to Bernard's.

Bernard nodded in agreement. "We can expect a counter attack at any moment. Prepare for anything that might come at us now." He turned his eyes to the far ridge. "General Howard should be up to us in a day or two. I'll send out a messenger to him after dark. No sense letting the Hostiles know what direction our support is coming from." A pause... "I've never seen so many Indians in one place at one time! I don't understand it! Tend to your companies, Gentlemen, and… Good work!"

"Thank you, Sir" answered the two officers as they saluted. McGregor and Bomus quickly returned to their companies, where sergeants and corporals were shouting orders. Troopers were hurriedly piling rock breastworks for protection, while others were drawing ammunition. It was going to be a long day.

Across the field, Umapine slowly arose to his knees. They were stiff and sore. He hadn't noticed it until now. He looked across to the now empty field before him. He'd killed. It felt good! He still had the power. He thrilled in killing men. Red or white, it didn't matter. He enjoyed the smell of gunsmoke. "This is where I belong," he thought to himself, standing. Around him, he saw warriors singing and shouting, waving insults to the soldiers on the opposite ridge across the field, where it bristled with Army activity. They had won! Oits reached down, grabbing a handful of earth. Screaming his elation, he threw the earth and pebbles into the air. Others joined in. They had dead and wounded. Warriors were lifting and carrying them downward to the creek. The women and children were now running to the village to give assistance to the injured. The blue coats could do no harm to them now. They had been stopped. Beaten! But they still had to be watched carefully. Any Army messenger sent out would be followed and killed. During the rest of the day, a strange quiet reigned between both enemies. Only an occasional gunshot came from the Army's ridge, followed by the high "zzzZZ-Eeeeeee" of the bullet passing overhead, above the warriors. The drumming had stopped and few, if any, warriors could be seen. But the soldiers knew they were there, as they peered nervously over their carbine barrels into the heat waves before them. Some troopers were allowed to get badly needed sleep, lying in their positions. Throughout the day, officers sat or lay in prone positions, scanning the Indian ridge for any sign of movement. It remained mysteriously quiet. It worried them.

That evening, as darkness began to creep across the Army's ridge, Bernard quietly ordered Officer's Call. Soon, the silhouetted shapes of company commanders and executive officers settled down amongst the rocks around him. Once he was satisfied with their reports about the condition of the men and their fortifications, he dismissed them. They slowly made their way back to their companies, disappearing into the murky darkness as a half-moon rose from the east, bathing the landscape in a faint silver light. "Damn!" thought Bernard, as he stared at the rising moon in the east. "What else could be against us?" His body gave a slight, sudden shiver. His thoughts raced to his young wife, Alice, for the first time since the day's action had began. She seemed so very far away from him right now. Yet, he swore he could smell her perfume, or was it her soap? He couldn't be sure, yet he felt her presence all around him on the lonely, deadly hilltop. The scent of dead horses and men briefly wafted passed his nostrils with its sweet-rotten odor. He gazed up at the climbing half-moon to the east. A familiar sudden sense of guilt ran through him. How he wished he could have one brief minute to apologize to Alice, for everything he'd done to hurt or disappoint her during their lives together in the Army. It was the lonely times without the security of his presence that probably hurt her the most, he thought. "I'll make it up to her, if it's the last thing I ever do." He shook his head slowly in the darkness. "How many times have I promised her that?" The moon had risen to its full height now. Camp and signal fires were blossoming higher on the ridge-top across from them; the drumming and singing never seemed to stop.

"Cap'n?" A low whisper spoke to Bernard in the darkness. The moon had rolled to the west now and was nearing its darkest period before sunrise.

The voice was that of his First Sergeant. "A trooper has volunteered to take your message through to Camp Harney, Sir. He says he knows the way better than most of us and he's served there recently."

Bernard answered quickly. "Bring him, Sergeant!"

Quietly a horse was saddled and untied from the picket line and led to Bernard's position by the young volunteer. "Come," whispered Bernard, as he led the trooper and horse through the darkness to where cavalrymen lay quietly behind their rock-piled positions. Once outside the perimeter, Bernard looked at the dark form of the young man before him. "Soldier, take this message to General Howard, or the Commanding Officer at Camp Harney. You may have to go on to Sheep Ranch to deliver it. The General should be there by the time you get there. Tell him that we need reinforcements and ammunition badly. Tell him where we are and what happened here today. I don't want to alarm him unnecessarily, but we're down on water and ammunition, and these people may attack at any moment. We will hold out as long as we possibly can,which may not be very long. The written message I am about to place in your safe keeping will not say all of this, so you must tell it directly to any officer in command or preferably General Howard himself. And one more thing, do not under any circumstances share this information with a civilian or newspaper reporter. Do you understand?" Bernard handed the envelope to the shadow.

A young hand reached out from the dark shape and took the envelope. "Yes, Sir," the voice whispered back in return.

"God's speed," whispered Bernard.

"Thank you, Sir."

The form moved out into the darkness walking the horse slowly, stopping now and then to listen. Soon nothing could be heard as the night engulfed them. As he slipped back through the perimeter, Bernard thought to himself "That voice couldn't have been more than eighteen years old. By the Grace of God, I hope he makes it."

An hour later, Bernard lay back on his saddle and brought his blanket up closer on his legs. The morning chill was beginning. He went over every word in his message to Howard, trying to reassure himself that he'd communicated properly. He hoped that Howard would understand the hidden meaning of the communiqué. He knew that the press would get the message soon enough. The Army didn't need a stampede of news reporters spreading the alarm across telegraph wires shouting that another Custer tragedy was in the making. The message sent to Howard read:

> After march of five hundred miles, attacked enemy on 23d instant; charged with pistols; drove enemy across slough to rocky bluffs; used carbines; enemy is in overwhelming numbers; troops withdrew to good position, having re-formed under fire after the charge; used carbines to good effect. Losses: killed, Corporal Grantzinger, Saddler Joseph Schultz, Scout William Myers; wounded, Wm. Marriott (mortally), Trumpeter Louis Feck, Private Christian Hanson, Private George Foster, and two scouts, (slightly). Conduct of officers and men deserve commendation; all behaved splendidly. About fifteen horses lost in action. Indian losses unknown, estimated variously from ten to fifty killed. Indians estimated at two thousand-men, women, and children-seven hundred fighting men. Shall locate their camp again tonight. They are moving leisurely, burdened with stock and many wounded.

Men were awake and ready in their positions. Suddenly the far ridge blossomed into an inferno, as the Hostiles set large clumps of sagebrush afire, lighting the faces of the troopers in their positions. A long hideous scream echoed over the roar and crackling of the fire from the ridge, sending chills down the spines of the soldiers watching and listening in the distance. The screams continued unceasingly, then abruptly stopped, as flaming fingers clawed into the night sky.

"Get ready!" shouted officers and non-coms; everyone stiffened and re-checked weapons. Many were making the sign of the cross as they prayed, making peace with God. The fires continued to burn across the ridge into the morning hours, then quickly diminished into a long solitary line of faint twinkling light that soon burned out, instantly cloaking it and its occupants in smoke-filled darkness. As the smoke drifted across to the Army's ridge, troopers began coughing and hacking with dry throats. The pungent smoke reeked of burnt flesh.

"JOE!"

The cry startled everyone within the Army perimeter. Private Marriott screamed again as he tried weakly to raise himself, groping outward with a fevered, hallucinating mind for his dead bunky, who was no longer there. Privates Hanson and Forster tried to calm the dying young trooper. Marriott moaned as the two gently pushed him back onto his blanket. As the full darkness before dawn blanketed the position, Marriott drifted back into the swirls of smoke and death in his nightmare. Comforting hands were near. Troopers swore quietly while others prayed for daylight and a reprieve from death, with the old repeated promises of abstinence from the vices of the world should their lives be granted.

Bernard's forehead shone damp with perspiration in the darkness. He removed the blanket and stood up stiffly. "God, that was close yesterday!" he thought to himself, as he wiped his forehead with a stiff handkerchief taken from a vest pocket. He recalled all too vividly Custer's defeat on the Little Big Horn River two years previous. The Seventh Regiment had been stopped and overrun, losing nearly three hundred men. He thought how the next day would be the second anniversary of that action. He tried to shake off the thought, realizing he needed to check the perimeter and men. "Must not let them sleep. Will they hit us now? Damn," he whispered to himself, his brain foggy from the lack of sleep. He carefully picked his way into the early morning darkness to check on the perimeter, continuing to ponder the question, as he knew everyone else was. He fought with another grim question. "Were the screams that had come from the flaming ridgetop last night those of Scout Myers?" An icy chill slithered across his back.

Lieutenant Bomus' body felt as stiff as dried rawhide, and sore, as were the muscles and joints of everyone around him. There was no way he could sleep, his brain was being assaulted with the scenes of the previous day's action. He couldn't get the horrific images to stop long enough for him to have a moment's rest. The adrenaline fatigued muscles and joints of his body had stiffened in the coolness of the night. He knew the men around him were suffering as well. Only the occasional cough or sound of someone relieving himself in the darkness indicated the presence of the weary battalion. He waited for sunrise. They all did, staring toward the distant ridge in the darkness. It lay silent in the smoke-shrouded early morning darkness.

The black eastern sky began to turn purple, then pinkish red, followed by tints of baby blue, blossoming into an aura behind the mountainous hills to the east, announcing the beginning of a new day. In a short time, the blue-pink light surrendered to the sun, its brilliant golden light suddenly flashing over the horizon, bathing the smoke-obscured far ridge and the sagebrush-covered desert in smoke-shrouded misty early morning daylight. Cavalrymen began to shift in their positions, cold and sore from the long night. Uncertain troopers sat up or kneeled, grunting and moaning. No one spoke. After a brief Officer's Call, Bernard sent out Robbins and a few of his civilian scouts to reconnoiter the surrounding area, especially the battlefield and ridge. It was too quiet.

Before long Robbins reported back, swinging off his horse and walking straight to Bernard. "Gone! Every last one of them. Skedaddled! Went north up the creek, Cap'n. Took their dead with em too. They musta lit out during those fires they built last night. I sent two of my best boys after em, I told em to keep in close touch with us, Cap'n." He paused and taking in a deep breath, spoke painfully. "Sir? We found William Myers." Robbins looked into the questioning eyes of Bernard. "They burnt him alive, must have been him we heard last night. There ain't much left of him, Sir. The only way we could identify him was by this." His grimy hand held out a charred piece of red and blue checkered shirt cloth, spotted with brown bloodstains. "He was wearin this colored shirt last time I seen him, the buggers took everything else from him. Truly sorry, Cap'n."

Bernard nodded, staring silently at the bloody piece of cloth in Robbins' hand. "Good work Rube," Bernard said in a unusually soft tone of voice. "Do you think it's safe to go over to the ridge and the creek on its opposite side? The men and horses need water badly."

"I reckon so, Cap'n, so longs as you keep a weather eye out for feathers and dust to the north of us up that creek," uttered Robbins, eyeing the mountains to the north of them. Bernard noticed a glint of uneasiness in Robbins' trail-worn eyes.

Bernard turned toward his Trumpeter. "Sound the General and Officer's Call!"

In the gathering daylight, Private Forster flexed his bandaged leg. "OWwww! Damit!" he growled painfully.

"At least we're alive, quit complainin!" blurted Hanson, as he stood up stiffly, flinching as he moved his bandaged arm. He glanced to where Marriott lay on his blanket. "How's...?"

He stopped midsentence. He could see Surgeon FitGgerald closing Marriott's eyelids. Neither spoke, oblivious to the bustle and activity of the battalion coming to life around them. Each man was trying to deal with death. FitzGerald motioned to his assistants to remove Marriott's body and place it with the others, which they did, in silence. Forster turned his head away, hiding the welling tears in his eyes. "He'll sleep better now, no more hurt. He's with Joe now," choked Hanson, as he busied himself gathering gear with his good hand.

Soon, the still ridge had come to life. Sergeants and corporals were shouting orders to their men, who by now realized that they had lived through the terrible, lonely night. The mules and packhorses were re-packed, mounts were saddled, and troopers stood to horse by company in ranks of fours. The dead, tied across horses, had been wrapped in their personal dirty, bloodstained gray Army blankets. Silence reigned briefly as the troopers stared at them. It could have been one of them. Bernard sent out Robbins and his volunteers riding slowly, toward the smoldering ridge across the field before them. The volunteers spread out in a fan-shaped pattern, four dropping back and waiting to ride as flankers at the sides of the column, while others continued riding well to the front as point riders, weapons at the ready.

From the rear of the waiting Army column, a commotion was running along its length toward Company G stationed at the front of the column. Trotting and panting wearily from fatigue and thirst, a small red dog was struggling towards Company G and its men. As he passed along the column, troopers' hearts lifted and happy shouts reverberated encouragement to the dog, increasing in volume as he approached the front of the battalion. Troopers in G Company turned in their saddles to see what the commotion was about and instantly began cheering even louder than the rest of the companies to their rear.

Bernard, distracted from his concentration of the volunteers before him, angrily snapped his head to search for the cause of the distraction. It was Jack! As the dust-coated Irish setter came alongside Bernard, the starving and thirsty dog let out a sharp bark of joy, looking up at him, wagging its drooping tail. "Well, I'll be damned!" blurted Bernard, losing his intended reprimand for the moment. The dog was the G Company mascot and had been accidentally left behind, locked in the company barracks. How any animal could have traveled that distance and found the company was a mystery. Yet, here he was, exhausted but overjoyed by being with his lost family. Bernard shouted to the Company First Sergeant. Immediately, gentle arms picked up the dog, placing him across the saddle of one of the beaming troopers. Bernard felt a small surge of energy from seeing the dog. With the reunion of the mascot and his company, morale had suddenly been boosted higher than anything he could have tried. Regaining his composure and turning to the front, Bernard looked to where the volunteers were now approaching mid-field in the direction of the mist-covered ridge, moving cautiously at a snail's pace. Robbins knew what he was doing.

Bernard raised his right arm. "Battalion!"

"Company!" followed from company commanders, their arms also imitating their commander's. Red-over-white Guidons were raised from their saddle sockets.

"Forward, march!" Bernard's arm lowered, pointing to the ridge before them. Trumpeters echoed the familiar call. The battalion rode downwards from the ugly red lava ridge, soft iron shod hooves clattering across the rocky ridge where they had spent the long, terrifying night. No one glanced back at it as they rode down onto the field below. As they began crossing the field, the battalion came upon dead mounts from the day before. The carcasses were bloated and stiffened in death, some with legs stretching skyward in the blue morning air. Already, hawks and magpies were busy with their morning feast. The younger horses became nervous and wide-eyed within the ranks of the passing column. Bernard noticed that no harness or gear remained on the dead mounts. The Indians had been on the field during the night after all, and within feet of the perimeter. "Damn!" he thought to himself. "They could have easily taken our position but didn't. Why?" The question nagged at him. Bernard returned his thoughts to the volunteers in the distance ahead of him. They seemed to dance in the warming, misty heat waves before him. "Lieutenant Pritcher!" he shouted.

Like a shot, a young second lieutenant left his position on the right front side of the company behind Bernard. Pritcher trotted to Bernard from the right side, coming up beside him, snapping a salute with a dirty, white gauntleted hand. "Yes, Sir!"

"Lieutenant," said Bernard, his eyes squinting to the front, not addressing the officer visually. "I want you to proceed to the front and contact Volunteer Scout Robbins. Tell him we'll be making a temporary halt at the Hostiles' most recent campsite. Tell him to swing right when he reaches that point. Inform him once we have watered, we will be proceeding northward up Silver Creek, on the heels of the Hostiles in one hour. Then report immediately back to me. Any questions, Sir?"

"No, Sir!" croaked Pritcher.

The young Lieutenant snapped Bernard a salute, and swung his mount around, spurring it toward the volunteers, who were now approaching the ridge in the distance. Some were already signaling "all clear" to the column.

The thirsty column crossed the field slowly, the only sound being the coughing of men and horses, rattling equipment, and the plodding of horses' feet, as the familiar gray-white dust rose upward into eyes and mouths in choking clouds. Once the battalion arrived at the bank of Silver Creek, picket guards were posted. Mounts were watered first, then walked and allowed another drink. Afterward, each company tied the horses to picket lines. Troopers carefully brushed and curried the horse's coats, removing dried and matted sweat-laced dirt and, in some cases, blood. When finished, the horses' coats shimmered and gleamed in the morning sun light. Wounds were dressed, keeping FitzGerald busy. Once done, the troopers rushed upstream for non-muddied water and began splashing the cold water upon themselves and drinking heavily. They drank, and drank some more, filling up. Canteens were filled and wounds were cleansed and re-dressed. Exhausted as they were, the fresh water had given them new life.

Bernard and FitzGerald walked to where Forster and Hanson were sitting. The two troopers were already sweating in the morning air from their wounds. Fresh blood showed brightly through the new dressings. "At ease, men," said Bernard as he saw the two men struggling to rise. "I'm told that your wounds are serious, but that you both want to travel with the battalion instead of returning to Camp Harney. Is that true?" Both men nodded, glancing at each other. "Good! It will go in your record. I'll try and take it easy on you. We're marching up this creek about ten miles, to where there is better water and camp wood. We'll soon have cooking fires started and hot coffee for you. Are you certain that you can stay up with us?"

Two weary faces grinned, looking at the two officers. "Yessir!" was their response.

Robbins and Bernard walked to the lava ridge to search for signs. Dried blood trails ran through and across the lava rocks. Some rocks were splattered with dried blood and bits of flesh. Brighter colored rock fragments from bullet strikes covered the ridge. Upon entering the Indian campsite, only scattered scraps of scorched and torn tenting were found. Empty cartridge cases lay in profusion all over the area. The charred remains of lodge poles burned in the attack were now smoldering or cold. An enormously wide trail of fresh earth, ground up by thousands of animal hoofs, headed due north up the confluence of Silver Creek and into the mountains in the distance.

Four graves had been dug in the sandy earth. Each crudely made cross had been fashioned from freshly cut willow branches from the creek bank. An empty carbine cartridge case had been shoved into the earth before each, just below the surface. Each case contained a piece of ruled notepaper taken from an officer's notebook. Upon it were written the name of the deceased, the date of death, and the officer's signature and rank. The case was then plugged with a dry piece of wood and shoved down into the earth before the cross.

Bernard ordered "Assembly." Soon the battalion had formed at attention. Nothing was heard, excluding the occasional whinny of a mount or a subdued cough from a trooper standing to horse. Infrequent puffs of air stirred through the willow trees near the banks of the creek. A seasoned, gray-haired sergeant walked slowly to where the blanket-wrapped corpses lay beside each of the four open graves. Reaching into the inside pocket of his dusty blue wool coat, he produced a pair of silver-wire spectacles. Cautiously, almost shyly, he put them on. He then opened the small worn Bible that he was carrying. His hoarse but robust voice flowed through the surrounding cavalrymen and upward into the bright blue sky above them. Soon finished, he slowly closed the tattered Testament and with disciplined smoothness back-stepped from the graves at attention. Bernard's trumpeter walked resolutely to the graves, left faced, and brought the trumpet to his lips. The long lonely notes of "Taps" drifted outward and back across the ugly field and blood-drenched ridge behind them and over to the ridge where they'd spent the long, agonizing night. When finished, the trumpeter snapped his bugle downward to his right side, right faced, and walked back to his position in the company. After a moment of silence, Bernard ordered the battalion dismissed. As the troopers walked their horses back to their companies, they raised small clouds of dust that drifted waist high. Each man walked with his own special thoughts, and in more than one case, fear. Quickly, the burial detail lowered the dead into their final resting places. The detail wore bandanas over noses and mouths because of the pungent stench of death and roasted flesh beneath the blankets. The metallic ringing of shovels pealed across the silence of the desert, culminating in the thumping sounds of spades tamping down earth. The names of those buried remained in the thoughts of those who knew them in life. It was finished.

Marriott
Grantzinger
Schultz
Myers

As he was adjusting the cinch strap of his saddle, Bernard saw Scout Robbins making a beeline towards him. He could see that he had something to report. Robbins spat a large cud of tobacco into the dust as he approached Bernard, wiping his mouth with a sleeve. Robbin's eyes narrowed, staring northward up the creek where it disappeared into the blue-green mountains and timber four miles ahead of them. "My men got back, Cap'n. They say they followed the Hostiles up this creek about ten mile up. They also say that these here Hostiles ain't afraid to be followed. Seen em up ahead, looking right back at em. As usual, it don't add up to nothin. They got some kind of medicine or power behind em this time and it's big!"

"Move your men out to the flanks, Rube," said Bernard, looking toward the timberline in the far distance. "But stay in sight of us. When we approach the timber we'll need all the eyes we have to our front and flanks. I want to travel at least ten miles before dark to set up camp and wait for the General. I want your men out scouting for any one who might try to circle back and hit us again," Bernard said, as he flipped the lava pebble he'd been rolling around in his hand.

"So long, Cap'n," said Robbins tiredly as he stood up from the kneeling position where he'd been studying the ground as Bernard had been talking to him. He looked into Bernard's eyes and for the first time in a long time he gave the officer a tobacco-stained grin. "This sojer just might know what the hell he's doin after all," he mused to himself as he walked stiffly to his horse.

The battalion cautiously moved northward, following the Indian trail along Silver Creek. They traveled fifteen miles, taking care of their wounded as best as they could. Troopers glanced left and right nervously as the column approached the dark green timberline. Seven miles from the site of abandoned Camp Curry, the battalion stopped and made camp for the night. Wood was gathered and men and horses watered. Bernard didn't wish to go any further. It was late afternoon and the sun was beginning to wane in the high desert sky when most of the duties were finally completed. Before long, timbered shadows began to stretch across the meadow. A meadowlark sang in the distance from the banks of Silver Creek.

As soon as the horses were picketed, an instant flurry of small sections of soiled white canvas shelter halves materialized, each a separate or double roof for the troopers' shelters. The wood-gathering detail finished splitting the last of its white pine for the morning cooking fires and returned to its company area. Cooking fires were started and soon the aroma of boiling coffee and salt pork mixed with the sweet smell of pinewood smoke drifted throughout the Army camp. It would be another night without campfires within the battalion's perimeter. The Hostiles were still too close, having entered the dark forest to the north of the battalion. The sun quickly slipped behind the horizon, bringing long blue shadows across the camp. The fires slowly burned down to coals as the last blue drifts of cooking fire smoke drifted away to the east. Guard details were posted close to the horse picket lines, the large animals concentrating on tearing at the sweet grass, chomping loudly as they savored each mouthful. There would be little grain for them tonight, as had been the case for the last four days. Their bodies needed grain, but there was little to be had.

Bernard walked slowly through the camp, quietly exchanging words with his officers and men. Once satisfied with the pickets, he returned to his bedroll, sitting upon it heavily. Soon, one by one, various officers discretely wandered towards him and sat down around him. Bernard cast a questioning look toward Surgeon FitzGerald with raised eyebrows. "The men are fine, Sir," said FitzGerald softly, responding to his commander's concerned look.

"Thank you, John," Bernard said, relieved.

The officers conversed in low tones for a period of time. As the gathering shadows turned to darkness, the small group of officers broke up and returned to their companies. To a man they pondered the questions digging at their insides. "Where are the Hostiles and where is General Howard?" Not a man had the courage to ask Bernard, so they had to wait. The coals of campfires soon died out, leaving everything in darkness. A half-moon raised itself in the inky blue-black sky. Stars began to twinkle brightly in the heavens. Weapons were kept close and ready. It would be another long night.

Sunrise dawned brightly the next morning in the Army camp. It was Monday, the 25th of June. Sunrays streamed through the smoke-hazed air from smoldering embers of breakfast fires. The battalion was tying gear onto saddles and placing shelters and cooking utensils into the wagons. Soon the battalion was zigzagging its way northward, traversing Silver Creek. The dark blue-green mountain range rose ominously in the distance, greeting the column. Bernard decided to march seven miles further to abandoned Camp Curry, where he knew there should be better forage and water for the animals, as well a good wood supply. He knew that it would be prudent to wait until Howard came up with reinforcements and supplies before entering the deep-forested canyons before them where the Indians had entered and disappeared. By late morning, the battalion had arrived at Camp Curry. As the battalion rode across the old parade ground, now overgrown with high grass and weeds, the troopers eyed the forlorn collapsing wooden buildings, all that was left of a once bustling Civil War Army camp. The column halted, dismounted, and began to set up camp. Troopers were detailed to clear brush and debris for a camp area for General Howard and the approaching reinforcements. Other details, carefully guarded, were posted to gather wood and water. Robbins and his volunteers kept up a deadly game of cat and mouse with the warriors guarding the rear of the Dreamers ahead of them.

Woodsmoke stung the nostrils of Egan, arousing him to full consciousness. He looked downward painfully at the dressing on his chest. The wounds had stopped bleeding somewhat, the leaden balls having been removed by the Old Woman. The small caliber shot hadn't penetrated deeply but had created serious bleeding. Egan's fever had broken and his left arm was tightly bound to his chest. He groaned weakly with a half-smile at the worried women kneeling close to him. His gaze turned to the small cooking pot as the aroma of stewing meat met his nostrils. He was hungry! Quiet tears of joy ran down Evening Star's cheeks as she softly kissed her husband's cheek. The Old Woman grinned toothlessly, cackling as Egan's two daughters crowded closer. Evening Star instantly instructed the older girl to run to Honey and tell her brother that his father was awake and going to take food. The tall, lean girl sprang to her feet like a mountain lion as she flew from the lodge, long braids flying behind her. Evening Star began stoking the small fire, sprinkling dried pitch-laden wood chips and shavings onto the embers. Immediately the coals sprang to life with a bright flickering flame, bringing the stewing meat and roots to a frothy boil. Deftly, she dipped a fire-blackened tin cup into the pot, removing some of the savory liquid. With the tip of her knife she expertly plucked a large piece of meat from the pot, shredding it with the knife and her fingertips until it was finely minced. Quickly the meat was dropped into the cooling broth and stirred. The steaming cup was brought to Egan's trembling lips as she gently allowed his lips to contact the hot cup and slowly sip the hot broth. Egan lay back stiffly with a low groan. He struggled to speak. "Evening Star?" he whispered hoarsely. Through blurred eyes he focused upon the familiar sweet face of his wife. His eyes opened and closed slowly as he smiled feebly at her.

"I am here, my love," spoke Evening Star quietly. "Rest, my husband."

The Old Woman had stopped fussing and cackling, her dark ancient eyes now boring into Egan's as she studied him from somewhere far away.

Honey and Charley had hurried to Egan's lodge once they'd been notified of his regaining consciousness. A very short visit assured them that he would live. Relieved, both men had gone to the other Paiute head men and passed the word. Honey knew that if anything happened to his father, the three Egan bands would look to him for leadership. The thought of that burden worried him deeply. But his father was alive, and above all needed rest and protection from those that would harm him. Honey had felt the uneasiness eating at Egan for days now and suspected that there were People who felt that he was no longer a believer in the Dreamers. Honey was secretly not a Dreamer himself and felt that his father wasn't either. He had come on this journey only to help his father protect their own three bands from Oits and the other Dreamers. Things were not going well and they could all be killed if they weren't careful. He would watch and listen and pretend for now. That is what his father would tell him to do. For now he had to see to his own wife and Hubert, their infant son.

Inside Egan's wikiup, through half-lidded eyes Egan whispered, trying to focus on the four women in the lodge. "What of the Numa people today?" The four women instantly stopped what they were doing and stared at each other.

Evening Star caught herself. Pausing as she took a deep breath, her shoulders began to tremble beneath her worn cotton dress. As her large, dark eyes met Egan's, she spoke in a low, hushed voice. "Many are traveling Gosipa (Milky Way Road of the Dead) this night, my husband." There was silence in the wikiup, except for the slight crackling of the lodge fire. Four sets of heavy-hearted eyes gazed at Egan from the half-lit shadows. In the darkness outside an owl hooted mournfully. A tear crept slowly down Egan's cheek, reflecting the fire's light. His eyes closed.

Elsewhere in the Dreamer camp, Oits glared at the Bannock sub-chiefs who glowered back at him with wolf-like eyes. One in particular unsettled Oits. War Jack stood staring at Oits unblinkingly as he gripped his rifle tightly. War Jack wore the traditional pullover warrior shirt, decorated with green, blue, and red Dreamer symbols, and tufts of horsehair. A dirty brown stained hole showed where a bullet had struck him in the upper forearm. The shirt was made of rough cloth, since game was so scarce. Oits knew that any of these men could and would kill him in an instant if they felt he or his Dreamer faith were a fabrication. It was all these men had left. Oits straightened his stooped shoulders and spoke in his gravely voice, "We should do as the Nez Perce Dreamers did last year when the blue coats followed them. When the soldiers stopped, the Nez Perce warriors would stop and rest. They would then move when the blue coats moved towards them. Egan is healing quickly and will be ready to ride again. The bullets could not kill him. The faith will keep us from the harm of soldier bullets." A murmur of satisfaction passed amongst the warrior leaders. Again Oits snarled, "We should attack the Army camp and take their horses or scatter them. They will be easy to take. The pony soldiers are too tired to fight now. They have been whipped!" Another murmur passed among the Bannock and Shoshoni men. Most of the Paiute and other tribal members stood to the rear or to the far sides of the council.

War Jack had stood unemotionally as he listened to every word Oits had spoken to the council. He looked at Oits' pouting smirk before speaking. "The soldiers are whipped? Does a whipped dog lie at the heels of the wolf, waiting to be whipped again? The soldiers know that we can kill them at any time, but they follow. Why? Why do their hairfaced scouts watch us from the distance? I do not think the soldiers know they are whipped, or else they wait for more soldiers coming from somewhere. I do not know what my heart wants me to do. We must sing and dance so that the dead spirits from the other world can tell us what to do and to guide us on the right path. These are my thoughts." All eyes were on him. War Jack was a powerful speaker at council. Oits glowered and turned away from the council, pointing his carbine into the darkness in the direction of the soldiers' camp below them. A sneer traversed his painted countenance as he stiffly walked away from the council. War Jack studied him quizzically, eyeing him as he passed into the encampment.

Morning broke gray and cool in the Hostiles' camp. The busy sounds of children, supplies, and utensils being tied to horses and the long double-poled travois being harnessed to the older, milder tempered Indian ponies rustled throughout the large Indian encampment. Small Cayuse colts kicked their heels at the barking, snapping camp dogs playing at their hind feet. The giggling, squirming smaller children were scooped up and placed aboard the strong Indian horses and secured with soft rawhide thongs. Infants snuggled in warm hand- fashioned wood and hide carriers either slung behind their mothers' backs or tied securely to the side of the trusted horses, within reach of their mothers. They were ready to move. The Messiah was waiting. Soon there would be plenty to eat and the children would be strong again. The thought of hot, juicy buffalo hump gave them the energy to walk more quickly as they followed their husbands and braves leading them out at the front. The rising sun's warmth quickly warmed their dawn-chilled bodies.

Communication received at General Sheridan's HQ, June 4, 1878.
"Hostile Sioux, Arapahos, Cheyenne and other Indians assembled at the eastern corner of the Cypress Mountains and known as "Sitting Bull's camp" contemplate an invasion south of the boundary line at an early date. There are now congregated, he says, at that location not less than 1,400 lodges, which can muster at least 2,000 warriors. Major Irving, the commanding officer Ft. Walsh, (Saskatchewan) when recently visiting Ft. Benton said he had no faith in the peaceable intentions of these Indians. They were fully supplied with arms and ammunition, carrying loaded belts around their waists, breasts and arms."

Major Guido Ilges. Commanding 7th Inf.
Ft. Benton (Montana).

Fort Harney, Oregon.
"We all like our good agent Parrish… There can be no better man than he, and why send him away? Oh, my good soldier-father, talk on paper to our Big Father in Washington, and tell him not to take him away."

Paiute Chief Winnemucca.

Chapter 2

Road of the Dead - Passing of the Pipe

Captain Bernard walked carefully through the knee-high grass of the overgrown parade ground, overseeing the hasty preparations for General Howard and the desperately needed reinforcements. His caution was not only for Indian sign but also for one of the many rattlesnakes the men had seen or killed. This would be no place to be snakebit. He paused briefly, sitting on a downed pine tree. He reached into the inside pocket of his blue woolen blouse, withdrawing a thick "U.S. Army" marked envelope. He removed the letter and began to read its contents for the third time since the fatigued courier had delivered it before daylight that morning. It was from General Howard. He recognized the slanted left handed scrawl of the one-armed general. The message read:

> June 25th, 2 a.m. Sage Hen Springs. I am delighted at your success, and congratulate your Officers and men with all my heart. The loss of their ammunition and baggage and stores bothers me. I am with Miles, and if you do not run them another ten miles, we will be up before night.

He felt relief as he returned the envelope to his coat pocket. He thought to himself. "No fuel for the reporters this time. The young trooper had done well delivering his message on the ugly morning of the 23rd. There's no substitute for youthful vigor and pride."

Rising sorely to his feet, he realized he'd shut out the noise and commotion encircling him. Looking skyward he spoke under his breath, "Clouds coming in, looks like rain. Damn!" He suddenly choked back a laugh as he noticed a young trooper stumble and fall over backwards onto his rump while dragging a dead pine tree limb. The limb had snapped from the tree with a "crack!" The trooper landed with a "Crrrummph!" landing heavily onto the grassy ground before Bernard. The trooper lay for a moment, then rolled sideways like an overturned beetle, trying to rise on tired legs. "Shit!" he blurted, not seeing Bernard approaching from behind him. A lone hand reached down to help the soldier. The soldier took it. "Thanks pard...." The trooper's eyes widened with shock as he stopped mid-sentence, looking into his commanding officer's eyes. "Sir? I'm...."

The Captain grinned as he pulled the trooper to his feet. "Let me give you a hand with that piece of timber you're trying to move, OK with you, soldier?"

"Yessir!" snapped the soldier with a grin, grabbing one end of the large limb. Together, they dragged it out of the clearing. As Bernard walked away, the trooper watched him, scratching the back of his head.

"Well, I'll be damned!" uttered the trooper under his breath, smiling to himself.

"Trooper!" yelled a sergeant. "Back to work dere!" The youngster scrambled off, searching for more dead limbs. Soon a clearing had been made and tents and shelters or "shebangs," as the soldiers called them, sprang up. Camp equipment was unpacked from the pack animals and company cooking fires were started. This would be as far as they would go today. Across the parade ground a threesome of crows began to scold the Army invaders from their perch on a rooftop beam of a dilapidated Army barracks in the distance. The Army mounts, secured to the picketline in the distance, raised their heads and pointed their dark furry ears at the commotion, then returned to chomping and tearing at the dark green grass at their feet. The animals were uncaring of the taunts of their noisy neighbors, as well as of the existing danger from their deadly foe camped a few miles to the north in the dark mountain canyon of Silver Creek.

Delaying his inspection tour temporarily, Bernard stopped to admire the beautiful landscape laid out before him. Green forest and mountains to the north of camp and green bushy desert to the south. "Oregon can be beautiful at times," he thought to himself as he inhaled the sweet scented mixture of pine forest and the pungent aroma of freshly crushed grass and sagebrush beneath his feet. His thoughts went to his wife, Alice, and their five children. His mind thought of each one individually. Harry was ten, Kate was eight, John, six, Mary, three, and little George, two. He likewise thought wistfully of little Fanny, whom they'd laid to rest nine years ago. He took off his dusty, sweat-stained campaign hat, staring at its weather-beaten condition. Has it been that long? he thought to himself, as he gazed into the vast distance before him. The thoughts brought Alice and the children over the distance separating them to this green virgin place where the children could play games of tag and hide and seek. He and Alice would sit in the shade of that pine tree over there, watching the little ones as they struggled to escape into the tall grass and frolic with their older siblings. Suddenly, almost in a panic, his heart rate increased and he desperately needed to hold Alice again, if for nothing else but to feel the reassuring warmth and strength of her young, strong body against his. Making her his and his alone. "God, I pray that they are all safe and sound," he voiced to himself. A deep, overwhelming, guilt-ridden sinking sensation in his chest and stomach nearly overpowered him. Lord, how he hated himself for not being with them now. Embarrassed at himself, he blinked his eyes and tried to shake himself back to the present. A sharp bark startled and abruptly awoke him from the dark mood. Looking behind him, he saw Jack wagging his tail, ears raised for any friendly word his captain might have for him. The red setter at once swapped ends and trotted back to the main camp, stopping once to glance back, assuring that Bernard was following him. Jack had summoned his battalion commander. They needed him as he needed them.

The G Company trumpeter was meticulously grooming the withers of his mount to a high glistening shine in the morning sunlight. The horses tied along the line stopped eating momentarily, sensing Bernard's approach. The musician came to attention and saluted. "Sir?"

"Sound Officer's Call," Bernard ordered calmly. Soon Bernard was surrounded by his company officers. "Gentlemen, are we ready for the General's arrival?" They were ready.

A sentry shouted to the corporal of the guard from the south camp perimeter. A lone rider was seen in the distance approaching the camp trailing dust. "Halt!" challenged the young sentry as the rider and horse drew near the camp sentries. The trooper brought his carbine upward in one smooth motion toward the incoming rider. In a cloud of alkali dust, the civilian volunteer reined in his sweat-caked mount before the sentry.

"Message for Captain Bernard, from General Howard!" barked the dust-covered volunteer hoarsely, the dust trail catching up with horse and rider, enveloping all in a gray haze.

"Dismount, the Cap'n is comin!" choked the trooper, nodding toward Bernard, who was walking quickly towards them.

"K-HAK!" coughed the trooper as he spat, still enveloped in dust. The volunteer swung down from the exhausted horse and remained motionless, grasping the mount's reins.

"Messenger from General Howard, to Captain Bernard, Sir!" blurted the volunteer through dried, parched lips.

"I'm Captain Bernard, report!" Bernard said to the sweating civilian volunteer.

"Sir," creaked the volunteer, "The General's comin bout two hour out, sends his compliments, Sir."

"Reinforcements?" Bernard questioned the exhausted man.

"We caught up with two companies of the Twenty-First Infantry, under Cap'n Miles, at Sage Hen Springs this mornin, Sir!" The volunteer slowly scanned the camp with narrowed sun- and dust-burned eyes beneath the brim of his hat. "Is this all aya, Sir?" He spoke without looking at Bernard, as obvious worry crossed his face like a cloud crossing the sun.

"Ask me that in two hours, mister," said Bernard, motioning the thirsty horse and rider toward the creek bank. "And by the way, well done!" yelled Bernard, smiling after the volunteer. The weary rider nodded his head, looking around the camp as he led his horse and himself to a welcomed drink of cold water from the creek. Both resembled snow creatures, covered in alkali as they were.

Two hours later, a dust trail was seen winding, then cutting a direct trail towards the Army Camp. "Bugler! Sound Assembly!" yelled Bernard.

"Yessir!" The trumpet's sound rang throughout the camp and outward, in the direction of the incoming column as it approached them. The assembled battalion stood at parade rest. Bernard mounted his horse, turned and took his place at the front of the formed battalion, his trumpeter to his left rear. The dust trail approached them and began to reveal dark images of mounted men and wagons. As the first two riders appeared from the dusty haze, it was apparent that one was missing a right arm.

"Ba-tal-ion! Ten-Hut!" commanded Bernard, sitting erect in his saddle. He touched his spurred boot heels ever so gently against the horse's sides. The large mount instantly walked forward to meet the general. As Bernard gently pulled the reins back, the horse stopped as if struck at attention before the two dust-coated Army officers now facing him and his rider. "Sir! Captain Bernard at your service," snapped the captain as he smartly brought his off-white gauntlet to a salute. He looked into the steely eyes of the older, one-armed Army officer facing him. Gold general's stars twinkled beneath the coat of dust on the shoulder straps. It was General O.O. Howard himself, commanding the Department of the Columbia. The general returned the salute with his left hand, bringing it down slowly. The general seemed pre-occupied for a brief second as he scanned the small, battered formation to the rear of Bernard. Both men were perspiring in the afternoon heat.

"My compliments, Captain," said Howard, his eyes returning to Bernard. "You know Captain Miles of the Twenty-First Infantry?" Bernard nodded to the captain at Howard's side. "You've done well and we have much to discuss. May we retire and talk a bit, Sir?" asked Howard.

"Of course, Sir" smiled Bernard, motioning his hand towards the newly erected command tent sitting in the shade beneath a large stand of pine trees.

Howard's Staff and Field Officers stood beneath a canvas tarp in a semi-circle around a small battle scarred field table. A territorial military map was spread across its top, secured from the occasional gusts of air by Bernard's revolver and Howard's binoculars. Present were captains George B. Rodney, Howard's battalion commander from Battery D, Fourth Artillery; Evan Miles of Company E, Twenty First Infantry, Commanding the Artillery and Infantry Battalion in the field; and William F. Spurgin of Company I, Twenty First Infantry, in charge of the battalion's wagon train. The officers stood in composed silence awaiting Howard's briefing.

Brigadier General Oliver Otis Howard, Commanding General of the Department of the Columbia, sat listening intently to Bernard's after-action report of the battalion's activities during its past four weeks in the field, particularly the battle at Silver Creek. Howard carried his forty-seven years, twenty of which on active duty with the U.S. Army, quite well. The amputation of his right arm at the battle of Fair Oaks, Virginia, in May of 1862 didn't distract from his energy or sense of purpose in the least. It had only inured him to physical and personal discomforts, supported greatly by his deep religious convictions. Recent exposures to negative political criticism and an occasionally strained relationship with his commander, William T. Sherman, had not diminished his enthusiasm for life or his sense of duty. He sported a beard, slightly sandy in color now, as was Bernard's. His complexion was fair. Reddened high cheekbones showed the effects of sun and wind in the recent outdoor campaign. His eyes were a brilliant hazel that flashed when excited. "O.O." had no tolerance for profanity or consumption of alcohol within his command. His deep compassion for all underprivileged peoples tended to get him into controversy with zealous commanders, as well as from the troublesome press and angry settlers and ranchers who wanted to be rid of all Indians. He had a social and military tightrope to walk, as did all military commanders of the time. Above all else, he was an officer and a gentleman to all who met him, and a compassionate Christian.

Howard did wrestle with the issues involving Indian Wars, however, knowing that the combatants fighting this new war really didn't hate each other. One side fought corrupt and inept government agents as they struggled to salvage what remained of their way of life; the other policed unlawful Hostile activities on and off the reservations, at times actually issuing their own Army rations to the Indians when no food was available to them. The government's inability to pass legislation quickly, authorizing payment to Indian agents, who in turn were required to purchase and issue rations to the Indians, was a hopeless situation. He'd found himself commanding scattered troops as far away as Arizona, where he'd singularly sought out and sat in council with the Apache Chief Cochise. He had grit.

The Nez Perce War the previous year had strained his relations with General Sherman. He certainly needed to control this new, unexpected outbreak. It could mean his last chance for future field action. He knew "Cump" Sherman and newly elected President Hayes would be watching him closely. From the field notes he'd examined over the past few weeks, he knew he might be facing the possibility of one of the largest, full-scale Indian outbreaks in U.S. history. Reportedly two thousand strong, these Indians were organized and were growing in strength by the hour. There was mounting evidence that the Indians joining them represented practically all of the tribes in the northwest and worse, that it might be a holy war. He suspected they might be planning to unite with the Yakima Tribes to the north in Washington Territory, which lay in their present path. If the Indians crossed the Columbia River dividing Washington and Oregon, and joined with the Yakima, the flow of blood could not be stopped. There simply were not enough troops available to restrain such a large number of Hostiles. The possibility of death and carnage on such a scale would reach beyond anything the United States Government could now imagine.

Howard opened the briefing and reported the latest dispatches from his immediate commander, General Irvin McDowell, commanding the Department of the Pacific at the Presidio in San Francisco. Once he'd finished with the preliminaries, he delivered his primary concerns regarding the situation they were in. Uneasiness began to show on a few of the newly arrived younger officers' faces. Howard concluded the briefing by assigning Bernard's battalion as the point element of the column. Bernard's battalion would probe ahead at the point, keeping as prudently close to the Indians as safety allowed. He wasn't to harass or force them into any contact. That could prove fatal to the entire command. Bernard would keep Robbins' scouts in constant touch with the Hostiles' camp locations, sending updated intelligence back to Howard, who would maintain his Headquarters Staff with the wagon train. Howard turned and looked directly at Bernard. His eyes blazed at the captain as he spoke in a solemn voice to all ears listening.

"We must stop them at the Columbia River, Captain, or we'll lose them. I cannot allow that to happen." His eyes continued staring at Bernard. "You will be the command's eyes and ears. We will stay behind but not push them, because we desperately need time for reinforcements to block their advance to the north. That should take them one and a half to two weeks. I shall need you to re-group your battalion and scout the be-devil out of them. I want you to hear them if they sneeze! But, the trick is to not alarm them. If they stop to fight us now it may certainly be to their advantage. We're some distance away from a base of supply or support. If they move too quickly, then we'll flank them and try to slow them, but right now that is all we can hope for. Time, Captain, time! That's what we need!" Howard's steely eyes bore into Bernard's.

Bernard nodded solemnly "Yes, Sir. Robbins should be back soon, he's watching the Hostile band closely as we speak. The Hostiles have camped two miles up the creek and their scouts are constantly watching Robbins' men from a distance and I'm sure they know where we are." Bernard turned his head to the north. "There is a better grass and water supply a mile north of us, Sir. We'll need it badly now that you have joined us."

"Agreed," said Howard. "But make certain that we know the location and activities of the Hostiles. They will probably move when as we do, but keep me alerted to any changes." Bernard nodded. Howard turned his attention to the other officers intently listening and watching. "Gentlemen, see to your men and animals. I do not have to elaborate anything that Captain Bernard has reported to us here today. See that you are prepared for an attack upon our camp or stock herds at any moment, as the Hostiles are only a few miles distant from us and have been watching us. Prepare to sound the General (bugal call) at four a.m. I shall keep you apprised of any pertinent intelligence information the scouts should bring into camp." Quickly the officers saluted, briefly exchanging friendly greetings with each other, broke into small groups, and returned to their assigned company areas where troops and wagons were still arriving.

"Riders approaching!" shouted a sentry from his post on the south perimeter of the camp. A cloud of dust signaled the approach of a small detachment of cavalry, winding its way towards the camp. Bernard and Howard walked quickly toward the sounds of the incoming detail. Howard's eyes squinted in the bright sunlight as he buttoned his blouse with his one hand. As the patrol approached the camp's perimeter, the officer leading it raised his arm, bringing the patrol to a dusty halt at the camp's perimeter. Seeing Howard approaching, the young second lieutenant quickly straightened to attention in his saddle as he brought his hand to a salute.

"Lieutenant Wood! I trust you've had a successful scout of the battlefield?" shouted Howard, smiling.

"Yes, Sir!" responded the lieutenant, dismounting from his horse. "A successful sketch of the battleground and also a surprise, Sir!" Wood ordered the detail to dismount and return to their units. Dismounting behind him were two young Paiute women. The smaller one quickly walked to a horse carrying a very old Indian woman, so weak that she only remained on the horse by grasping onto the animal's thick main. Both women gently eased the emaciated woman, who resembled more a tattered bag of bones than a human being, from the horse and into their arms, supporting her as her feet touched the ground. The women spoke to the ancient one in low tones, a combination of song and words that the officers could not understand.

"Sarah?" greeted Howard to the older and larger woman. "Who do we have here?" The pre-occupied woman nodded to the general as she and the younger woman gently lay the old woman on the ground before them. Bernard barked an order to a sergeant standing close by. Surgeon FitzGerald was immediately summoned. Soon medical orderlies had gently carried the near dead woman to the headquarters area in a blanket. Howard's smile had abruptly vanished from his face as he awaited the response from the Indian woman he'd addressed.

The two women stood holding their horses' reins, looking at the three officers before them. "General Howard! It is good to see you," said the Paiute woman known as Sarah, brushing her long black hair from her sweaty face. "Lieutenant Wood found the old sister on the battle field, nearly dead," Sarah said to Howard, continuing to brush her hair from her face.

"Lieutenant?" questioned Howard, turning now to Wood, his adjutant.

"Sarah is correct, Sir. I was sketching the Silver Creek Battlefield as ordered when I found the old woman. When I found her I thought she was dead. I watched her for a long time before she moved, that's when I called for Sarah and Mattie. They can communicate with her and I thought she might be valuable to you if she were questioned about the Hostiles. She seems to be a member of their band. I'm surprised she's lived this long, Sir."

"Come," directed Howard courteously to the women as they began walking to the tent where Bernard had ordered the detail to take the old woman. "Sarah, did she say anything to you?"

"Yes, General Howard. The old sister is a Bannock and she says that the others left her to die on the battlefield. She also tells me that she is the aunt of Chief Buffalo Horn of the Bannocks."

"My Word! Buffalo Horn?" blurted Howard, obviously upset. He remembered Buffalo Horn when he had scouted for him the previous year, chasing Chief Joseph and his Dreamers. He recalled Buffalo Horn, who with his scouts had gone back and dug up the graves of Nez Perce corpses for their scalps. Howard was now beginning to see what he might have on his hands.

"That is what she says," continued Sarah. "She also tells me that white men far away to the east, at a place called Silver Mountain, killed her nephew Buffalo Horn, less than one moon ago. The old sister told me something else, General. She says that these Indians are Dreamers and are led by the Paiute Dreamer-Prophet Oits, and that her people, the Fort Hall Bannocks, are with them as well. The old one says that Indians are coming in from everywhere and all the tribes will soon join with them and seek the new power and medicine of the prophets. They go to meet with the great Lakota Sioux medicine man Sitting Bull who lives in the white queen's land to the north." Sarah seemed out of breath from the excitement she felt in relaying the information to her general.

Upon hearing the names of Buffalo Horn and Oits, the two officers, Wood and Bernard, standing at either side of Howard, flexed as if struck by lightning. Howard's brain shifted into another realm, as he began to analyze the escalated danger he now found himself and his command in. If the old woman were telling the truth, this was something he'd never expected and certainly something Washington was not prepared for. The possibility of fighting the tribes of the northwest! And here he sat in the middle of nowhere, facing a religious war against hardened war warriors like the Fort Hall Bannocks.

Sarah paused, taking in a breath. "General, we must take care of the old sister, she is blind and cannot see."

"Of course, Sarah, we'll care for her as well as we can here and then return her with the next detail returning to Camp Harney." Sarah nodded her thanks. There was something else. Howard could sense it.

"General?" Sarah spoke to Howard in a whisper, as she stepped closer to him. Howard stood his ground.

"What is it, Sarah?" asked Howard nearly as quietly, realizing that Sarah had something of confidential importance to share with him.

Sarah placed her mouth close to Howard's ear and whispered. "General, the old one told us that my little sister Mattie's brother Egan is also with the Dreamers, but that his heart may not be against the whites as the others are. This is what she was told by her people."

"Oits? Egan?!" muttered Howard softly to himself, turning to stare at the mountains in the distance as if he were trying to see inside the Hostile camp itself and into the brains of the two men Sarah had just mentioned. The two names struck a chord. "Sarah, you and Mattie can water your horses in the creek where you see the Army animals being watered. When you've taken care of your horses, please come to my tent and we will get you and Mattie settled. Are you hungry?" asked Howard with a smile.

"Oh, yes, General!" chimed Sarah. "Little sister Mattie and I have not eaten in quite a while. We are very hungry!"

Howard chuckled beneath his beard, "Very well, hurry back and I will have a hot meal ready for the both of you. You ladies have earned it today." He watched as the two women led their horses away. "Sarah is always hungry."

The two women led their horses through the maze of inbound faded blue Army wagon teams driven by cussing, dust-soaked infantry and artillerymen. Where the first wagons had stopped, teamsters had already unhitched the teams, cooled them down and were now leading them to water, leaving the large wagons and canvas-covered mountain howitzers behind. They seemed to be the only things not moving in the camp. The two Indian women's horses were noticeably smaller than the large Army horses around them. They were Cayuse, Indian bred. Grass eaters, not requiring grain as the Army mounts did. Sarah was dressed in a dark brown full-length skirt and a brightly colored man's shirt and was of short stature. Her rounded face housed large, dark brown eyes and full rounded lips. Her shiny black hair fell past her shoulders and was cut in a square fashion, framing her face. Her facial expression was one of concern and frustration. It shone with perspiration. Sarah's given name was "Toc-Me-To-Ne" or "Shell Woman." To the whites she was known as Sarah, daughter of the Paiute Chief Winnemucca, whom she'd just recently freed as a hostage from the clutches of the same Hostiles ahead of them. She was a paid contract interpreter for Howard, whom she trusted and thought highly of. She also had close friends and relatives amongst the Hostile bands they were following. She had very mixed feelings about this whole affair; however, the sixty-five dollars a month for her services temporarily suppressed many ambivalent feelings. Her tired, somber facial expression betrayed her age of thirty-four.

Walking beside Sarah was a much thinner and younger woman in her twenties. She wore the same style clothing as Sarah, but her long black raven hair shone bright in two braids that reached the small of her slim back. She stood taller than Sarah did. Her unusual narrow face presented high cheekbones and a small upturned nose, giving her a youthful schoolgirl look. Her dark eyes had flashed as Howard had spoken to them. Her quick smile showed a brilliant row of white teeth. Her name was Mattie and she was Sarah's sister-in-law, being married to Sarah's brother Lee. More important now was the fact that Mattie was the adopted daughter of Egan and also his sister-in-law. Egan had adopted her years ago, at the dying request of Chief Shenka her father. Egan's wife Evening Star was Mattie's older sister. That made Mattie and Egan as close as blood.

As the two women walked their horses toward the creek they gaped in wonder and disbelief at the soldiers around them, especially the small groups of soldiers sitting or lying on the ground. Some of the soldiers were wearing bloody bandages, others seemingly stared at nothing at all through wide red-rimmed eyes, detached from reality. There were "Walk-A-Heaps," or infantrymen, stacking their long Springfield rifles and unloading canvas packs from their backs with grunts of relief, then sitting where they could, waiting for the arriving wagon which contained each man's canvas shelter half and extra clothing and cooking gear. The dirty, sweating infantrymen stared at the two passing women. Some of the men grinned at them, others wore the grim expression of hardened, determined regular soldiers, which unsettled the two women as they quickened their pace to the creek. They looked straight ahead, avoiding eye contact with the sea of men encircling them, paying no attention to the crude comments made by some. Many of the soldiers had immediately started poker games and paid the two women no attention whatsoever. Once the two arrived at the now muddy creek, they had to thread their way around and through the horde of drinking Army mounts until they found a open space away from the clamor of soldiers and animals. As their horses sniffed, then noisily sucked in the cool water, the two women cautiously turned their heads back to the bustling Army camp, then turned towards the dark mountain canyons in the distance that contained their people.

Three volunteer horsemen, Robbins and two scouts, rode into the Army camp from the north. Robbins suddenly reined in his horse, looking for something. Once he'd spotted the Headquarters flag and the G Company Guidon hanging limply in the hot air, he nudged his mount, gently winding it through the throng of soldiers, who were shouting and yelling as they assembled their off-white canvas shelter-halves and ingenious lean-to's. All was organized pandemonium. The scout noticed the blue Army wagons with their dirty white canvas tops. Some were unhitched, the horses being watered at the creek. Others were still coming into camp, their dust trail seen far out onto the prairie. As they came to a stop, blue-clad infantrymen jumped down from the high wagons with a "ugh!" raising more dust for everyone's benefit. The infantrymen carried long Springfield 45-70 Trap Door rifles, and bayonets hung from their belts.

"Infantry, by God!" Robbins muttered to himself. Once arrived at the Headquarters tent, Robbins reined in his mount and swung down, removing his shotgun from its scabbard in one fluid motion. He handed the reins over to one of the two volunteer riders, who wordlessly turned and led the horses to water.

It was getting warmer as the sun slipped slowly across the powder blue sky. "Scout Robbins, Sir!" announced Lieutenent Wood, Howard's adjutant, through the opening of the command tent. Howard appeared through the tent's doorway immediately, with a broad grin as he thrust his left hand towards Robbins.

"Scout Robbins! How good it is to see you again. Please come and sit down, I'm sure you are tired, forgive the heat inside but we must speak in confidence, Sir."

"All the same, Sir, I been sittin astride that razor-backed nag of mine for the last four hours. I swear, his backbone is sharper than a mountain ridge!" Feeling the strong grip of Howard's left hand in his, the two men entered the large tent that had its door and window openings rolled up and tied, allowing some air to circulate. At the moment there was none. In the center of the tent stood a small wooden table and collapsible chairs. A bunk had been set up on one side and a worn trunk sat at its feet. One side of the trunk, in chipped white stenciling, read "O.O. HOWARD. GEN. U.S. ARMY." A coal oil lamp hung from a wooden overhead tent support. The general had removed his blue tunic, which now lay on the bunk beside his black campaign hat. White suspenders supported his blue uniform trousers. He wore boots and a white uniform shirt with a shortened and sewn right sleeve. His left sleeve was rolled to the elbow.

In the distance the choir of crows resumed its mocking litany high in the pine trees. "Caw-Caw-Caw." Upon entering the tent Robbins saw that Captain Bernard was sitting in one of the chairs, nodding to him as he entered. "Robbins, are those crows trying to tell me something?" asked Howard with a slight, nervous chuckle. His eyes were serious.

"I'd guess they'd be talkin about that crazy group what's camped north of us, General," answered Robbins. "But I don't know if they're yellin at us, or them." He looked directly at Howard through his red, dust-stung eyes.

Howard pulled a chair away from the table and sat down. His eyes stared out through the doorway into the bright shimmering sunlight. The tent's interior was getting very warm. Bernard's chair creaked as he squirmed to get comfortable. "Gentlemen," spoke Howard. "After reviewing Captain Bernard's after action-report, I believe we have a full scale Indian outbreak on our hands. For now, the newspapers haven't gotten a full understanding of what is going on here and that is just as well. Here is the way I see this. One, the Bannocks under Buffalo Horn left Fort Hall. Secondly, they split into two separate groups. One group striking mining camps and ferry crossings on the Snake River, killing and burning anything they can pitch into. The other group crossing westerly into Oregon doing the same thing. Why?" Howard kept his gaze through the open tent fly as if alone. "They stop temporarily at Steens Mountain, where they meet together and proceed west to our present position and here meet with the Paiutes, supposedly led by Oits. That may be understandable, but Egan? We now have evidence that there are also Cayuse, Umatilla, Yakima, and Shoshoni with this group, some of whom are still coming down from the north to meet these people. Why?" asked Howard. "No local Indians will scout for us as they did so vigorously during the Modoc War. Why? Too much Power they tell us. What power!" pondered Howard, face reddening.

Robbins cleared his dry throat. "We got a taste of that Power two days ago, General. They coulda, but didn't counter-attack us when they had us on the field, and later when we made a stand on the ridge. We're lucky we're not all crow bait right now!" Robbins' eyes were beginning to show fire, his forehead shone with sweat. Bernard shifted in his chair with a creak.

Bernard spoke, looking straight at Howard. "Sir, what do Sarah and Mattie have to report?"

Robbins also looked straight at Howard, shaking his head with a resigned air, then surrendered himself to a chair, sitting down with a "umph."

Howard turned to Bernard. "Sarah's family has been torn apart with this outbreak, Captain. She rescued her father and brother from these Hostiles less than a week ago, at great personal risk to her own safety." Bernard nodded acknowledgment of the affair. Robbins' expression remained unchanged, waiting.

Taking in a long breath, Howard continued. "Sarah and Mattie are closer to them than I would prefer, however, as long as they are with us they can be of no use to the Hostiles and they are presently the only means of communicating with the Hostiles should the opportunity present itself."

"General?" Robbins spoke, clearing his throat. "Could Sarah turn on us? I mean Mattie is her sister-in-law and I hear that her pappy is ol chief Egan himself, if he ain't dead yet. It just seems to me that we mite be courtin the devil himself."

Staring at Robbins in disbelief, Howard's voice suddenly arose deep and thunderous, "Scout Robbins! While you and your volunteers are a great aid to our success, I cannot and will not tolerate any questions regarding my selection of contract interpreters without cause. Every man under my command is important to our success and if you'll recall, Sir, Egan was the only Paiute chief who attempted to bring his bands into the reservation system at Malheur. And he nearly made it work. If he is with that group north of us, he just may be the only chance we have in talking with them. Only God in his wisdom knows whether or not Egan is dead or alive. Please leave Egan to him, Sir." Howard's voice softened.

Awe-struck by the unexpected intensity coming from Howard, Robbins bit his lip, trembling with pent-up frustration. Taking a deep breath, he stood slowly to full height. Bernard rose also. The two men watched each other apprehensively. "General," Robbins said in a more submissive voice, "I just come back after spendin most part of a night up there in them mountains watching at least two thousand hostile Indians dancin an makin plans to lift somebody's hair. They be dancin somethin I ain't never seen before but heard tell of a few times. It's called the Dreamers dance, I think. It's an Injun holy spirit thing. They dance till they drop and then others drag them away, talkin to em all the while. They got em a new religion of some kind, I think, and it's about killin every livin white or non-believin redskin that tries to stop it or don't believe in it." Robbins stood silent now, waiting for Howard's reply like a scolded child.

Howard arose stiffly from his chair shaking his head, eyeing Robbins. "Colonel Robbins," referring now to the scout's unofficial volunteer rank, "Let us not get off on the wrong foot, here and now especially. We need the services of each other if we are to succeed in this campaign. We must buy time for Army reinforcements to get into place to the north and east of us on the Columbia River and block these Indians from advancing any further northward." Howard's eyes flashed, his face still reddened from the recent heated exchange. "We must watch these Hostiles closely, but from a distance. I realize they grow in strength as we wait; however, once we have our commands in place we will try to pin them down and fight them on our terms. We must be the ones to choose when and where to fight them." His eyes softened. "Containment and the protection of their women and children, and those who wish to surrender is imperative. We must insure that, whenever possible, Sir."

Howard's eyes looked deeply into Robbins', who sighed and nodded head. "Will that be all, General?"

"Yes, Sir, for now, but please keep me apprised of the Indians' every move." Robbins nodded again and walked out into the bright sunlight. The fingers grasping his Winchester were white.

On June twenty-sixth, daylight broke across the mountaintops as the battalion formed into a long column. The smoke of extinguished breakfast campfires drifted off to the east. The tents and equipment had been stowed inside the narrow wagons. The cavalry formed into position at the column's front, rear and flanks protecting the mountain howitzers of the Fourth Artillery's Batteries D and G. Companies B, D, E, G, H, I, and K of the Twenty-First Infantry "walk-a heaps" marched along the center of the long column, their Springfield rifles carried or slung over shoulders. The column now consisted of nearly four hundred and eighty soldiers. From the head of the long column orders were shouted, followed by the high pitched notes of bugles. The column began its slow crawl, resembling a long, hungry serpent searching for its unseen prey. Billowing clouds of dust drifted upward into the ranks of cavalry, infantry, and artillerymen. Robbins' civilian volunteers fanned outward at the point and flanks of the column, sniffing and watching for Indian sign. General Howard rode at the head of the column. Beside him rode Sarah and Mattie. Behind rode Lieutenant Wood and the rest of Howard's staff. Robbins' scouts reported that the Hostiles had broken camp and had moved several miles further north into the mountains and were encamped in the heavy timber high above the deep canyon of Silver Creek. The column would move only one mile today, taking it easy, not wanting to bother the Indians or alarm them. Robbins' scouts had reported a wide grassy meadow just ahead of them that promised a good camping spot. The command needed the advantage of water and grass to fill the bellies of their horses with nourishing bulk, saving their precious grain for the hard work and the possibility of little grass or time in the days ahead.

Two hours later found the column making camp. Tents were going up and wood and water details were busily moving throughout the campsite. Out on the large grassy meadow divided in its center by the creek, scattered bands of closely guarded Army horses grazed peacefully. The individual herds of dark and gray colored horses crept slowly, devouring the fresh grass. Each band of horses belonged to its own company or battery. An officer assigned to the grazing detail directed each group of horses from camp. Through field glasses he watched the movement of the herds. Periodically he issued instructions to a signalman at his side, who quickly waved a colored signal flag. Upon seeing the signal, the officer in charge of the herd would issue orders to the corporals or sergeants guarding the horses and the herd would be moved. If the signal officer wished a band of horses to pull in closer to the main band of horses, a signal was given and the band was moved closer to the main herd by its detail. This was necessary in such a large meadow with so many animals. It also created better security, insuring that a herd didn't stray too far away, allowing them to be attacked.

Howard sounded Officer's Call. Officers quickly came from every direction to his Headquarters tent. In front of the tent sat a table with Wood, pen and paper ready. Once the officers were assembled, Howard allowed them to sit down upon the grass if they desired. A few stood. The officers' low chatter and murmurs quickly ended when Howard cleared his throat. Robbins stood off to Howard's left, looking worried. The taunting crows from the day before were conspicuously absent. Captain Bernard stood among the officers in the first row.

"Gentlemen," opened Howard. "As you know we've marched to this location in order to take advantage of its abundance of grass and water before we begin our advance in earnest. Robbins' scouts tell me that the Hostiles have moved several miles further into the mountains. I believe that they are preparing to depart from this location and begin their advance. I believe that this band is fueled by a religious energy that we have not seen before, and one that is highly dangerous to anyone before it or behind it. We still have not identified it clearly, but we are endeavoring to find that answer. Our command is stronger now and the enemy will be less inclined to attack us. But if they should, I must tell you that they will be a formidable foe. Captain Bernard can attest to that. They possess a power that is highly unusual. In spite of all this, we are going to begin following them as they move before us. Company commanders will personally check their men and equipment. Post your herd guards well and apply hobbles one half hour before sundown. The Hostiles may try to attack the horse herd tonight, so be alert. Support forces are now moving towards the Columbia River to our north to block the Hostiles' approach from the south, and we have increasing support arriving from the east. We will move as the enemy moves, at its own speed of march if possible. Buying time is of the essence in order to prevent the Hostiles from gaining the Columbia River before our support forces are in position."

Howard cleared his throat before continuing. "Gentlemen, we are in for a long and hard campaign. I believe that these Indians are heading northward to join with the Yakima Tribe to our north across the Columbia River, and then to meet with the Sioux Chief Sitting Bull in Canada, which, as you recall, the Nez Perce tried to do last year. Most of you know how difficult that campaign was. Well, I believe that this one will be as hard or harder because of the difficult terrain ahead of us. I will ask for all of the devotion and energy that you can muster from yourselves and your men. If you can do this, then with the grace of God we will succeed. In conclusion, I must add that in all cases of encounters with these people the safety of non-combatants must be insured. Are there any questions?" No hands were raised. "Then God go with you." After a moment of silence the officers saluted their commander and returned to their companies. Howard turned to Robbins, who nodded in approval. Wood dropped his pen and, neatly folding the note pages, placed them in a leather dispatch case. Howard entered the warming interior of the tent, drawing the flaps closed behind him. He dropped to his knees before his bunk and silently began to pray. Outside, Wood nervously looked at the closed tent flaps as he finished securing the dispatch case.

A dull half moon had risen in the black sky, casting dark shadows across the meadow where the Army horses were grazing. Their dark, hobbled forms speckled the scene in the moonlight, merging and emerging within the shadows in the meadow. The occasional movement of a horse head rising with a mouthful of grass could be made out in the half-darkness. The dull ripping sound of teeth tearing and chomping the tall grass was the only sound save the low, lonely humming of a soldier as he rode amongst horses. Soothingly he sang, "Good bye ol Paint, I'm a leavin Cheyenne, I'm a leavin Cheyenne, I'm goin to Montan." Extinguished cooking fires sent curling columns of smoke into the black sky as air currents caught them and pushed them out into the horse-filled meadow, catching the nostrils of the slow riding troopers as they gently wove through and around the herds of horses. The guards routinely met and passed each other as they completed each circling perimeter patrol.

"Sarge, is that you?" whispered a trooper as he and another other rider approached each other in the darkness. No response. From the pitch black timber at the edge of the meadow came a low wailing coyote call, startling the private, causing him to instinctively rein in his mount. Another chilling coyote call broke the night, resonating from the darkness at the north end of the meadow. The private turned his head quickly in the direction of the second call. Nothing but darkness. A low rumble instantly traversed the moonlit meadow as the now spooked horses nervously began to mill.

Something was wrong. The big Army horses sensed it. The private blurted "What the hell?" as he turned his attention back to the approaching rider. Something hissed past his right ear, making him reflex. Instantly something thudded into flesh and a horse screamed behind him in the darkness. Things rolled in slow motion as the private shouted, "Sergeant of the guard!" The other rider screamed a war cry not fifteen feet from him in the darkness, drowning his voice out, followed by the blinding flash and roar of a revolver in the trooper's face, stunning and blinding him.

Another shot roared as a another bullet snapped past the private's head, this one so close he felt the heat of the deadly missile. The trooper struggled with his mount as he tried to draw his own revolver from its holster while fighting to control the terrified horse. Another war cry ripped the night, followed by a crashing sickly thud as the charging Indian's pony collided straight into the flash-blinded trooper, knocking him from his shocked and frightened mount like a rag doll. The trooper was slammed to the ground with a "Ugh!" knocking his breath away. Paiute Warrior Whisker screamed and galloped his pony through the frightened and confused Army horse herds, waving his blanket, whistling and snapping over his head as he tried to stampede the animals. Bugle calls split the night air as "Boots and Saddles" rang from the camp, accompanied by shouted commands within the confusion. There was little firing from the meadow because few targets could be identified. As quickly as they'd attacked, the Indian raiders disappeared into the darkness like ghostly phantoms. Lights flickered, then sparked to life in the camp as lanterns were lit. Details galloped toward the meadow.

The trooper sat on a stump holding a towel to his bleeding nose. Surgeon FitzGerald stepped back, admiring his work in the dim lanternlight. "He's all right, just a little worse for wear," he said, grinning. "You still have your scalp, Son, and that is more than some have these days." FitzGerald turned from the trooper, walking into the darkness to treat others. His aid stumbled along behind, holding a lantern aloft.

"Report, Captain!" ordered Howard to Bernard, who stood before him out of breath.

"A horse raid, Sir, unsuccessful, with few injuries reported. No mounts lost." He re-holstered his revolver. He stood in his undershirt, suspenders hanging down the sides of his trousers. "I've posted additional guards for the night, Sir!"

"Very good, Captain, have the column form at four-thirty a.m. Are you ready, Reuben?" asked Howard.

"I was born ready, Sir!" responded Bernard, saluting tiredly. "With your permission, Sir, I'll call it a night."

Howard returned the salute. "Good night, Captain." He pulled his pocket watch from his vest and snapping it open, tilted the watch towards the yellow light coming from the lantern hanging from his tent beam. "Eleven-thirty." He snapped the watch cover closed and stood looking out into the darkness of the mountains. He prayed silently to himself, "God, prepare us for that which is to come." Wearied, he entered the tent and closed the tent flaps behind him. As he closed his eyes, trying to sleep, his thoughts were anything but peaceful. They were mixed with the faces of frightened soldiers and of his wife, Lizzie, and, their daughter, Grace, who had four days ago celebrated her twenty-first birthday. He hadn't been there; it hurt him to think of it. She'd have missed her "Papa," but the Army had come between them again. He felt it more these days. The twisted and bloodied faces of wounded and dead soldiers that he'd seen during his career swarmed around and through the faces of his family, causing a shudder in the darkness of the tent. A troubled sleep came slowly.

Miles to the north in the darkness stood a large clearing on the banks of Silver Creek. Giant bonfires were crackling and popping, shooting large, brightly burning yellow and red sparks and embers into the black starlit sky. The chilling combination of flickering light and shadows was accented by the thundering drums and high-pitched singing of warriors and women, as they danced in unison left to right. The steps were simple and stately. Scarcely lifting the left foot from the ground, it was advanced a step, with the right foot following into its spot, in unison with the song. Slowly the ring of dancers revolved, circling left to right. Eagle feathers worn by warriors fluttered from the rhythmic dancing and the heated currents of air from the fires as they met the cold night air. Singing and chanting voices shattered the solitude of the pine trees and dark mountains surrounding them.

"Dombi'Na so'wina', Dombi'Na so'wina', Dombi'Na so'wina', Kai'-va so'wina', Kai'-va so'wina', Kai'-va so'wina."

The rocks are ringing...
The rocks are ringing...
The rocks are ringing...
They are ringing in the mountains...
They are ringing in the mountains...
They are ringing in the mountains...
The snowy earth comes sliding!

Shrill voices sang towards the heavens, singing down the deadly storm of their power upon their enemies, white and red. The thunderclap "k-Bang, k-Bang" of the drummers echoed out into the darkness and downward into the deep canyons beneath them. Frequently, a dancer would collapse from exhaustion. The messages from the spirits of the dead would give them counsel and direction.

At the edge of the clearing, amongst the other lodges, stood the huge Medicine Lodge where an important counsel was being held. Inside the lodge the only light was a brightly burning council fire at the center. Encircling the fire on robes and blankets sat the war chiefs. From the Bannock Tribe were Bannock Joe, Big John, War Jack, Boss, and Ploqua. The two main Northern Paiute bands led by Oits and Egan were represented. The Oits band included Oits, Surger, Whisker, George Oits, Wa-Ah-Gah, George Pony, and Paulina. Egan's band and two sub-bands were represented. Supported by a wood and rawhide backrest with his wounded arm wrapped in a sling, lay Egan. To his left and right sat the sub-chiefs of his Paiute bands: Patch, Wad Jah, Siwash, Jake Springer, Hoo-Doo, Doctor Johnson, Fort Hall Jim, Wahzee-Twenty-Battle, Sergeant and Widow. Behind Egan stood his son Honey, rifle ready beneath his blanket. Standing in the dark shadows to the rear of the chiefs and sub-chiefs were warriors from the various other tribes, filling the lodge to capacity. The pungent smell of sweating bodies mingling with acrid tobacco smoke, dried blood, and the smoke from the council fire made the lodge uncomfortable and stifling. The occasional metallic glint of a rifle barrel flashed amongst those standing in the shadows. Faces were solemn and determined beneath bright paint. Unhealed wounds lay hidden by clothing and blankets.

Egan's eyes shown brightly through his fever as he cleared the phlegm from his throat. "I am pleased that none of our men were lost in the horse raid against the soldiers." A murmured agreement rumbled around the lodge. Oits sat staring at Egan. "I do not wish to see any more Numa (people) lost. I have seen too many Numa walking away on Gosi'pa (The Milky Way, Road of the Dead). We have shown the bad agent Rinehart that we have power to resist and will use it again, if necessary. I am told that the Army Chief Howard is here now with many Taivo (white man) soldiers. He brings with him

Walk-a-Heaps (infantry) with their long rifles. He also has brought the large wheel guns that can bring Takwu'kwij (lightening) down on us." Egan's chest trembled as he drew in a long painful breath. "I do not believe the soldier Chief Howard has seen the Nanigukwa (Ghost Dance) but he will hate it." Oits' eyes narrowed, his mouth sneering like an angry wolf as Egan continued. "I say this. We should ask for a talk and smoke with the Soldier Chief Howard. He has always been fair with the Numa and will listen to us if we speak the truth to him." Egan wheezed weakly, his face glistening in the flickering light of the lodge fire. He winced with pain and closed his eyes.

War Jack stood up. He was strong and stocky as a bull. Shedding his blanket, he proudly showed his war scars and paints in the vibrating firelight. Another low murmur coursed through the lodge. War Jack turned slowly as he spoke, so that all in the lodge might hear him. "Paiute brothers! We whipped the blue coats. Did no one see it? My warriors and I saw it! Have the blue coats attacked us again? I have not seen it! Have you? They have felt the sting of our bullets and arrows. They have felt the power of the prophets and dare not attack us, even with more soldiers. They are women; their drying scalps hanging from our pony's manes prove it. They are afraid of our medicine! We can take the old war trails through this country to the north with the aid of our Paiute Brothers who fought with us bravely today. The great queen mother's red-coated pony soldiers will protect us from the white father's blue coats. But, we must first fight our way to join our Yakima Brothers across the Great River. Then we will be too many and powerful for any blue coats that we come across. Our way must be one of destruction and death as it has been done to us by the white settlers that push us out! The great prophet Smohalla says that this must be the way!" A rumble of agreement reverberated throughout the circle. War Jack sat down, glaring into Oits' dark beady eyes, as he drew his blanket over his shoulders. More dried twigs were added to the fire, creating sparks and smoke that spiraled upward and exited the vents of the large teepee into the night sky.

Oits rested his eyes on the ceremonial pipe lying across his lap. The pipe was thirty inches long. It had a spiral hide wrapping on the stem. Black horsehair was inset into the center, with six human teeth. Golden eagle feathers and small carved, wooden half moons and stars dangled from its bowl. Oits reverently picked up the pipe. All eyes in the lodge were on him. The drumming and singing outside seemed to grow in intensity. The Pipe Bundle contained sacred articles, the fetus of a deer and bird and squirrel skins. He withdrew a small tobacco pouch. With three fingers he took a large pinch of tobacco and carefully filled the pipe bowl. The tobacco contained a mixture of sumac leaves and the dried inner bark of dogwood, which made a pleasant-smelling combination, called "Kinnikinnick." With a forked stick he carefully withdrew a hot ember from the fire and lit the pipe. He exhaled a puff of smoke upwards, extending the pipe stem toward heaven in a prayer to God, then pointed it to each of the four winds. He then passed the pipe to Surger on his left, who repeated the procedure until the pipe had gone around the circle, returning to Oits. Oits tamped the pipe ashes into the fire and solemnly returned the pipe to its bundle, wrapping it in a beaded-fringed bag. He began to hum a low song, swaying back and forth as he drew his blanket over his head. The drumming and singing outside penetrated the lodge.

Oits carefully picked up the Pipe Bundle and stood, keeping the blanket wrapped over his head. He held out the Bundle, offering it to War Jack, who stood and accepted it. Accepting the Bundle made War Jack the Pipe Holder, or co-leader of the entire band of Dreamers.

Egan's eyes were open now, wide and disbelieving. He didn't speak. He felt the sudden tenseness among his warriors sitting to his left and right. He could have handled Oits by himself, but War Jack was something entirely different. Honey was noticeably surprised and angry, standing behind his father. With War Jack leading the Fort Hall Bannocks and Shoshoni as well as carrying the pipe for the Paiute, it was like signing a death warrant for anyone wanting to leave the group of Indians.

Oits let his blanket drop to his shoulders, looking upward to where the smoke drifted outward into the night. He began to sway back and forth in the flickering firelight of the lodge, his feet silently lifting and dropping in unison with the drumming and singing outside.

"The Rocks are ringing! The Rocks are ringing!" he cried, "See the snowy earth come sliding! Oits the Prophet sees the white man sliding from the earth. Hear the rocks are ringing as they see the snowy mantle glide from the earth!" His voice rose to the top of the highest lodgepoles, as others joined in. Soon war whoops shattered the enclosure with a deafening sound. Rifle barrels shone in the firelight.

Unnoticed amongst the chanting warriors of the lodge, Umapine the Umatilla grined slyly to himself. His teeth shone brightly in the low, flickering light. The time would come when he would enact his revenge on Egan for an old grudge that could be satisfied only in blood, one that he hoped Egan had forgotten. When the time was right he would strike. But for now, he would show only obedience and friendship towards the wounded Paiute Chief. Besides, the thought of getting rich on stolen settlers' horses appealed to him.

Only Egan and his warriors seemed less than enthusiastic about what had happened. Egan shivered, thinking about his family and the others. They were trapped. His heart

77

sank, re-fueling his growing hatred for Oits. For now though, he and his bands must go along until the time was right. To move now could be fatal to all of his people. He had to get his strength back.

After the council had terminated, the warriors returned to their wikiups or joined in the dancing and singing. Charley and Honey carried Egan to his wikiup. He was exhausted and his wounds showed fresh signs of bleeding through the dirty bandages. Hours after Honey and Charley had returned Egan to his wikiup, the moon was long gone, leaving only the stars blinking in the dark late night sky, when a sound outside awoke the old one.

Silently, the Old Woman crawled on all fours to the entrance to the lodge. Evening Star suddenly stirred from a light sleep. Her body instinctively froze in her position beside her husband. Something was wrong. She quickly reached upward beneath the blankets as her fingers gripped the handle of her razor sharp Green River skinning knife. Without a sound she quietly slid it from its leather scabbard. She then lay back like a rattlesnake, coiled to strike. She watched as the Old One poked her long bony nose out of the door flap into the cold morning air. Her wrinkled nose raised upward, sniffing for any scent of intruders, as she'd seen badgers do. Suddenly the Old Woman cackled to herself in a toothless grin and scampered backwards across the lodge floor in the dim light. Bringing her crinkled mouth to Evening Star's ear she whispered loudly enough for everyone in the wikiup to hear, waking the slumbering girls. "A daughter comes with medicine tonight," she spoke through her two remaining teeth. Egan moved slightly from his deep sleep, slipping back into unconsciousness again. All was dark in the early morning sky.

"Old One?" came a deep male whisper from outside the wikiup. Instantly Evening Star and the Old Woman were at the lodge entrance, skinning knives in hand. It was Charley. The door flap was pulled back carefully and Mattie entered the lodge swiftly, followed by Sarah. Both carried baskets and full, Army marked ration sacks. Blankets covered their heads. The Old Woman retreated to the rear of the lodge, her two teeth showing through a wide grin. The two girls sat upright and scrambled from their blankets to see the visitors. They smiled when they saw Mattie and Sarah. Charley and Honey remained close outside in the darkness, guarding with the others. Sarah and Mattie quickly removed the blankets covering their heads. Hushed greetings and tears of joy were exchanged among the women as they squatted down beside Egan, hurriedly opening the containers they'd brought with them. Mattie began to sing just above a whisper as she removed the bloody dressings from Egan's wounds. He stirred and groaning, opened his eyes. His eyes focused on the two women and he tried to rise. Gentle hands pushed him back.

"Father, do not speak, rest and let us help you." Sarah gently moistened the dirty rags and slowly peeled them off. Egan grimaced. Once the rags were removed and the shot wounds were cleaned, she produced a powdery substance and carefully applied it to the wounds. Clean bandages were then placed over the wounds and the arm gently re-wrapped in a sling with the assistance of the Old Woman and Evening Star. The two younger girls watched from across the lodge with stoic faces. Removing the cork from a tiny glass medicine bottle, Sarah placed it to Egan's lips. "Drink this," she ordered. Egan weakly sipped the liquid from the bottle. He choked upon it, but got it down.

"Good," Sarah said with a sigh, looking at the Old Woman and Evening Star. "Give him a small amount from the bottle each morning and night. Clean his wounds once each day and apply the powder each time. Cover the wounds with the clean bandages that I leave with you and keep the bandages dry."

"We must go now or we will be discovered," whispered Mattie to the Old Woman, smiling at her as she gently squeezed her bony arm. "We will be back when we can. The medicine is from General Howard. Tell my father that I love him and will come to him as I can."

"Thank you," whispered Evening Star through silent tears, as she quickly hugged the two women who had risked their lives to aid them, wishing she had the time to ask her many questions of them. Both women grasped the aged bony hand of the Old One. Suddenly, they were gone as swiftly and quietly as they had come.

The dawn on Thursday the twenty-seventh began with a steel gray overcast and a cold rain drizzling on the moving Army wagon train. Robbins and several Army scouts continued their probing of the mountains ahead of them while Captain Bernard rode the point. Scouts had reported the Indians had broken their camp and were traveling northward in the deep winding canyon of Silver Creek. After the wagon train had traveled for an hour, the road disappeared, leaving the train on its own for direction. Howard turned the column to the northeast, leaving the canyon floor and beginning the slow ascent upward into the mountains, crawling from one ridge to another as the wagons and artillery began to mire down in the mud in the narrow canyon bottom. It promised to be a long, hard day for man and beast. Wagons were mired in the mud on the sidehills and slid sideways in the red sticky clay on the steep hills. The animals fared no better in their traces. Infantrymen's shoes and boots were soon covered with the sticky goo, making even walking difficult. Cursing, they marched alongside the wagons as they coursed their way over the hills in the cold drizzle. Toward late afternoon a shout was heard from the rearguard of the column far below Howard's position at the front. Howard brought his binoculars to his eyes quickly.

A bright red and white Guidon appeared out of a stand of timber that they'd passed through earlier. The shrill sound of a cavalry trumpet reached Howard's ears, as a cavalry troop came into view, heading upwards along the column towards Howard. It was Company K. Over thirty minutes passed before the hard breathing mounts and their riders reached Howard. A rain-soaked Army captain straightened in his McClellan saddle and saluted a smiling Howard. "Captain Bendire reporting, Sir," said the weary officer, returning Howard's smile. Condensation steamed from horse and rider, making them appear as if they were smoldering from a fire.

"My compliments, Captain, on your endeavor to locate us in this difficult country. You and your men are desperately needed here. Did you see any Hostiles on your way, Sir?" questioned Howard.

"No, Sir," responded Bendire, twisting stiffly in his saddle. "We made a forced march to get here, the only sign we saw was on the battlefield below and your recent camp." Bendire's eyes spoke as they scanned the long column with cavalry wounded. "It looks like Bernard had a go at them, Sir," the young officer addressed Howard.

Howard nodded. "I want you to join Captain Bernard's battalion at the point of the column, Charles. And take it slowly, save your mounts. They are about played out." Bendire nodded, saluting. His Army saddled creaked as he twisted, facing his Company K troopers and waving them forward.

Howard carefully eyed the horses and men of Bendire's company as they passed him. "It's a wonder they can carry anything at all, let alone riders," he thought, as he turned his attention back to his column.

At the end of the day, the last daylight was slowly fading in the west as tents and shelters were set up; since they were close to the enemy only small ground fires were permitted. They were built in holes deep enough to hide open flames. Everyone and everything was soaked. It had rained all that day during the tortuous climb into the mountains. The temperature had dropped to forty-two degrees and had made men and animals miserable. They had marched thirty long miles. Amongst a small group of A, Company First Cavalry troopers, huddled in the darkness around the nearly ineffective, but welcome fires, sat privates and non-coms, sipping hot coffee from fire-blackened U.S. stamped canteen cups. Tired, dirty hands wrapped around the hot tin cups for warmth, some trembling from the cold and dampness. First Sergeant Richard Barrett sat with his back to the west, where in the blackness far below ran Silver Creek. From his favorite briar pipe he thoughtfully inhaled the sweet and mellow smoke of his special order "Pure Yellow Bank" tobacco, allowing the smoke to mingle with the wet mist surrounding them. The small fire spread a red hue to his already sunburned face.

"First Sergeant?" came from a private among the group, the youthful voice trembling slightly. No answer came except a quick glance from the wolf eyes of the first sergeant, boring into those of the private. Barrett's eyes softened as he nodded. The private cleared his throat, as if addressing the Lord himself. "Sergeant Barrett, what do you think the chances are of us catching up with em?"

Barrett stared back into the flickering fire, as if he'd never heard the question. A puff of smoke slowly exited his lips, drifting upwards, then abruptly vanished in a cold breeze. He drew a long breath, slowly let it out in almost a sigh. "Well, Son, I'd say about the same chance lightening has of striking a shithouse as a castle." Silence, then laughter burst amongst the group. Another private slapped the trooper on the back with a guffaw, his teeth shining with a grin in the low firelight. Suddenly a driving rain began, driving swearing soldiers beneath their ponchos and blankets. It was going to be another long, cold night.

The command awoke at four a.m. the following morning, the twenty-eighth. It was Friday to the outside world, but to the Army it was waking up under a mantle of white snow. Curses burst along the rows of tents and shelters as puffs of snow erupted from awakening soldiers. Artillerymen poked their heads out into the snow-covered darkness from beneath canvas shelters, which had been laid over the cannons, making a rather comfortable, but airy shelter. "Shit" seemed to be the word of the moment. Small cooking fires were quickly started and within the hour the trumpeters sounded the "General," ordering the command to strike tents and prepare to start the day's march. Dark muddy trails in the snow showed where the scouts had left the column much earlier in the misty darkness. Snowflakes fell as fog-laden snow squalls passed across the mountain sides, reducing vision to fifty yards, then alternating with blue skies and clear vision. The command began its trek in the snowstorm. The thermometer hovered in the low thirties. Men shivered beneath their rubberized ponchos and blankets. The wagons being pulled by oxen faired better in the freezing slush, due to the animals' larger and more powerful legs and hooves. The poor Army horse teams stumbled and slid over the hills and hogbacks as they wove back and forth through the mountains, slowly gaining altitude.

Two miles ahead of the crawling train, F Company had dismounted and was adjusting its mounts cinch straps. The troopers in their black rubberized ponchos resembled swaggering bats as they fussed over their horses. Clouds of condensation steamed upward from the mounts and the breathe of the men. Most of them looked around nervously as they worked with stiffened fingers. Snowflakes drifted amongst them, landing on hats and faces, some hanging onto the long eyelashes of the horses as they stared, eyes and ears pointing downward into the gray fog and mist-shrouded canyon far below. Occasionally, an Army horse would whinny, the sound echoing into the canyon's mist. The animals sensed the invisible horses and riders traveling in the same direction in the creek bottom far below them. They smelled Indians. Captain Bernard stood on a rock ledge looking through his field glasses into the snowy mist below them. "They're down there, but how far are they ahead of us? Damn this weather, luck seems to be with them." Lieutenant Bomus stood to Bernard's right, also glassing the fog. Suddenly, Bernard's head shot to the front and he raised his arm. The bugler quickly trotted to Bernard's side. The sound of carbines and revolvers being brought close at hand sounded throughout the company of alerted troopers. No one moved. Through the snowy veil to their front came the sounds of shod horses, kicking rocks and shale as they came closer. Suddenly, the noise stopped. The only sound was that of heavy breathing of horses and men.

"Ha-Loooo, Army!" came a voice from the misty curtain before them. It was Robbins and a scout.

Bernard let out a sigh, "Come on, Robbins," he shouted. The two riders appeared out of the mist, riding towards Bernard.

Robbins spoke first through a grin. "Cap'n, how goes the hunt?" He spit tobacco juice into the snow at his horse's feet, then dismounted stiffly, dropping his horse's reins into the snowy slush.

"Can't see much in this damned pea soup," Bernard said, returning his field glasses to their leather carrier.

Robbins depressed a nostril with a finger and blew his nose into the snow, at the same time pulling a dirty rag from his back pocket and wiping the cleared appendage. "Damndest weather I ever did see this time of year!" he growled, looking around them at the surrounding grayness and snowflakes. Bernard stared into Robbins' face, patiently waiting for any news. Robbins withdrew a plug of "Old Horseshoe" chewing tobacco, not wavering from his stare now into the fog to the west, concentrating on something unseen beneath its gray cloak. He thrust his hand and the tobacco towards Bernard, who declined by shaking his head. The chew was returned to its pocket. "I cut their trail a few miles in front of us bout two hour ago, Cap'n."

"My God!" Bernard whispered, out of earshot from the others. "Do you mean they are in <u>front</u> of us, and not down in that canyon!"

"<u>They are </u>in front of us, Cap'n. They came out of the creek bottom sometime yesterday, as I figure it. They come up here and camped right in front of us last night. It looks like they broke camp and then returned to the canyon bout daylight. They left a good-sized trail goin back down, still ain't afeared of us. I'd recommend their old campsite to the General; it's well protected. And Cap'n?"

"Yes," answered Bernard.

"Well, Sir, I ain't never been lost in my life, no-sir, but there was a few times that I was powerful confused for a week or two. I got to admit it now. This is one of those times."

Bernard nodded. "Lieutenant Ward!" Ward strode quickly to Bernard. "Ride back to the column and tell General Howard with my compliments that he'll be entering the evening campsite in about two hours. Guide the column directly two miles from this position to the north. We'll be waiting for you there."

"Yessir!" saluted Ward. He mounted up and selected three troopers to accompany him. Within seconds they disappeared into the wall of fog and slowly falling snow.

That evening, after the cooking fires had finished heating the meal of salt pork, hard tack, and coffee, everyone was cold and wet. Nearly all of the men not on details or guard duty were rolling into their bedrolls. It was too cold to sleep. They'd only covered thirteen miles. The wagon train had made its night camp at the site of the recently abandoned Indian camp. Signs seemed to be everywhere.

"Sir?" Lieutenant Wood's voice called outside of Howard's tent doorway.

"What is it, Lieutenant?" Howard spoke as he exited the tent, buttoning his coat.

"Scout Robbins would like you to see something, Sir," said Wood as he led the way, holding a glowing lantern in the foggy night air. The two men walked to where a scout was seen holding a burning firebrand, giving off a low flickering ghostly light in the darkness. Howard pushed his way through the small group of soldiers and scouts as he approached Robbins. All were staring at a small altar, fashioned from wood and rawhide, sitting upon a fallen tree stump. A bow of bent sticks rested in the center.

Attached to the inside of the circle, stretched by rawhide strips, hung a human scalp. The hair was a light brown in color and fresh, not having dried.

"It's white, Sir," Robbins said to Howard, his own eyes transfixed on the object. "I'd have to guess it's Scout Meyers'. That was his hair color and its age is about right. I believe it's a message, Sir, warning us not to follow them."

"Please bury it, Gentlemen, we must respect the remains," said Howard sadly, closing his eyes briefly, then turning to walk back to his tent. Wood's lantern glowed eerily as the two forms disappeared, enshrouded in snowy darkness.

In Howard's tent sat Robbins, captains Bernard, McGregor, Bendire, and Whipple, and Lieutenant Ward of the First Cavalry. Captain Rodney, Lieutenant Chapin of the Fourth Artillery, and captains Spurgin, Downey, and Boyle, plus lieutenants Farrow, Haughey, and Cornman of the Twenty-First Infantry were also present. Bernard had just finished reporting that he had seen fresh pony tracks in the canyon below them, first coming toward him, then abruptly turning back, during a brief scout that afternoon.

Howard spoke. "This is where we stand at this time, Gentlemen. Mr. Robbins, my compliments to you and your men for staying up with the Hostiles. Do you have anything to add to Captain Bernard's report?"

Robbins cleared his throat. "Well, General, the size of their abandoned camp across the way there looks like it held from fifteen hundred to two thousand Hostiles all right. Most of the inner tree bark has been removed as high up as a man can reach. They're plannin fer a long trip. They're storin up. They smelled the snow comin last night and headed back down into the canyon before it got here. They'll go out that way, through that mountain range to the north. For now I think all we can do is keep in touch with em and follow em. I hope this weather breaks for us."

Howard nodded in agreement, turning to Captain Bernard. "Captain Bernard will leave camp momentarily with his battalion and camp as far away from us as he safely can in this darkness. It will conceal his exit from camp. He will, at the safest moment, drop down into the creek bottom below us and to the rear of the Hostiles, following them at a safe distance. I'm not comfortable with the idea, so please keep me regularly informed as to your location as well as that of the Hostiles." Bernard nodded in affirmation. "I will try to locate a crossing at the divide," continued Howard, "and I will join you as soon as possible. God willing, I will remain only one to two days to your rear until we meet. Hopefully, you and your animals can subsist on short rations until you reach the John Day River, where supplies are coming from Boise City. I will rendezvous with you at the river, or shortly beyond. God speed, Gentlemen!" concluded Howard, as he and the officers exchanged salutes. The officers exited the tent, into the drizzling cold.

The next day proved to be a repeat of the former one. They were cold, wet, and lost. The long column slowly crawled and zigzagged its way northward in the pink-blue dawn towards the distant summit, climbing from ridge to ridge. Howard had to guess as to where a summit crossing might be in this world of cliffs, jagged rocks, precipitous slopes, and deep canyons in a place where the distance from a crest to the mountain stream that tumbled over the rocks far below was sometimes four of five miles. He tried to keep his fears from showing to his men. He prayed.

"It is estimated that the whole force of the savage warriors numbers 2,000; 103 camp fires were counted. The Indians will be pursued, and there is every prospect of a protracted campaign. The Stein Mountain country is well adapted for defensive operations."

The (Pendleton) East Oregonian, Saturday, July 6, 1878.

From Canyon City.
Indians all around the Place- -Fighting for Three days.
Following is an extract from a letter from Mr. E.E. Turk to C.B. Bellinger, Esq:

Canyon City, July 1, 2 a.m.
"I have just returned from carrying dispatches to Col. Grover's command. Everything is disorganized; Indians all around us. Carrie and the children are in tunnel taking care of the wounded. We have been fighting for the last three days. Can't tell how many are killed. We know of eleven of our men. I have been in the saddle for three nights. All the business houses are closed. Fighting and burning – Oliver Aldrich killed and E. Schults wounded.

The Sunday Oregonian, Saturday, July 6, 1878.

Chapter 3

Ranchers and Wolves

Saturday, the twenty-ninth, found the forward scouts of the marching Indians riding downward into the deep canyon of the South Fork of the John Day River, far to the north of Howard and the Army wagon train. They had easily passed through the mountain range during the night, leaving behind the main column of Indians riding through the deep canyon of Silver Creek.

In the semi-darkness Oits and War Jack stood as motionless as the canyon walls surrounding them. The only sound was the cold, swift water of the South Fork. Nearly invisible in the murky darkness, two stealthy figures wearing wolf-headdresses, sitting astride their Cayuse ponies, were approaching them.

"Ho! War Jack!" smiled Paddy Cap, through his painted face and white teeth. "The way is clear in this canyon, until you get to the white man's lodges at its mouth. The white men have taken their families from their lodges to the city in fear of our power! He leaves cowards to watch his lodges!" The two chiefs' teeth gleamed, grinning like hungry wolves. War Jack twisted on his pony, raising his open hand to the side of his face. A coyote bark drifted up the draw behind them. Instantly, where there had been none, sixty warriors emerged from the shadows. Two assistants carrying long crooked wooden staffs wrapped in animal fur were selected to help lead the advancing war party. They instantly disappeared into the dusky ravines and coulees, heading northward in the blue-gray darkness.

To the north in the canyon of Murderer's Creek, above where the small flowing creek enters the South Fork of the John Day River, thirteen civilian volunteers from Canyon City to the northeast, sat shivering around a fire. The aroma of coffee and cigarette smoke hung in the cold air. The rippling sound of Murderer's Creek over-rode their voices, requiring them to talk louder than usual, betraying their presence to anyone in the area. Some were nursing sore heads from their rowdy send off from one of the saloons in Canyon City the night before. They'd left Canyon City near midnight. The men mused about the proud speeches and the friendly slaps on their backs when they had volunteered to leave town and verify the reports of Indians coming from the south. In the saloon, a grizzled old miner had slugged down a shot glass of whisky and slammed the empty glass on the bar, staring into the large glass bar mirror which reflected the faces of the other men at the bar around him. He wiped his walrus mustache clean with his fingers. "Boys, I've been trappin and minin in these here parts since the sixties and I'll tell you all right here and now, if there're Injuns comin from the south they'd be followin their old trail, pushin right-smack-dab down the South Fork!" Those around him stopped their banter for the moment and nervously eyed each other. The bartender poured another shot of rye whiskey. A general murmur of agreement flowed through the saloon crowd. Someone shouted, "Who wants to volunteer?"

"Damn it's cold!" growled Bert Williams, as he thrust his left hand closer towards the small fire on Murderer's Creek, his coffee in his right. Gray daylight had begun to show on the high rocks above the canyon.

"Hurry up!" mumbled Frank Aldrich at the sunrise, shivering beneath his coat. The glowing flame from his hand-rolled "Bull Durham" cigarette reflected upon his cheeks.

"I don't think they're comin!" blurted Joe Burnham. "I don't think there's an Injun within fifty miles. Hell, they're probably sleepin in warm blankets inside a warm teepee with a hot squaw where we otta be!"

"Spek-so," agreed Bob Hall, watching the condensation from his breath in the cold morning air. The creek gurgled and rippled in the darkness.

Jim Clark stood up stiffly, tossing the remaining coffee from his cup into the fire. The "hiss" of ashes and steam plunged the scene into semi-darkness. "Well, let's git, we got a ways to go to the Stewart place, maybe Grandma Stewart left us some johnny cakes before she left," he said, chuckling. The others followed Clark, finishing or throwing their coffee onto the campfire. They arose and walked to where their horses were hobbled. The men carried their rifles and carbines. Their gunbelts were heavy with cartridges and most of them were still sporting hangovers.

The volunteers rode eastward up the canyon of Murderer's Creek, allowing their horses to pick their way in the semi-darkness, riding in a column of twos with one man in the rear. The only sounds were those of their shod horses' hooves clomping and clacking on rocks in the narrow canyon, echoing from the sides of the canyon walls above them. Blue-pink sunlight began to creep down the crests of the canyon, not yet reaching the bottom. Aldrich rode at the front beside Clark. "Jim, do you suppose we could lick any Indians we might come across?" asked Aldrich in a low tone. "I mean, if we see any here at all?"

Clark, studying the ground before him, answered, "Hell, yes, Frank, from what I hear, they're just a bunch of digger Injuns pissed off at their agent. They've run off the reservation just to make him look bad in Washington. Believe me, the last thing they want is a fight, I know these Injuns."

"Jim! Look!" exclaimed Aldrich, grabbing Clark's coat sleeve, his wide eyes locked to the front as he jerked back on his reins. In the canyon before them, standing like rock statues, stood the raiding party stretched across the canyon, blocking it. The warriors' burning eyes and nostrils smelled blood. No one moved.

"Damn!" Immediately Clark brought his rifle up to his shoulder and fired, then jerked his horse around yelling, "Get the hell out of here! Ride!" wide-eyed with fear. The volunteers, confused, crashed and jolted their horses into each other as they fumbled for their rifles, while at the same time trying to spin their mounts in the opposite direction. The thirteen men rode for their lives, galloping wildly back down the canyon toward the South Fork. War whoops erupted as the warriors burst after the fleeing volunteers. The retreating volunteers fired a few hasty, ineffective shots. For six miles the race of life and death continued. The volunteers' large quarter horses began to play out, while the small Cayuse ponies kept up the chase unwinded. As the chase slowed, four of the volunteers turned and futilely fired their Winchesters, then spurred their sweating horses onward into lather.

The volunteers galloped down and out of the canyon, turning north down the South Fork of the John Day River. By the time they reached Jackass Mountain on their right, Aldrich's horse had become completely winded and he slowly fell behind the other volunteers. His eyes were wide with fright and he'd dropped his rifle along the way. He turned in his saddle to see if the Indians were still behind them. Sam Foss yelled, "Come on, Frank!" Aldrich frantically tried to catch up, spurring his numbing horse. Suddenly, the left side of his head blew away, driving wet bits into Foss's face. A warrior's bullet had found its mark. Aldrich jerked forward in his saddle, then fell onto the road behind Foss with a sickening thud. Foss spurred his horse. Clark's horse screamed as a bullet entered the rear hindquarter of the chestnut. Horse and rider fell. Clark was thrown over the horse, landing on the road and rolling across it. Colby and Davis's horses floundered and fell beneath their riders out of sight, behind a curve in the trail. They scrambled to their feet and ran into the rocks beside the road. Seconds after passing the three men hiding in the rocks, Andross felt a bullet slam into his right leg and the warm sticky blood quickly spread beneath his saddle. He kept riding. Burnham was suddenly thrown forward in his saddle, as a bullet struck him in the back, exiting out the front of his chest. He gripped his saddle horn, grasping the reins with blood-slick fingers as he fought to stay in the saddle.

The warriors had lost interest in their pursuit and stopped the chase after six miles. There was easier game to catch and their horses were tiring badly. They would need them. Many hours later, the remaining volunteers, exhausted and bloody, finally reached the Cummins Ranch and protection, twenty miles from their first meeting with the Hostiles. They'd found their Indians.

Meanwhile, miles to the south, Howard and the Army wagon train hadn't traveled more than an hour when the general spotted a sergeant trotting from the skirmishers marching at the front of the wagon train. The sergeant reined in his mount in front of Lieutenant Wood. "Beg yer pardon, Sir, but I have two civilians at the front wanting to speak to the commanding officer."

Wood turned in his saddle, looking at Howard, who nodded. "Bring them up, Sergeant!" ordered Wood.

Soon, two civilian riders approached the column at a shaky, clamorous trot. Metal pots, gold pans, and a myriad of camping accessories clanged and rang in the morning air, sounding like a church bell on Sunday morning. Howard grinned slightly behind his beard at the approaching souls. He greeted them, trying hard not to show his humor at such a moment. He thought jokingly to himself, "They remind me of my own predicament right now." He greeted them. "Gentlemen, to whom do I have the pleasure?" His eyes studied every detail of the two scraggly men before him, one of whom was having difficulty holding his skinny horse in one place.

"It's our pleasure, Gener'l!" The cleaner of the two vagabonds spoke through yellowed teeth and a scruffy dirty beard that shone with grease in the morning sunlight. "I'm Clem Jackson, and this here be Shorty Pruitt." His companion was unable to greet Howard at the moment, having his hands full controlling his bony steed, which apparently wanted to show Howard and its rider how it could rotate in circles without being told, while thinking up other nice tricks, one probably being ready to go anywhere else than here at this particular moment. "We're headin north to the John Day country to do a little minin! Cold enuf for ye, Gener'l?" chuckled the vagabond, quite pleased with himself and his audience with the general.

Howard noticed that both of the men's horses looked like they would drop at any moment, whether from old age, questionable breeding, or both. Someone had made a good horse deal. He was somewhere else now, counting his money and good fortune. Howard shifted in his saddle. "Would either of you gentlemen happen to know where the crossing is up there?" pointing to the summit ahead of them in the distance.

The two miners shared greedy glances with one another, as the unruly horse stopped his gyrations for the moment, facing in the opposite direction. The talker turned to Howard, smiling, "Shouldn't be too hard to find 'er, Sir. We sure could use us some grub money though."

"Very well," said Howard, "I'll hire you as guides at the regular rate of a scout provided you are successful."

"Done!" said the miner, wheeling his raw-boned charger around as he shouted, "Come on!" to Shorty, who was pre-occupied again, trying to get his own charger turned in the right direction. Howard shook his head and turned to Sarah and Mattie sitting on their horses behind him. Both women shrugged their shoulders and grinned.

After three hours of slow travel towards the summit, a single rider was seen approaching the column at a shaky trot. It was Jackson on his bony charger. As he rode closer his eyes were white circles of fear. He shook in his saddle and not from cold. As Jackson reined in before Howard with difficulty, the general noticed a large rusty Remington cap and ball revolver had been stuck into his waistband. "Kee-rist A-mity! Gener'l, why in the HELL didn't ya tell us how m-<u>many</u> Injuns you w-wuz lookin fer?" he stuttered. "That g-g-gawd-damned canyon down there is fairly well crawlin with em! With all due respects, Gener'l, Shorty and I are lost too and want to save our hair, what's l-l-left of it, and you sojer boys had b-better too! S-Shorty has crapped his b-britches and I gotta try and find him! D-<u>Damn</u>!" With difficulty the frightened miner turned the bag of bones, kicking its ribs madly, and trotted jerkily northeast. Although he was soon out of sight, the clamor and clanging of his equipment could be heard long after losing sight of him in the green timber.

Behind him, Howard heard shrill giggling coming from Sarah and Mattie. Both women were holding their hands over their mouths in typical Indian fashion, trying to stifle their laughter as they listened to the metallic clanging far below them in the timber. Howard turned in his saddle, facing the two with a feigned stern "that's enough, girls" expression on his face. Both women had to turn their faces away from him and he from them since all of them were unable to stop laughing at the poor white soul they'd seen disappear into the trees. Howard, again filled with worry about the pass, shook his head and carefully studied the terrain before him. His experience following the Nez Perce the year before had taught him much. Selecting a long, wide ridge to his north, he drew in a large breath and pointed the Army train towards it. Again, he prayed quietly to himself.

In the canyon far below, Bernard's battalion carefully made its way, following the muddy tracks behind the main group of Indians. The white foamy rapids boomed over giant boulders. The water was a bone-numbing snow run-off. The horses were showing serious signs of fatigue from lack of grain. The cavalrymen's bellies growled with hunger. Evening shadows began to crawl across the mountainside as Howard's wagon train was making camp on the top of a high hogback at the summit. As the dying sun was setting, Howard could see the North Slope of the range, where the sloping foothills descended into the head of the South Fork of the John Day River. He bowed his head in the dusk, removing his old worn campaign hat. A thin, silvery slice of moon was rising in the east. He'd found the crossing.

At eight that evening, volunteer Jim Clark limped into Canyon City. He was at once surrounded by frantic townspeople, yelling and shouting questions about the Indians and where the rest of the volunteers were. As Clark shoveled food and coffee into his mouth, he related to those surrounding him the details of their engagement with the Indian that morning. Soon, a group of volunteers were outfitted to head straight to the Cummins Ranch, where the other survivors had decided to spend the night awaiting help. It would be easier to defend than the Stewart place, which was on Murderer's Creek. The Cummins place had better water and forage for the horses. J. Cummins, who owned the ranch the volunteers were holed up in, left town after midnight leading the rescuers. They left as quietly as possible; eyes could be watching out in the darkness. The moon had set, plunging the fourteen men into an inky night.

On Sunday, the thirtieth of June, the first gray daylight began to show in the east at the Cummins Ranch. Not a sound came from the house and the usual lamplight and smells of a family breakfast were non-existent. Inside the ranch house, the volunteers stood silently by each window, weapons at the ready, fingers squeezing rifles with white knuckles. They were jumpy. It had been a long night, filled with mysterious sounds and imagined shapes moving around. The stock had been let out of the corrals, making it unusually quiet. Inside the house only the occasional moans and groans of the two gravely wounded men and the squeaking floorboards of the house were heard. Men's whispers were heard occasionally within the darkness of the house.

"Riders!" hissed Bob Hall, bringing his Winchester rifle up to the window from which he was watching. Weapons were immediately brought to shoulders and the metallic clicking of carbine hammers being drawn back filled the still house. Then silence.

"Hello the house!" shouted Cummins from the darkness outside.

"It's Cummins!" Everyone let out a breath of relief.

"Come in!" shouted Sam Foss from the darkness of the house. As the riders approached, Foss could barely make out the fourteen riders dismounting in the front yard, tying their mounts to the picket fence.

"Boys?" Cummins said as he entered the house and looked around the dark living room, seeing the dark forms of Andross and Burnham lying on the floor. He could smell blood. He wondered what his wife would say when she returned from Canyon City and saw the mess in her living room.

"We had a bad day yesterday," said Foss. "We'd better get the hell out of here while we still can! I've never seen such fighters in my life. They sure as hell aren't from around these parts and they mean business, Cummins!"

Cummins caught the twinge of fear in Foss' voice and Foss certainly was no coward. He nodded his head. "Let's go, boys! Can they ride?" he asked, nodding towards the two forms lying on the floor.

"You betcha!" wheezed one of the forms in the darkness. It was Burnham, gasping for air. Cummins turned and walked back outside, while the others hurriedly picked up the two wounded men. Soon horses were saddled and the two wounded men lifted onto theirs. A movement in the dark shadows near the corral caught Joseph Shultz's attention briefly. He froze on the front steps, staring into the darkness. He shrugged his shoulders and continued down the steps towards the horses and men.

"Ka-Pow!" A gunshot roared from the corral. The bullet struck Schultz high up in his back, throwing him forward to the ground, squirming and coughing blood. Flashes of gunfire erupted from all around them, spitting flame out of the darkness. They were surrounded. The volunteers quickly organized and returned a crashing volley towards the muzzle flashes coming from the barn and corral. No gunfire returned. Schultz was dragged to his horse in a hail of bullets now coming from the dried creek bank to the north. He was lifted into his saddle. Covered with sticky blood, he was only half-conscious and reeled in the saddle. A volunteer held his reins. The volunteers spurred their horses, riding for their very lives. As they galloped through the ring of firing Indians, the sagebrush seemed to come alive with deep red flashes and booms of gunfire. The blue shadows of dawn had made the volunteers poor targets. The Indian attack had been sprung prematurely because of the quick abandonment of the ranch house. As they galloped eastward towards Canyon City, a single gunshot flashed from the sagebrush, this time the bullet striking Nick Thorton in the right leg, breaking it. When he screamed, his horse crow-hopped briefly, then headed after the others, saving his life. A piece of glistening bone showed through his pant leg in the dawn light.

The Indian warriors stopped their chase and returned to the abandoned ranch house. Even though their trap had been sprung prematurely, their magic power had protected them once again, their wounds being light. They knew they must not venture too far from the approaching main group, which depended upon them as their eyes and ears. As the volunteers' horses began to play out, Cummins turned in his saddle and looked backward toward his ranch. A long column of greasy black smoke spiraled upward into the early pink-blue dawn. "Haaa!" he shouted, spurring his horse towards Canyon City, not looking back again.

When the volunteers limped into Canyon City, they saw near panic and terror on everyone's faces. Eight hundred citizens, men, women, and children, were climbing and struggling up the high slope adjacent to the city where the mine shafts sat gaping on the side hill. Some shafts were one hundred to three hundred feet in depth. Trenches and rifle pits were hurriedly being dug for the defense of the shaft entrances, which were filling up with refugees. The trail winding up the slope was littered with personal possessions dropped by their panicked owners, who failed to retrieve them in their haste. Many believed this would be their last day on earth.

The kitchen door sprang open at the Small ranch, three miles north of the Cummins place. As the door squeaked open, a boy shuffled down the back wooden steps of the house, lifting a suspender strap over one shoulder. His auburn hair sprouted out, wild from a fitful night's sleep. He and his brother had volunteered to guard the ranch and its livestock, consisting of sheep and a few cattle belonging to their cousins. The thought of raiding Indians didn't worry them. The Small family had gone east to Canyon City for protection from the possibility of marauding Indians. With the family gone, the two boys had slept late.

The boy turned his head back towards the two-story white framed ranch house, where his younger brother was probably still sitting on the edge of his bed, trying to wake up. "It's daylight in the swamp, brother!" he shouted. "Get up and start the stove!" He walked by the small whitewashed woodshed, automatically picking up the double bitted axe from its usual place where it leaned against the shed. Nearby stood the splintered chopping block, stained with the dried red-brown blood of butchered chickens. Flies were beginning to buzz around it in the warming morning air. The boy picked up a split piece of dried yellow pine and placed it on end on the chopping block.

As he began to split off the narrow pieces of white kindling, a thought slowly entered his foggy brain. "No dogs?" "Ol Joe," the collie, and the other four stock dogs were always around his feet during this time of morning, begging for a kind word or a rough pat on

96

their wiggling sides. He stood up straight. "Ol Joe!" he called. Silence. The livestock were in the corrals, milling around nervously. Something had spooked them. "OL JOE!" the boy called again, louder this time. Silence. Nothing but the sound of the livestock's milling feet reached his ears. His eyes glanced towards the log barn. He noticed that no barn swallows were flashing and chirping around the hayloft as usual. Something was wrong. The hair on the back of his neck began to bristle. His heart began to pound in his chest, trying to exit through his throat, almost suffocating him as he stood there looking at the open kitchen door of the house. It appeared to be a hundred miles away from where he stood. From the barn came a sudden clinking sound of metal against metal.

Taking a breath, he slowly picked up the kindling, dropping a few unnoticed pieces on the ground at his feet. Cradling the kindling in his left arm and the ax in his right hand, he began to walk quickly towards the kitchen, passing the woodshed, not leaving the axe in its familiar place. As he approached the steps, his heart pounding, he heard a mysterious rapid "whirring" sound behind him. "Thud!" An arrow instantly struck him at the base of his neck above the shoulders, the iron point protruding through the trachea. He felt nothing at first, having been thrown forward, dropping the axe and spilling kindling over the ground at his feet. The only sound he could emit was a gurgling squeak as two more arrows struck him, one in his stomach and the other entering his skull through the left ear. He never heard his brother running to him down the steps or the sound of the double bladed axe as it split his brother's back apart like a butchered beef. Nor did he feel his brother's last remnant of blood pumping onto his own lifeless form.

As the sun rose higher in the cool morning air, the war party slowly moved out, looking for more spoils and blood. They left behind them two naked, bleached white forms lying side by side at the back of the ranch house steps. The two lifeless forms were smeared with their own blood and excrement. Their scalped heads glistened in the morning sunlight. Inside the ranch house, the family cat floated inside the syrup keg, drowned. The feather bedding had been cut open, exposing its contents, then smeared with syrup. The front door was hacked into splintery ribbons. The table was set with kerosene poured into cups and glasses. Outside in the corral, a white pyramid stood high within one of the pens. It consisted of slaughtered sheep, piled one upon the other. The flies were feasting today. The cattle had been herded along by the Hostiles, as a mobile source of food.

By noon, June thirtieth, over two thousand Indians had reached the mouth of the South Fork, where it emptied into the John Day River. The river was running high and swift from the recent rains and snow in the mountains to the south, from where they had just traveled. As they spilled out of the steep canyon and fanned out, it seemed that every Indian in the world had burst from the deep South Fork canyon. The large dust cloud following them stopped at the river's edge and slowly drifted across the river, flowing upwards into the blue sky. They came to the mighty river, spreading out for hundreds of yards in both directions along the riverbank. Men, women, children, and thousands of animals watered everything and everyone in the cold water. Children squealed with delight at the very thought of running into the sparkling river before them; some were already splashing into its cold refreshment beneath the watchful eyes of their mothers, as they supervised the watering of thirsty horses.

The warriors riding point were returning from the east, riding single file. They shouted and sang their victory to all. Dripping women and children stood up from the river to look. Soon their own shrill singing and calls joined those of the warriors. Big John carried a double bladed axe stained with dark blood. He held it high at arm length over his head. "Eeee-AAhhh!" he screamed at the top of his lungs.

Another warrior, carrying the long medicine pole, held it high so that all could see the three fresh scalps dangling and dancing from its tip. "The Taivo have no medicine!" he shouted to those running towards him, thrusting the pole towards them. The wet scalps shook with his gestures.

"We will have a great 'Nanigukwa' dance this night!" shouted Oits. "We have fresh beef! Fat! For the Numa! tonight! The prophets have spoken!" Everyone shouted and screamed at the victorious warriors, who struggled to control their excited war horses, as others untied loot tied to the horses. From the stolen horses they removed a shotgun, several revolvers, and rifles. Traditional medicine men stood back and lightly tapped their drums, not wanting to intercede with the new "Dreamer" medicine.

Egan stood at the riverbank, weak but able to stand on his own now. He raised himself from the travois with the assistance of the Old Woman and Evening Star. His eyes gazed at the six dark smoke columns trailing skyward from ranches to the east. He spoke quietly, "What will the Soldier Chief Howard and the great white chief in the east say of all this?" Not looking at the two women standing beside him, he continued, "We must not offend the whites any further, yet, we must not allow the bad people amongst us to know what is in our own hearts. We must find a chance to speak to the Soldier Chief Howard. His heart has always been true." The Old Woman grinned and cackled something and went about preparing for the river crossing. Evening Star's eyes turned moist as she watched her husband.

"Wo! Egan! You will live!" The unseen approach of Oits startled Egan, who slowly picked up his gunbelt and holster, putting them on. He winced as he adjusted the belt buckle. He stared deeply into Oits' eyes, seeing that small flicker of cowardice that he knew so well.

"Yes, I will live. We should not stay at this place very long. The Taivo soldiers are coming."

"As soon as we have watered!" shouted War Jack, his chest thrust out as he swaggered towards the two men. Egan could smell the pungent smell of fresh blood and sweat emanating from War Jack, whose eyes and flaring nose showed that he hadn't yet recovered from his killing passion. He was still very dangerous.

War Jack was much different than Oits. He was a warrior in every respect. Egan and War Jack's eyes locked, each trying to read the other. War Jack glanced at the revolver resting in Egan's holster, lingering for a moment in deep contemplation. War Jack broke his trance and looked at Oits.

"Come, Oits! We have scalps to stretch!" He tapped Oits on the shoulder. "Another time, Egan!" Egan didn't miss the sneer War Jack gave him through his painted face.

"Soon," Egan thought to himself, as the two men swaggered away, laughing to themselves.

In the distance, Egan could see and hear Indians crossing the swift river upstream. They had chosen the widest part of the river where the current wouldn't be as strong. It was deep from the run off and the current was strong. It would be a long swim but it had to be done, and nearly everyone had done it before. He could see horses and riders entering the water, goaded by men and women who also had the children to contend with. On the bank of river, Egan painfully mounted his old friend the buckskin. The large horse stood rock still as Egan struggled, finally mounting his beloved horse.

It felt good! The Old Woman gave him a toothless grin as Evening Star helped the older woman upon her own Cayuse mare. Evening Star thought the old one felt like a bag of dried twigs as she carefully helped her mount.

Egan's two daughters rode up on either side of their father, bright eyes and smiling white teeth shining as they giggled at the adventure of crossing the river. Egan didn't miss the glances from the younger men toward the two attractive girls, nor the quick return glances and shy girl whispers from the two sisters.

The water sparkled in the bright sunlight, as Egan's bands made ready for the crossing. Evening Star smiled and nodded to Egan as she fell in behind him, on her short Cayuse mare. Egan nodded to her and wheeled the buckskin into line with the others who were now beginning to cross the river. Some had already crossed the mighty stream and were riding northward. Egan eased the buckskin into the river. The water reached the belly, *then the shoulders of the horses, quickly pushing them downstream. "It is stronger than it looks!" thought Egan, turning around to see where his family was. He motioned Evening Star to bring the Cayuse up close to him down river, so that the buckskin's size would protect her and their daughters from the swift current. Within minutes the women were beside Egan and the large buckskin, enjoying the protection from the current. Soon their horses' front feet struck the river's edge and climbed onto the north shore. Egan was exhausted and out of breath. His wounds were bleeding again.*

Once on firm ground, Charley, Honey, John Bull, Sergeant, Widow, and Patch joined Egan, riding alongside him. A meadowlark sang from its perch on a side hill above the riders; no one heard its song. After crossing the river, the Indians traveled northward over the foothills and into Fox Valley. Small children shivered dripping water droplets from the river crossing. At the point of the column, the warriors rode, sitting upright on their horses as they fanned outward on the prairie for miles. They were convinced of their immortality. Egan rode at the head of his bands of Paiutes in silence.

Behind the Indians, approaching the mouth of the South Fork, one of Robbins' volunteer scouts approached Captain Bernard, tipping his hat. "Body, Sir, white. Up ahead!"

"Lead the way," Bernard said, wondering if his mount would survive the next few hours, as weak as it was. The scout led Bernard down the rocky trail beside the bubbling creek. Soon Bernard could see another scout dismounted on the road, resting on one knee, rifle pointed northward toward the Indians' direction of travel. Fifty feet behind the scout lay a naked white corpse. Bernard dismounted.

"No identification, Sir, didn't even leave his boots," said the Idaho volunteer.

Bernard studied the bloated body. "It looks like he was killed yesterday morning, Frank," he said to Lieutenant Ward.

"Yes, Sir," Ward responded.

"Get a blanket and we'll take him out with us. Perhaps someone can identify him when we reach the river," Bernard said. Ward saluted and issued orders to a sergeant. Bernard mounted his horse and waved the battalion northward, riding past the body without further notice.

Three hours later, the battalion reached the John Day River. Everyone in the battalion was astonished at the number of human and animal footprints spreading along the banks of the river. It looked as if an army had watered there.

Bernard pointed the battalion towards the closest column of smoke, coming from a ranch house upriver on the opposite bank. Once a scout detail had secured it, the battalion entered a field beside the smoldering house and barn of the Cummins ranch. Bernard ordered Officer's Call immediately. "We'll make our camp here, Gentlemen. Post tight security measures. Water the horses carefully and bring drinking water inside the perimeter quickly. I want the river at our backs. A supply train should be here shortly from Boise City. Tell the pickets to keep a keen lookout on that road. Any questions?" asked Bernard.

"Sir?" said Captain McGregor. "My men have reported a large blood trail in the front yard of what used to be the ranch house. Someone must have put up a bonny good fight."

"But no bodies?" asked Bernard. McGregor shook his head no. "That will be all, Gentlemen." Bernard removed his dusty hat, taking a handkerchief from his pocket. He wiped the grime off of his forehead. "That river looks inviting," he thought to himself as he walked to the riverbank and, leaning down, trailed his handkerchief in the water. Army horses now lined the bank for several hundred yards in either direction. The scene made him feel good. He couldn't explain the feeling. The troopers were alternately walking the mounts back and forth from the river, per Army regulations. "They are good soldiers," Bernard said to himself as he wiped his face with the wet handkerchief.

In the mountains far to the south of Bernard's battalion, Howard's column had crossed the mountain range summit near Snow Mountain and was struggling downward, zigzagging down the north face. They had entered Grant County. The long wagon train camped that night on a smooth hill nearly three-quarters of a mile in length. Their campfires twinkled in the clear night sky.

"General Howard?" A woman's voice sounded outside the general's tent. Howard opened the tent flap. Outside stood Sarah; at her side stood Mattie.

"Good evening, ladies, won't you come in? I'm afraid it's still a little cool this high." Both women entered the tent. Howard arranged chairs for them. "Now, what is on your minds?" he asked as he sat down in the creaking chair, obviously fatigued. He had a weak smile.

Sarah spoke first. "General Howard, I know that we have been a burden to you, and I see the anger in the faces of some of your soldiers. I have asked to come along because perhaps my Little Sister Mattie and I would be able to help you talk to the bad Numa that we follow. But I do not believe you trust us to talk to them. All we do is follow far away from them. May we go to Captain Bernard and ride with him?"

Mattie's eyes raised from their lowered position, looking at Howard, who was waiting to hear them both out. Mattie then spoke in her soft singing tongue, "General Howard, you are a great soldier general amongst the 'Taivo' (white) soldiers. You are my dear friend, as Mrs. Parish at the Malheur Agency School was. I love and miss her very much. I too have friends and relatives among these Numa that we follow. I do not believe that they are all bad and I wish to tell them that they must stop the killing and come home now and that you are here to help them."

Mattie gave Sarah a quick fearful glance. With anxious eyes, Sarah pushed at Mattie to continue talking to the general. Howard took notice of the glance. They were holding something important back from him. Mattie, in her singsong voice, struggled as she continued, "General, we have received word that my father Egan is with them and that he has been badly wounded by your scout Robbins at Silver Creek and may die." Howard's eyes shone in the lantern light, body stiffening. "His two daughters, my little sisters, and my mother Evening Star are also with him. His son Honey, my brother, and his wife, Hattie, ride with him; she carries their new baby son Qua-See-Ah (Herbert)." Mattie shivered as she wiped away the tears forming in her dark, fawn-like eyes, which glistened in the lantern light. Howard sat ramrod straight in his chair, scarcely breathing as he watched and listened to the small woman sitting across the table from him. "General, my father wants to come out and bring his people with him, but Oits and War Jack will kill them if they try. We know this because we have been in the Indian camp, against your wishes, to help Egan." Howard sat transfixed.

Sarah gently placed her arm around Mattie and looked directly into Howard's eyes. She cleared her trembling throat. "General Howard, will you let my little sister and me go to Egan and continue to treat his wounds? It is said that he may die."

Howard stood upright in the tent. Sarah and Mattie thought they could see his eyes glisten as he withdrew a handkerchief from his tunic and blew his nose, then returned it to his pocket. He walked slowly to the open tent flap, staring out into the dark sky. Mattie and Sarah stood watching him in the dim light. He spoke so that both women could hear him. "Sarah and Mattie, there are no two people in the world who have suffered and given more to your people, than you both have. I too know there are Numa with good hearts in the group that we follow. The time has not yet come when I will ask for everything you can give to this campaign. I did not believe that Chief Egan would take his family and his three bands on this fool's errand without cause. In my heart, I believe that he knows now that he was wrong and will try to speak to me, if it isn't too late. He may be in more difficulty than we know. This news disturbs me terribly. You both have betrayed my trust, yet it was not a selfish betrayal in that it was to render charity to loved ones in need, at the risk of your own lives. The information you have brought back to me is very valuable." Howard turned to the two women. "Yes, I am a Taivo chief among my people, yet there are other Taivo chiefs who want all of the Numa destroyed. But we must not let that happen!"

Both women sat watching, listening. "To do that, I will need your help, loyalty, and patience. Yes, some Numa may soon die. But together we must save the children and build a safer future for them. We must try. And with the help of God Almighty, we will accomplish the impossible for the Numa. Yes, Egan may die, as have many before him." Howard paused, taking in a breath as he turned to the two women. "Go to Egan and do what you can, ladies, but keep in mind that I may not be able to help you should you get caught by the Hostiles in the camp. We can spare medicine and bandages, but you must not breathe a word of these things to anyone. Is that understood?"

Both women stood up, nodding. Mattie wiped the tears from her eyes and was comforted by Sarah's arm around her shoulders. As the two women passed by Howard as they left the tent, they whispered, "Thank you, General," and disappeared into the night.

Miles below Howard's campsite, Bernard's camp on the John Day River was beginning to extinguish evening campfires. Robbins' scouts had reported there had been no signs of war parties attempting to leave the Indian camp to raid the battalion. The Indians seemed contented for the present, feasting on the fat beef they'd stolen from the ranches. The rawhide drums were again booming as singing accompanied the sound. The presence of the battalion didn't bother them. Only Egan and his followers stood outside the ring of celebration, in the darkness. His eyes searched across the brilliant starlit heavens high above him, searching for answers as to why his world had been shattered, asking if his wife and daughters would survive this dangerous journey he'd brought them on.

Bernard sat with other officers around the campfire. The flowing John Day River gurgled and hissed in the darkness at their backs. The conversation had dropped off, leaving the river and the popping fire as the only sounds. He was worried about the patrol that hadn't arrived yet, as the others had. A sudden "Corporal of the Guard!" rang out from the north perimeter. Instantly, the officers sprang to their feet.

"Go see, Peter!" snapped Bernard to Bomus. "To your companies, Gentlemen!" The order wasn't necessary; the officers were already running to their companies in the darkness. "Bugler, stay close and follow me!" ordered Bernard to his close companion. Lieutenant Bomus trotted in the direction of the sentry's call, soon finding him looking nervously into the darkness. A Company's first sergeant, Richard Barrett, stood beside the sentry. Both soldiers grasped their carbines tight. "What's up?" asked Bomus, breathing heavily.

"Sentry here says someone called the camp, might be the last patrol reporting in, Sir," said Barrett, buttoning his blouse with one hand.

"Who is there!" called Bomus.

"Lieutenant Galbraith, F Company, returning from patrol. Permission to enter camp," came the tired response from the darkness.

"Advance and be recognized!" shouted Bomus. A lantern was lit and held high by Sergeant Barrett.

Out of the darkness rode Lieutenant Galbraith, followed by the rest of the ten-man patrol. The officers saluted each other as the riders entered the camp. The troopers were haggard and dirty, much worse than when they had left the camp. Their shapes cast ghostly shadows as they passed by in the yellow lantern light. "Report, Lieutenant," said Bernard, as he approached the two officers. The patrol had dismounted and was walking its mounts to the river, disappearing out of the lantern light. The last trooper in line was leading two broken-down horses that they'd managed to catch, left by the Indians because of their poor condition. As the trooper approached the officers, he stopped as the horses came up to them. Each of the two horses carried a cargo wrapped in soiled blankets. Galbraith walked stiffly to the first odd-shaped load tied to the horse. Bomus and Bernard both knew what they were. Galbraith took in a breath of fresh air, holding it. He then untied one end of the soiled blanket and threw back the covering, stepping back. Sergeant Barrett came closer, holding the lantern high. The men looked into the empty eye sockets of a blackened, blood-covered corpse. The cheeks had been cut open, exposing teeth and jawbone. The throat had also been cut, exposing the spinal column at the back of the stiffened body. The sentry began to hack and gag as the stench reached him, powerless to stop.

"The other one is the same, except for the severed back and ribs, Sir," said Galbraith. "We found them at a ranch, north of here about three miles. They were lying side by side outside the back of the house. We found three dogs that had been killed and about forty sheep stacked up in the corral." He continued, "They didn't burn the house though. We found signs of looting. No arrows were present at the scene, probably took them to use later. Both bodies had the remains of small fires on their chests, Sir."

"Thank you, Lieutenant, good report," said Bernard. "Have these bodies placed with the other one, beside the house. Captain Bomus will show you the way." Bernard drew in a tired breath. "I'll have the cook start coffee for you and your men. I'm sorry there isn't more. My compliments, Sir." He saluted Galbraith. The lieutenant returned it with a tired look. It had been one hell of a day for him and his men. The smell of death stuck in his nostrils.

Daylight on Monday, July the first, found Bernard's men finishing their meager breakfast rations of coffee and a few crumbs of hardtack. The metallic clinking of utensils being returned to saddlebags that rested in long lines upon the grass rang throughout the camp. Blankets were rolled and tied upon the black saddles. Morning coughs mingled with other sounds of preparation. The smell of freshly lit pipes and hand-rolled cigarettes wafted throughout the camp. A few troopers slowly sipped the last of their coffee as they gazed upon the three covered corpses, some distance away. The bodies were long past the time when they should have gone into the ground. The bloody, blackened foot of one of the corpses stuck out partially from beneath the blanket, as if it were begging for notice. It needn't have begged. The bugler sounded "Assembly."

At the head of the South Fork, the sounds of Howard's cursing teamsters and infantrymen echoed in the steep canyon. The nearly perpendicular red-brown lava rocks loomed down upon Howard's column as it snaked its way northward. Infantrymen were out of the wagons and were playing tug-of-war against gravity and the heavy wagons and disassembled Hotchkiss cannons. They slowly lowered them downward by ropes into the depths of the canyon below. Men sweated and cursed (out of Howard's earshot) in their labor. Ropes had been wound around tree stumps, using them as a windlass with the other end tied around wagon axles and sides to keep them from tipping over on the steep incline above. Brave "volunteers" sat upon the wagon seats, operating the wheel brakes. The scene resembled ants carrying their gigantic trophies back to the anthill. Men had stripped off their shirts and their sweating bodies shone in the morning light.

One set of stubborn mules was refusing to proceed downward, digging their hooves into the rocky ground, pushing red shale before them. A red-faced sweating teamster shouted, "I'll fix those sons o bitches! Here, you men!" as he glared at the young sweating faces of infantrymen. "Give me a hand here, Gawd damn it!" The youngsters jumped to his assistance. As the teamster swore at the mules, the soldiers, the Army, and a woman from his past, the two mules were unhitched from the front of the wagon. Curious sweating faces looked on, not wanting to get caught in the teamster's wrath. As the teamster re-hitched the stubborn animals to the rear axle of the wagon, he shouted. "Now! Release the Gawd-damned brake, soldier!" Infantrymen bolted away from the wagon, running for their lives. As the wagon's nervous young driver released the brake, the wagon rolled and skidded forward, gaining dangerous speed. The driver, eyes large and terrified, looked forward to certain death on the rocks below him, too frightened to jump. Suddenly, the wagon slid to a grinding stop. Behind it, hitched to the rear axle, the mules in their stubbornness had deliberately pulled in the opposite direction, their hooves throwing shale,

105

rock, and dust in every direction as the obstinate animals, unknowingly, allowed the wagon to roll downward safely. Young infantrymen peered from behind trees and soon were rolling with laughter at the scene. A sergeant's bark sent them back to work. As the last of the wagons was lowered into the canyon, artillerymen quickly re-assembled the artillery pieces. Wagons were reloaded and they were finally on there way again, down the South Fork. Howard, with Sarah and Mattie beside him, smiled from his horse. He would be seeing Bernard soon.

"Corporal of the Guard!" shouted the sentry from Bernard's perimeter on the John Day River. Bernard could see First Lieutenant Frank Ward's patrol returning from the east. The patrol's red and white Guidon fluttered in the distance. As the patrol came closer, Bernard saw that two civilian wagons were following the patrol. As the patrol arrived, it formed a line and dismounted, walking the horses towards the river to water. Lieutenant Ward walked to Bernard with two worn looking civilians following him.

"Lieutenant Ward reporting, Sir," the tired, dust-covered officer addressed Bernard with a salute.

"Lieutenant," said Bernard, returning the salute. "Report."

"Sir, these men are volunteers from Canyon City." The two men introduced themselves to Bernard, who shook their hands. Ward continued. "They've brought grain, beans, and fresh beef, Sir."

"What's the state of affairs at Canyon City, gentlemen?" questioned Bernard of the two men.

"Well, Sir, every man, woman, and child has taken to the mineshafts in the side hill across from town. They took what they could drag up with them, mostly food and water. We got a few guns among us and could put up a good fight for a short while I reckon, Cap'n."

"What about the telegraph, is it working?" asked Bernard.

"Been on and off for a week now," answered the man, his partner nodding in agreement.

"Thank you, gentlemen, for your kind assistance in helping us. We certainly did need these provisions. We'll see to your payment. Also, gentlemen, General Howard will be here in a day or so and will be in need of provisions if there are any to be had. Frank, let's get these wagons unloaded fast." The foursome walked towards Bernard's shelter.

After Bernard had reimbursed the two volunteers with promissory notes, he spoke. "Gentlemen, I have a very disagreeable request to make of you. Will you please follow me?" He led them to the side of the charred farmhouse where the three blanketed corpses lay. "Can either of you identify these people?" asked Bernard. A trooper untied the blankets, pulling them down, exposing their heads. The two volunteers hurriedly drew their bandanas over their noses.

One nodded and pointed a dirty finger at the three corpses. "These two boys here are the Small brothers, they was watchin their uncle's place, while they was in town! Lord a mity!"

"Oh my, God!" blurted the other man, through his shaking bandana. "That be Frankie Aldrich. We figured he was a goner," said the man sadly.

"I need to get these men into the ground quickly, gentlemen," Bernard said.

"I reckon you'd best bury the Smalls here, Cap'n, but I'd like to take Frank back to Canyon City. I think the family would want it that way, if you don't mind, Sir."

"Of course," replied Bernard. "Lieutenant Ward, have a burial detail take care of these two at once and assist in loading the other one into the wagon."

"Yes, Sir," responded Ward.

As dawn began to show over the misty canyon of the North Fork of the John Day River, many miles to the north, it was Tuesday, July second. A Umatilla Indian was hunting deer. Having not come across any fresh Indian sign, he had stopped his scouting duties momentarily to hunt for fresh meat. His heart was pounding in his chest because he had been stalking a giant mule deer buck for over an hour. His breathing was heavy from the long climb up the mountainside and now the buck was moving downhill, in front of him. The Umatilla was sure the buck could hear his heart pounding. He stopped and knelt down to study the dark fresh deer droppings steaming in the grass. His nose and eyes stung and watered from the crisp morning air. He was close! He drew in a deep breath and stood up slowly. "Crack!" came from just below him in a thicket. Something large had stepped on a dead limb, snapping it. Suddenly, the faint sound of loose shale sliding behind him caused him to wheel around. Above him he saw a large buck deer as it walked into a thicket out of sight. "Two of them!" he thought in astonishment as he turned his attention to where he'd heard the limb snap below the ridge where he stood. He raised his rifle to his shoulder and walked carefully to the edge of the rocky ledge. As he peered downward into the thicket, expecting to see the large buck at any second, his heart suddenly stopped. Below him, on a

107

game trail, stood five painted warriors on horseback. They seemed to be preoccupied with the huge river canyon below them, looking for something to the south.

The scout froze, not moving a muscle. He could see the Indians weren't Umatilla, but probably Bannock. He recognized one of the warriors, who wore an Army cap with a feather tied in it. He'd seen the Indian at his agency not more than a month ago near Pendleton. Others had been with him then, including the Bannock Chief Buffalo Horn and Chief Egan of the Paiutes. He'd suspected that they were up to no good then and now he was sure of it. Here he was, alone and dead meat for sure if they saw him. He was shaking. Suddenly, sounds of sliding rocks and shale high above the Umatilla caught the warriors' attention. They brought their rifles up quickly and briefly conversed in whispers and sign language. Soon they cautiously rode upwards along the game trail to where the sounds had come from in the thicket, where the Umatilla had seen the buck disappear only moments before. "That damned buck saved my life!" he thought as the Indians disappeared over the ridge, heading northward. "Point riders! sure as hell! They really are coming," he thought, as he quietly back-tracked to where he'd hobbled his horse. In seconds he was trotting toward camp with his two companions. Soon they were riding cautiously, but speedily back to the Umatilla Reservation to spread the alarm.

On the John Day River, Bernard broke camp and pointed the battalion to the northeast, following the Hostiles' trail. Robbins' scouts had reported the Indians' camp had been abandoned early that morning. A day of travel over the rolling, grass-covered hills of Fox Valley found the battalion making night camp at a good spring, located in a copse of pine trees. One of Robbins' scouts had found a lone steer and killed it. At an abandoned ranch house he'd discovered a large cache of tobacco. That night, the battalion ate and smoked well.

Howard's column continued its march, traveling down the South Fork of the John Day River south of Bernard. Things had gone smoothly and he camped again on the South Fork in the darkness of the deep river canyon. By Wednesday, the third, Howard had exited the mouth of the South Fork and, after crossing the John Day River, had watered the stock and established a defensive perimeter where Bernard's camp had been at the burned Cummins ranch. He quickly made camp, awaiting the arrival of the pack train coming from Boise City. As Howard was washing himself inside his tent, Lieutenant Wood caught his attention by showing him the rolled up pieces of note paper taken from the cartridge cases that had been pushed into the ground behind each of the crude crosses found near the charred house. Howard dried himself off and walked outside where the light was better. He rolled out the small pieces of paper, praying that it wasn't an acquaintance in his command. The papers each had the same message written on them in pencil:

"One of two Small family brothers.
Killed near here. Unidentified.
Reuben F. Bernard
Capt. U.S. Army"

To the east of Howard in the mining town of Canyon City, men were shouting to their families to hide further back in the dark, candle-lit mining shafts, as they scrambled to their rifle pits above the shaft entrances. There was a column of dust coming from the east, directly towards the false-fronted buildings in the town below them. At the outskirts of the mining town, a young Army lieutenant raised a dust-covered arm, shouting "Halt!" to the long column of pack mules wagons and the cavalry escort. As he raised in his stirrups, Lieutenant William Brown gazed at the apparently abandoned town before him. Through the dust drifting past him, he could just make out a few people, not the large population he had expected. Something was wrong. "Sergeant!" he called for the detail sergeant at the rear of the column.

"Yes, Sir?" The dust-coated sergeant was immediately by the side of his young lieutenant.

"You remain here with the train. I'm going into the town to see what's going on." With that, Brown spurred his Morgan at a walk toward the deserted town, stopping at the saloon where two men were leaning against the building's swinging doors on the front porch. He turned the Morgan with ease, as though they were on a parade ground and stopped, facing the saloon and its two occupants. "Lieutenant Brown, First Cavalry. Is this the town of Canyon City?" he introduced himself to the two men whose red eyes bespoke of liquor and hard times.

One of the men, large and red bearded, removed a stained toothpick from his mouth. Brown noticed the large revolver stuck inside his waistband. "Howdy!" slurred the man. "Didn't expect to see any Army comin from the east. Where's the rest of ya?" He gazed at the awaiting pack train in the distance.

"I'm to meet them to the west of here," Brown said. For the first time he looked at the map in his hand. As he looked sharply in the distance, he saw dark black smudges of smoke hanging in the air. His jaw dropped. West Point suddenly seemed far away. This was his first campaign since he'd graduated.

"Yup, Sonny Boy, that's Injun sign yer lookin at!" blurted the man. "Take a good look at that hillside over there! Every swingin dutchman and woman has gone there! Feared of dyin! Ha!" he smirked. Brown's eyes scanned the hillside before him. It was covered with debris and dark muddy streaks where people had climbed and scratched themselves up the steep slope, terrified of the evil coming to kill them. Bedding, clothing, and children's toys lay scattered along the muddy paths leading upward towards the black mine shafts.

A woman's shrill scream shattered the silence. She ran down the city street, hair streaming around her face, hands held to her ears, eyes wide with terror. "Here come the Indians!" she shrieked to no one in particular, as she ran in circles from one side of the street to the other.

"Don't mind her, Sonny, that's crazy Carrie. Injuns kilt her husband and little ones back in the sixties over on Murderer's Creek!"

Brown looked to where he'd left his pack train, which was now rapidly trotting into town. "Either they're spooked or they're thirsty for a cold beer, maybe both!" he said to the two men on the saloon porch. A wild-eyed man carrying a shotgun ran after "Crazy Carrie," taking her by the arm as he struggled to get her out of the street. Brown turned in his saddle. "Let's have that beer, sergeant!" Brown said to the sergeant, as the pack train dismounted in the street.

Late that afternoon, Brown's pack train entered Howard's camp on the John Day River. Cheers rent the air as the pack mules and wagons trailed into camp. Howard greeted Brown, who kept his distance, hoping to keep Howard from smelling beer on his breath. Perhaps, though, Howard might have understood? "No chance," he thought to himself, "better safe than sorry." Brown watched as preparations were hurriedly made. Teamsters and infantrymen busily exchanged the horse teams for mules, and re-shod animal's hooves. The portable blacksmith bellows huffed and puffed and the sharp ringing of the anvil carried up into the hills around them. Grain was issued and rations were loaded into the wagons. Howard personally commended Brown for his ability in purchasing oats, flour, and barley as he'd traveled towards the column.

Bernard's battalion, moving northward, found itself riding in open green grassland, surrounded by blue-black timbered areas. Some troopers were even able to catch a quick catnap in the saddle. The weather was growing cooler again and gray-black clouds were approaching from the west. The serenity was broken as a scout in the distance galloped towards them. Bernard had the bugler sound halt. Soon the rider reached them, reining in his mount in front of Bernard. "Body, Sir, looks fresh," the volunteer reported, his chest heaving from the ride. Bernard waved the column forward. The column soon found the body.

The young sheepherder was lying on his back. Empty, unseeing eye sockets looked skyward. Various round bloodied holes in the corpse indicated where arrows had

110

punctured it and had then been removed. The scalped head had been crushed and the remains of a small fire, cold now, rested upon its chest. Coyotes had eaten at the body. A chorus of buzzing flies sang its song. Troopers looked bewildered at the nearly one hundred head of dead or dying sheep surrounding the scene. Those pitiful creatures still alive had had their forelegs cut off, some dangling. The coyotes had been feeding on them as well. The herder was buried and the long column rode solemnly past the burial detail and dead sheep. It began to snow lightly. Troopers reached back and removed coats and ponchos from their saddles, putting them on. Low grumbling reverberated along the column.

Pendleton East Oregonian, June 29, 1878.
"The settlers are building a fort on Long Creek in which to flock in an emergency. We are told that the settlers are better armed there than any place in the county."

The Grant County Times.

Army Navy Journal, July 6, 1878.
The following dispatches have been sent to Gen. Wheaton:
Silver Creek, near Camp Curry, Ore., June 25, via Baker City, Ore., June 27.
"The hostiles increase in number as they advance. At the beginning of the outbreak the Bannocks formed a junction with the discontented Indians north of them, then with the Paiutes under Oits and Egan, near Juniper Lake, and now some Klamaths have joined them here. Some Umatillas have been endeavoring to form a junction with the hostiles; some have succeeded and are now with them."

Howard, Commanding.

Chapter 4

Long Creek Stockade

Twenty-seven miles to the northeast, ahead of Bernard's column, the small town of Long Creek was preparing a defense against the approaching Indians. The town was nestled in a beautiful green meadow, surrounded by pine forests. At the east end of the small town sat a large, hand-hewn log stockade, built in haste by the citizens and surrounding ranchers. The stockade's walls were fashioned from large ponderosa pine logs, with firing ports cut for defense. Inside the walls stood a building with rooms full of supplies. There was a good well located within the stockade's walls. A special sally port had been designed to allow access only through it, then through another heavy door that led into the stockade's interior. The settlement was filled to overflowing with refugees, some having come far distances for protection. The long columns of black smoke surrounding them from burning ranches attested to the threat approaching them. Some of the people bore the look of shock on their faces from recent encounters with the Hostiles, having just run for their lives as flames and war cries roared behind them. Business was good in the town's general store. Empty shelves, where ammunition boxes once lay, stared back at those who needed them. "Indians! Here they come!" someone shouted. For a second all was silent. Time stopped. People suddenly realized that the Hostiles were actually here. Instantly, everyone headed towards the stockade. Once inside, men manned the walls and firing ports, looking for the reason for the alarm. They didn't have to look far.

Directly to the south ran a long pine-covered ridge, the tree line stopping approximately one half mile to the south of town and in front of the stockade's entrance. From out of the tree line, five Bannock and Paiute Warriors rode towards the stockade, painted for war: War Jack, Boss, Surger, D.E. Johnson, and Bannock Joe. The defenders of the stockade gripped their guns with whitened knuckles, as praying was heard from within the stockade's interior. Onward came the five Indians, seemingly out for a morning ride, pretending to be oblivious to the stockade in front of them. Occasionally, one of the horses would lower its neck, stretching to the limit as it tore off a mouthful of green grass, not breaking its stride in the movement.

"Steady, boys," a leader spoke to the nervous men manning the stockade's firing ports and walls. They watched mystified, as the warriors rode towards them, nearing the stockade.

"They sure as hell aren't dressed for pickin berries!" someone said quietly.

The five warriors stopped within fifty yards of the fort's entrance, their cunning eyes taking in every detail of the stockade and its inhabitants. Boss spoke, "Speak, talk outside!" The warriors on either side of him were studying the stockade's sally port entrance with deep curiosity, their rifles pointed skyward, loaded.

"No, come out! We talk <u>here</u>!" came the reply from a firing port.

The warriors' eyes continued to study the fort's construction, apparently oblivious to the conversation at hand.

"No talk in! Talk <u>out</u>!" demanded War Jack. His eyes bored in on the door latch mechanism of the sally port. He had never seen one like it. He wanted to see how it worked.

"Talk <u>here</u> - No talk!" came the voice from within. Bannock Joe's black flat-brimmed hat tilted downward on his head, concealing his war paint and searching eyes. His black boots were scuffed now, but the silver spurs still shone in the overcast light. Then as one, the five warriors turned their horses around and nonchalantly rode back toward the distant timber from which they had emerged.

Inside the stockade, a breath of relief was heard. Some were joyful and cheered, "By God! We showed em, didn't we? They seen we was prepared for anything! Didn't they! Wa-Hooo!" Soon the five warriors disappeared into the blue-black timber.

"Praise the Lord!" shouted a woman, holding a baby in her arms, her husband allowing her to get a look at the disappearing warriors.

"Wait!" shouted a man from another firing port.

"Oh, my God, look!" shrieked the woman, looking outwards through the firing port, her husband pulling her aside. From where the five warriors had disappeared into the timber there came spilling out of the dark trees the point riders riding four abreast, followed by all of the raiding bands, riding towards the stockade.

"Don't fire, unless they shoot first, men!" came the order from inside the stockade.

116

"What good would it do anyway?" someone asked, as they watched the long, brightly colored column of Indians parading towards them.

"We're dead," someone said. Stifled screams could be heard from within the building where the women and children were. As the column of Hostiles approached the small stockade, it didn't stop but continued on past the building. Indifferent stares came from the men and women in the long column; the children looked at the strange fort and people with wide, questioning eyes. The Numa were proud this day. The Indians stretched out across the wide, grassy meadow, continuing on for what seemed an eternity, especially to those watching from inside the stockade. The Indian column had swelled in numbers now, many Umatilla, Yakima, and Walla Walla Indians having joined along the way. A herd of stolen horses numbering in the hundreds accompanied the Hostiles. The stockade's defenders had never seen so many Indians in their lives. Not a sound came from within the fort, as the last of the Indian column drifted out of sight to the north. Over an hour had passed. It seemed like forever to the stockade's defenders.

To the north, a group of mounted volunteers coming from the towns of Pendleton and Pilot Rock rode across a large meadow, coming to Bentley's sawmill which had been abandoned by its employees hours earlier when alerted of the approaching Hostiles. James Wilson and the fifteen armed volunteers were cocksure confidant that they could handle any Indians they might come across. As the volunteers approached the sawmill, Wilson raised his hand, signaling the group to halt. Instead of employees, the mill was surrounded by painted horses, their riders raising a clamor inside the company buildings. Wilson turned in his saddle towards one of the volunteers. "Umatillas?" he asked. The volunteer nodded in agreement, as Wilson signaled forward. As the group approached the bunkhouse and storeroom, an Indian emerged.

The Indian was tall and wore a beaded buckskin shirt and leggings. His hair was loose about his shoulders and his face was painted in bright colors. He carried a Winchester carbine in his right hand; in his left he carried a soiled bed sheet containing cans of food. He froze, looking at Wilson and the volunteers. It was Five Crows of the Umatilla Tribe.

"Hey, Wilson! What you doin here?" he grinned. "We thought we'd better take these things so that the bad Injuns would not find them!" More Indians pushed by Five Crows standing in the doorway, walking to their horses. They also carried blankets and canned goods.

"Now, Five Crows, you know better than to take Mr. Bentley's goods without his say so," said Wilson, as the volunteers seemed more at ease in their saddles. They knew some of these Indians. But why were they here. And why now?

117

"OK, Wilson," said the Indian, "We'll put back the things, but you need to be careful here and now. There are bad Injuns coming from the south who would not greet you and your men as friendly as we have today.

"Why you wearin paint, Luke?" asked Wilson, leaning on his saddle pommel.

"If bad Injuns wear paint, we must let them know that we can fight too!" Luke said, as he swung onto his Cayuse pony, wheeling it around.

Five Crows grinned, "See you later, Wilson! Hah!" he shouted, as the group of Indians trotted into the timber.

"How did he know the Hostiles were reported coming from the south?" mused Wilson to himself as he waved his volunteers forward. He noticed far more fresh horse tracks around the area, more than the ten or so Indians at the building. "Must be from the mill workers' horses, he thought as he turned his horse around. He looked towards the timber where the Indians had disappeared. It was only then that he noticed where the majority of the horse tracks went. A chill ran along his spine. He shook it off.

Late in the afternoon, the alarm was sounded again at the town of Long Creek. This time, however, it was Bernard's battalion who approached the town. Cheers and handshakes met the column as it entered the small town. The troops quickly set up camp as Bernard took reports from the citizens and in turn passed on information regarding the Army's close watch on the Hostiles. "Ol 'Yesterday Howard' missed another fight!" seemed to be the political sense of humor coming from the citizens. "Every chance he gets for killin the red bastards, he ain't there. How does he expect to catch em, if he's way the hell behind em?"

Bernard could sense the anger of the citizens against Howard, but he did his best to smooth things over. After all, he needed their grain if they'd sell it. Supplies were purchased. As usual, the prices were inflated much higher than market value. After meeting with the townspeople, the battalion quickly started cooking fires and a defensive perimeter was put out around the town. Townspeople were allowed to visit the troops briefly before nightfall. In the distance, the dark stockade showed a faint candle light behind the firing ports. Someone didn't trust the Army completely. After evening meals had been consumed, fresh firewood was placed on the smaller fires for heat, as the night was quite cold. It had snowed earlier that afternoon in Fox Valley and the men were chilled. Around one of the fires sat Bernard, Ward, McGregor, Whipple, and Bendire. They were sipping their first real coffee in days. Bernard had allowed a small ration of "medicinal spirits," purchased from the town's saloonkeeper, to ward off the chilly night. The hot metal cups warmed their hands and bellies. Robbins sat amongst them, slowly puffing his pipe, staring at the flames in the crackling fire.

Bernard was thinking of Alice and the children. "Odd," he thought to himself, "they seem like a dream now. Did they ever actually exist in my life? Nonsense!" he shook the thought off. Much had happened. He was exhausted. "Good night, Gentlemen." he said tiredly, as he got up stiffly and walked to his shelter and bedroll.

Daylight on Independence Day, Thursday, July the Fourth, found Howard and a small escort of mounted infantry moving northward out of the John Day Valley. The infantry and artillery companies were still being issued rations and breaking in mounts, as the infantry would now be mounted. He'd left orders with Captain William Spurgin of the Twenty-First Infantry to take charge of the wagon train and to break camp the following morning and join him as soon as possible. Howard was worried that Bernard might be pushing forward too quickly, leaving his support dangerously far behind. Sarah and Mattie rode beside Howard. They knew that they would be vulnerable to any attack with such a small detail accompanying them, but Howard needed to move light and fast if he intended to reach Bernard quickly. Howard's plan was rapidly coming to its climax and he was ready to go into action. By now, the river gunboats and Army field support must be getting close to their positions on the Columbia River to block the Hostiles from crossing to the north. His plan was to trap the Hostiles between his commands, forcing a surrender or if need be, a fight. Quietly he had planned to leave an escape route to the east of the Indians, to allow the defeated Indians a means to return to their tribes. The last thing he wanted was a wholesale slaughter on his hands. He knew that the citizens wanted the Army to completely destroy these Indians, but he was not going to let that happen if at all possible. He would be unpopular but he could live with that, if it meant saving lives.

North of Howard, near the Middle Fork of the John Day River, Bernard's breakfast fire was smoldering as he looked at McGregor. "Thomas?" McGregor's eyes snapped to Bernard's. He knew something was up if Bernard spoke to him that way. "I don't like the feeling I'm getting from these Hostiles that we are following. I think they are tired of us nipping at their heels and are thinking about doing something about it, and soon. Robbins' scouts have reported Indians coming in from the north. That spells more trouble. If we engage them now, they won't allow us to disengage as they did on Silver Creek, Thomas." McGregor nodded silently. "They are gaining strength in numbers each day, with Umatillas coming south to join them." Bernard gazed into McGregor's eyes. "I don't want to, but I feel it is necessary to contact the General and bring him up as soon as possible. I want you to take as many men as you think necessary from your company and I will expect to see you and the General in a few days. Don't alarm Howard, just tell him what we have in front of us, Thomas. Understood?"

After a pause, McGregor took in a large breath, smiled and threw a jaunty salute to Bernard, who returned the smile and slapped him on the arm. McGregor immediately walked towards his company, barking orders. He had some dangerous traveling to do. Bernard watched him assemble his company for the march to Howard; he felt uneasiness in his stomach. His many years of fighting Indians told him something was about to happen. It seemed as if someone in the Hostiles' camp was speaking to him, trying to tell him something. But what!

The large Indian camp had been struck at daylight for the march northward. Rear guard scouts were instructed to stay in constant sight of Bernard's column behind them. The sun promised a warmer day. The Indians hadn't traveled far when a shout came from the point warriors. Something was wrong. A rider was galloping toward the front of the column, straight toward War Jack and Oits. "The Umatillas come!" he yelled as he approached the column.

Even before he'd slid to a halt before War Jack, Umapine the Umatilla had arrived at their side from the rear of the column. War Jack nodded to Umapine, who galloped towards the timber where the point riders had seen the approaching Umatillas. Soon, seventy painted Umatilla warriors rode out of the timber, riding in parade fashion towards the Hostiles' column. They shouted and yelled out their successes in war, raising rifles and carbines as they paraded towards the other Indians. Umapine had a sinister grin on his face. "HO! War Jack and Oits! See how your brothers the Umatilla have come to ride and protect you against the white snakes. Is it not good?" he shouted.

Once Umapine made introductions, Five Crows, the leader of the Umatilla warriors spoke. His long hair shone in the sun beneath the eagle feathers tied on it. "We are the mighty Umatilla. We have known the lies and bad treatment from the whites. We are here to help our Bannock and Paiute brothers during their journey. Who knows, maybe if we fight well our brothers might let us keep some of the fat ranch ponies waiting for us ahead?" There was laughter and whooping among the Cayuse and Walla Wallas. Five Crows shouted to the Indians behind War Jack and Oits. "The white volunteers found us stealing food from the sawmill north of here. They were so afraid of the Dreamer Medicine that they asked us to put it back and help protect them from the Bannocks and Paiutes coming their way. They are cowards and deserve to die!" All laughed, especially Umapine.

Egan had gone through the formalities and introductions. They weren't needed. He knew Five Crows; his only loyalty was to the Umatilla Tribe at Thornhollow. He watched Umapine and Five Crows closely. This meeting was not an accident. It had been planned, yet nothing was said of it when Five Crows and Buffalo Horn had talked with him about the plans for the journey several months ago in the Umatilla camp. Egan didn't trust either of the two men, especially Umapine, who seemed to live for bloodletting and carnage. Umapine was always at the time and place of murder; his eyes would blaze at the scent of blood and death. Umapine had reason to hate Egan. Egan had reportedly killed his father during a bloody argument years before. Yet Umapine had never spoken of it or raised an eyebrow when in Egan's presence. He wondered why, and now here was Five Crows, smiling and laughing with Oits, War Jack, and, yes, Umapine. A shiver ran down Egan's spine. He had to be very careful now. He needed to get his three bands away from this group soon. His shoulder ached in its sling and his mouth tasted of sour bile.

As the warming sun climbed skyward, the time was nearing nine a.m. Bernard's column had stopped to adjust cinch straps and to rest the mounts. The country around them was green and fresh, with multi-colored wildflowers creating a painted carpet stretching for miles. Only the blue-green of the Blue Mountains broke the colored meadows around them. As the sun warmed, a halt was called. Troopers removed their coats, tying them to the backs of their saddles. Along the column troopers were stretching their legs and relieving themselves. Private Thomas gazed out towards a large stand of pine trees to the east. Standing there at the edge of the timber astride his Cayuse pony sat a warrior looking directly at him. The warrior's feathered headdress fluttered in the breeze. Neither horse nor rider moved a muscle as they stood staring at the Army column. Nothing else moved.

Thomas blinked his eyes to be sure. "Sarge!" he shouted towards the front of the column, not taking his eyes off the warrior staring back at him at the tree line.

"I see him!" said the sergeant. "Lieutenant!" he called up the line. Suddenly the warrior vanished.

Captain Whipple of L Company ran to the two men. "What's going on, Sergeant?" he asked.

"Injun, Sir, he was standing just this side of that timber, Sir, just looking at us just as you please. Then he disappeared, Sir." As the sergeant finished his report, a column of gray-black smoke suddenly billowed into the air on the opposite side of the stand of timber.

"What the...?" Whipple blurted as he turned and ran to his horse. He jumped into the saddle and galloped to the head of the battalion towards Bernard, who by now was in the saddle himself. Shouted voice commands and shrill bugle calls ordered the troops to mount and Officer's Call. As one the battalion swung into saddles, everyone watching the smoke. Officers galloped along the column to the front of the line and Bernard, raising dust trails behind them. Bernard faced the stand of timber, carefully glassing the trees and the meadow at its side. Nothing! The smoke column grew in intensity, rolling upwards into the blue morning sky. The fire's roar and crackling could be heard in the distance. "Gentlemen, I want the battalion to left oblique around the left side of that timber," Bernard ordered, pointing a gloved finger to where the stand of timber stopped and surrendered to the green meadow. "I want to go around that timber. God knows what's in it!" His eyes flashed left to right. His blood was up. "Oblique at the trot! I want to see where that smoke is coming from! Robbins' scouts will swing wide through the timber. Tell your men to be careful, Rube!" Bernard ordered, trying to control his horse in the excitement.

Robbins nodded as he broke open his ten-gauge shotgun, checking it. The two brass shells were in place. He closed the gun's action with a sharp "Snap!" He was ready.

"Frank!" Bernard called to Lieutenant Ward, who was watching every move of Bernard's eyes and mouth. "I want you and your Company G broken down as a line of foragers to probe those trees. I will wait until you and Robbins have cleared the trees before I start my advance, just in case you get into difficulty." Ward nodded grimly.

"Charles," snapped Bernard hurriedly to Bendire, "You and your Company K will support Ward mounted." Bendire nodded, eyes narrowed beneath the brim of his black hat. "Good luck, Gentlemen, we'll see you shortly!" Salutes were given and Robbins and the officers galloped to their posts. Soon the foraging G Company troopers had dismounted and formed their line, walking toward the timber, carbines carried at the ready. They were several hundred yards from the battalion. The troopers and volunteers disappeared into the trees. Fifteen long minutes later, the company trumpeter exited the timber and blew the "Advance."

Bernard gave a sigh of relief and turned to his trumpeter. "Oblique Left. March!" As the shrill notes carried across the meadow, the battalion trotted at a left angle around the timber. G Company had cleared the timber, remounted, and had formed a line. Bernard's trumpeter sounded "Left Front Into Line" and the battalion formed into a line and was brought to a halt. Lieutenant Ward's company returned to the column and fell into line with the battalion. Before them in the middle of a large meadow stood the flaming house and out buildings of a ranch. The fire had practically burned out. It hadn't taken long.

The battalion approached the burning ranch as close as the horses could stand it, then dismounted. Scouting parties were sent out in every direction, looking for signs of life. Bernard and Bomus walked towards the smoldering buildings, also looking for survivors. Walking with the two officers was O.P. Cresap, who had been hired on at Long Creek to guide them through the country. Troopers walked around the area carrying carbines at the ready, looking for signs of life. There was none. "They're probably back there at Long Creek, Captain," Cresap said to Bernard as he holstered his revolver. "What's this?" he exclaimed, walking to a large pine tree away from the smoldering house. Bernard and Bomus followed behind him, curious. Before them on the ground was a dead lamb. The lamb had been stretched between two wooden stakes, so that it couldn't move. Then a fire had been built beneath it, slowly burning it alive.

"My God!" hissed Lieutenant Ward "Who in the name of creation would ever torment an innocent animal like that?"

"The people we are following, Frank," Bernard said as he headed back to the falling, blackened timbers of the smoldering house crashing to earth in a shower of sparks and flame. He turned his head toward Ward. "Be glad it's not you!"

The farmyard was littered with broken furniture and other household goods. Flies swarmed around a shredded feather pillow that contained the bloody remains of a cat. Syrup had been poured over the mess.

"Rider coming in!" shouted Lieutenant Ward from the area where the barn had once stood.

One of Robbins' scouts trotted in, horse lathered with white flecks of froth. Stopping before Bernard he repeated, "Another ranch attacked, Sir. Just two miles north of here. No signs of life though. They sure killed one hell of a lotta stock! Ransacked the place. You should see it!" The scout's shirt showed white perspiration stains, as did everyone else's.

"Thank you, Sir," answered Bernard. "Water yourself and your mount and we will follow you to that ranch." The scout stiffly dismounted, his boots thudding as they touched the ground. He led his horse to the well, which hadn't been poisoned as the others had.

The day felt as if it actually were going to get warm. As the column moved towards the next ranch, the trail and surrounding meadows were littered with dead and dying blood-splattered sheep, cattle, and horses. Magpies and coyotes were feasting as never before. Dying sheep bleated as the column rode by them. Their forelegs had been cut off, or hamstrung by the Hostiles. Time and ammunition could not be spared to stop the pathetic animals' pleading and suffering. It only added to the troopers' misery. Cresap rode beside Bernard, explaining the terrain ahead and answering the captain's questions as they rode along. Cresap was someone new Bernard could talk to; he'd read recent newspapers and at least had some current news. Cresap was amazed at the professionalism displayed by the men in Bernard's battalion. They were a breed apart. Cresap explained to Bernard that the

Indians they were following confused him. He'd lived in Grant County for years and had never experienced anything like this outbreak. As they rode along, eyes moving constantly, Cresap related to Bernard how he and his partner, Tom Meyers, had left Elk Creek on Tuesday the second, unaware of any Indian Hostiles in the area. The two had stopped at the Dribblesby Ranch for a bite of dinner and had found everyone gone. Other ranches they went to also were abandoned or burned. They went to Canyon City and then to Long Creek, where Cresap had offered his services to Bernard. So here he was in an Indian War.

As the column crossed the green meadows and timber, it soon came upon the ranch reported by Robbins' volunteer. The ranch buildings sat at the edge of a large meadow, with the timberline three hundred yards to the rear. As the column approached the ranch buildings, they seemed untouched at first. However, once they reached them, evidence proved otherwise. The battalion dismounted and scouts again searched for survivors. Its owners had abandoned the ranch. Frightened chickens were roosting in the trees in the front yard. "Cap'n!" shouted Robbins to Bernard, waving him over to where he stood on the front porch of the house. Bernard saw the dead lamb tied and burned in the same manner as the other had been. Robbins and Cresap squatted down, carefully studying the dusty, trampled ground around the dead animal. "Well, I'll be damned!" blurted Robbins with amazement, standing upright as he removed his dirty hat and scratched the back of his head. Cresap stared at the ground, nodding in agreement. "Kids! Gawdam kids!" sputtered Robbins.

Cresap looked up at Bernard, who was standing above him. "Moccasin tracks, Captain. Little ones. This here were the work of Injun youngsters." he said, shaking his head. Robbins spit into the grass.

Bernard blinked his eyes; McGregor and Lieutenant Edwards looked on in amazement. The ranch's yard was strewn with broken furniture. A shattered music box lay by the porch, torn women's clothing hung on the broken picket fence. A carpet had been dragged from the house and cut to shreds. All of the windows were broken out. "Mount, Gentlemen!" ordered Bernard.

A letter from Bismarck, D.T., June 5, reports a conversation with Father T.B.M. Genin, the noted missionary to the Sioux, who has personally known Sitting Bull for ten years:

"Sitting Bull has 300 scouts, and has full information as to every garrison on the Canadian side, and knows the situation thoroughly and is quickly informed of every movement on either side of the line. Their plan is to ask for food and not getting it hunger will drive them to war, annihilating the mounted police and taking the territory north of the Missouri. Father Genin says we must let them have the country north of the Missouri or there will be war, the worst in the annals of our country."

Army Navy Journal, June 22, 1878.

Chapter 5

Alarm Bells on the Columbia

Far to the north, a group of volunteers from Pendleton were combing the meadows and timber of the Blue Mountains south of the town of Pendleton. They'd decided to come and "have a look" at the so-called Hostiles coming from the south. They were certain that they could whip any reservation Indians that they might come across. John "Mac" Whittmore and twenty men were riding across the mountain ranges and meadows, looking for sign of Indians. So far they'd only seen an occasional lone rider passing in the distance. The men were nearly asleep in their saddles, tired from a sleepless night. They soon came upon a large band of sheep grazing peacefully on Little Camas Prairie. The sheep dogs watched the group suspiciously at a distance. The riders approached the three herders near the band of sheep. Mac Whittmore greeted John Vey and his herder, Crisp.

"Howdy, Mac!" said Vey, looking over the riders and their gun belts heavy with brass cartridges. "Looks like you are going to war, boys!" chuckled Vey.

"Now, John, there's talk of Indian trouble in the country and you had better take heed. Leave the band and come with us or at least go back to your ranch for protection."

"Hell, Mac, if I ran home every time I heard a rumor of Indian trouble, you wouldn't get that nice wool sweater for Christmas, now would you?" joked Vey. "Just the same, I'll keep a eye peeled for Indians and let you know if we see any, all right? Vey condescended.

"All right, John, but you boys be damned careful now. Have you seen Campbell's band of sheep?" asked Whittmore as he turned his horse away.

"Just east of here, Mac, the other side of the prairie, past the trees. Take care now, you fellas," shouted Vey as the riders turned and rode east. "Come on, let's bunch these woolies together," he said to Crisp as he gripped his wooden staff a little bit tighter than he had before.

Whittmore had found and alerted the Campbell outfit not far away and the volunteers were again riding along lazily. "Mac, look!" blurted one of the men to Whittmore, startling him. Riding across the meadow before the volunteers, two hundred yards away, rode a lone warrior wearing a large war bonnet. The warrior was riding westward in front of the volunteers, seemingly unaware of their presence.

"Git!" spat Bailey, as he spurred his horse towards the Indian, Dellivan following on his heels. The warrior suddenly kicked his horse into a gallop as he rode across the meadow. Meanwhile, Whittmore's men were drawing a bead on the galloping Indian. A volunteer's Sharps rifle roared in everyone's ears, horses reared. In the distance the warrior's head snapped back as he fell from the galloping horse, bouncing like a rag doll into the grass. The painted horse never broke its stride and continued galloping across the prairie.

As the volunteers approached the fallen Indian, someone yelled "Watch out!" The warrior, bleeding profusely from his chest, mouth, and nostrils, was struggling to get to his rifle, lying in the grass twenty feet away from him. A young volunteer riding up to him shouted, "I got him!" and fired his revolver into the side of the warrior's head, spraying blood and matter. The dying man dropped over on his left side with a grunt. As the youth approached him, the dying warrior kicked his leg convulsively, startling the youth who reacted by shooting the warrior once again in the head. "Will you look at this!" said the youth as he jerked the eagle-feathered war bonnet from the dead Indian's splattered head. "Wow! Wait till they see this in town!" he exclaimed, as he placed it on his head, chuckling.

"Come on men, let's go," said Whittmore to the laughing group.

"Oh, God, Mac!" shouted a volunteer behind Whittmore, pointing his finger toward the tree line from where the Indian had ridden.

The volunteers watched in horror as a line of over one hundred warriors slowly emerged from the treeline. Suddenly, with a screeching warhoop, the warriors charged the small group of volunteers.

"Ride like hell!" screamed Whittmore to his men, not looking back as he spurred his horse across the meadow towards Pendleton. The Indians chased the volunteers for about a mile, then broke off the chase. They had other plans. The volunteers scattered like quail over the landscape, running for their lives. The warriors had easier game to catch.

Nightfall found Bernard's battalion camped high above the Middle Fork of the John Day River. The high mesas around them reminded the Arizona veterans of the Apache campaigns and the landscape of the southwest. The pungent smell of juniper pine trees perfumed the evening air, mingling with wood smoke. Sitting around a fire were Bernard, Bomus, Robbins, and Ward. Each looked as worn and weary as the next. All knew that part of the reason was due to the stress of pent up energy, wanting to engage the Hostiles north of them. The fire popped and crackled, emitting hot airwaves that mingled with the cool night air around them. "Feels like it's clearin up a bit," mumbled Robbins as he sniffed the air.

Bernard stifled a chuckle, thinking that Robbins resembled the battalion's mascot Jack, the dog, sniffing with his long nose pointed upward into the night sky above them.

"Good weather is what we need!" said Ward through watering, smoke-stung eyes.

Robbins nodded his head, puffing on his pipe, staring into the fire. He removed the long stemmed pipe from his mouth. "Be glad when Lieutenant Mac gets back. Hope he made it OK." He returned the pipe to his mouth, and continued staring into the fire.

Bernard stood up to full height, stretching his arms. "Who here is as tired and sore as I am, Gentlemen?" he said to the fatigued ring of men sitting around the fire. A series of guttural agreements and nodding heads answered him. Suddenly, without warning, Bernard exerted a full cartwheel on his hands and feet in the grass, coming to a full upright position without blinking an eye, a wide grin on his face. Everyone sat awed, mouths open. "Good! Then we are in fine condition to fight these people if necessary. Good night, Gentlemen!" Bernard disappeared into the night as he went on his regular routine inspection of the perimeter before retiring. Jack found Bernard, as he usually did at this time of night. The two disappeared into the darkness, a man with his faithful companion trotting at his heels.

That evening, McGregor, having located General Howard, again camped at the small town of Long Creek. They were ready to move northward before dawn to join Bernard's column. Howard ordered Officers Call. As his officers sat or stood around him, he spoke. Sarah and Mattie sat together. "Gentlemen, Captain McGregor has brought me up-to-date about the enemy's progress. It seems that other Indians have been joining them for several days and that perhaps they are Umatillas and Shoshoni. Bernard is in a precarious position right now, being so close to their rear, making it necessary that we join him tomorrow at the latest. He could never withstand a full engagement with the Hostiles and we certainly do not want a repeat of the tragedies of the Little Big Horn and White Bird." Some officers cleared their throats in the smoky tent, eyes darting back and forth, some looked down at the floor of the tent. Sarah and Mattie felt stares from some of the officers. It made them uncomfortable.

Howard continued, "My mail couriers have been getting in and out quite well, against very dangerous odds. The messages from General McDowell at Headquarters in San Francisco and from Fort Vancouver advise me that steamers are being prepared with ordnance on the Columbia River and will soon be on station, patrolling between Umatilla Crossing and Wallula near Fort Walla Walla. When that happens, we will have the Hostiles between us and can force them to fight on our terms. The important thing right now is to restrain ourselves from starting a premature engagement. That would allow the leaders of this group to escape and would cost unnecessary lives. It is my estimate that we will engage them on or before the tenth. If there are no further questions, then please see to your men and animals. We march at daybreak. Good night, Gentlemen."

Before midnight, armed civilian sentries in Pendleton shouted a challenge into the darkness. They could hear horses approaching the town's south perimeter. Their answer came from Whittmore, the leader of the volunteers that had been attacked while taking the feathered headdress from the warrior they'd killed that morning in the mountains south of Pendleton. The volunteers led their winded and played out horses into the yellow lights of town, the townspeople slowly edging out of their shanties, wrapping themselves in coats and shawls. They were shocked at the sight of the dust-covered men and horses limping in. One or two women ran to their men, thankful for their return. The horses were caked with dried mud, dust, and sweat lather. The volunteers didn't look much better. No one had to ask what had happened; the men's faces showed it. As one of the downtrodden horses limped past the small crowd of people, they noticed a tattered feather headdress tied to the saddle horn. It flopped up and down with the rhythm of the horse's gait. Dried splattered blood covered it. It was Independence Day, 1878.

At one the following morning, Friday, July fifth, Captain W.P. Gray and Chief Engineer Samuel Gill of the Oregon Steam and Navigation Company were preparing to disembark from the steamer Idaho that they'd just docked at The Dalles, Oregon, on the Columbia River. A company messenger ran up the gangplank waving a telegram. The messenger scampered up the ladder, reaching the pilothouse where Gray and Gill were signing off the boat's log for the day. The last passengers had gone ashore several hours before, after spending the Fourth of July on a picnic excursion voyage along the Columbia River. They'd arrived late, having gone aground on various sandbars because of the unusually low river. The two boatmen were tired.

"My God! Simmons, what in duce is wrong with you anyway?" asked Gill, looking up from his writing.

"Telegram, Sir!" Simmons puffed out the words. Gill stopped writing and turned to both men. Simmons thrust out the telegram toward Captain Gray and stepped back, his chest heaving.

"Well I'll be damned!" Gray said, holding the telegram closer to the lamp. "It says we've been commissioned by the War Department to go up river to Celilo and get steam up on the Spokane and get her underway to the north shore to take aboard the Army and its brass tomorrow. It seems as if we are in another Indian war, Mr. Gill."

Gill frowned in the dim lamplight of the pilothouse. "Well, so much for shore leave, Captain. Damn! I'd made plans to go fishing Saturday. Oh well, let's get packed and catch the donkey engine up to Celilo." Gill snapped the log closed and placed it in a drawer. The Spokane was docked at Celilo and there wouldn't be any sleep for them riding the noisy steam engine as it puffed its way along the railroad tracks up river.

"Indians. Humph!" thought Gray, as he climbed down the ladder to the main deck and walked down the gangway of the Idaho. "If it ain't one thing, it's another!" he mumbled to himself, shaking his tired head.

As the first gray of daylight entered the eastern sky, Howard's column, with McGregor, filed out to the north, leaving a smoky mantle hanging over the campground in the meadow near Long Creek. Soon only the sounds of a few barking dogs disturbed the early morning silence.

At Celilo on the Columbia River, the sounds of hammering and cussing rent the morning air as men hastily worked to reconnect the engine on the steamer Spokane. It had been "winterized" and had been disconnected with no water in the boiler. "How's it going, Gill?" shouted Gray from the pilothouse above the sweating engineer.

"It's coming, Sir! We're onloading boiler water now. We should have fire in about an hour!" shouted Gill through the shiny brass voice tube in the boiler room.

As Gray was bringing the Spokane's log up to date in the wheelhouse, he heard the whistle of the donkey engine blowing an alarm as it traveled towards the dock from the west. Gray dropped the log and scrambled down the ladder to the forecastle, to see what was happening. Soon Gill was standing by his side, wiping grease from his hands. From the dock, a boat hand shouted that Indians had been seen on the track west of them and that the donkey engine had returned in a hurry. After conversing with the ten Oregon Steam and Navigation (OS&N) employees, it was decided that in light of the information they already had, it would be safer to cross to the Washington shore for protection and to wait for the Army there. It was their only chance if there were hostile Indians near. They would take the fifty workmen, mechanics, and their families with them. Within the hour the workmen and three families were safely aboard the boat. Children were crying and the adults wore anxious faces. They had few guns amongst them.

Captain Gray ordered the American and company flags raised. The wind caught them quickly, making them snap and crackle in the bright sunlight. Gray's gold buttons shone brightly against his dark blue captain's coat. "Mr. Gill! Do you have steam up, Sir?" shouted Gray through the voice tube to the boiler room, watching for Indians on the tracks.

"Aye, aye, Sir, I'll give you all we've got!" yelled Gill, as he shouted to his firemen Stockham and Tom Monoham, to keep throwing the large chunks of wood into the firebox. Soon the gray smoke traveling out of the large black shiny stack turned black and began to belch out in billowing clouds. The mate, Dave Clapp, was hauling in the gangplank with the assistance of the boat's seventeen-year-old watchman and lamp trimmer.

"Cast off bow and stern lines!" shouted Gray. The ropes securing the boat to the moorage were thrown off and Clapp jumped aboard. A jet of white steam followed the shrill boat's whistle, echoing from the high rock walls of the north and south sides of the great Columbia River Gorge.

"Back-Slow!" yelled Gray to Gill in the engine room. Gill immediately began to pull iron levers and open gate valves as he constantly watched the boiler pressure gauge on the bulkhead before him. He said a small prayer that they had enough steam up to make headway. Slowly the large red wooden stern wheel began to turn, churning up mud and grass from the shallow moorage bottom. The red wheel buckets shone and glistened in the sunlight as they turned and dipped into the river water.

The long steamboat gracefully swung its stern out into the Columbia, its white paint bright against the steel blue water. Captain Gray ordered Mate Clapp, who was also the company watchman at Celilo, up to the wheelhouse to navigate the boat across to the Washington side of the river. The teen-aged lamplighter replaced him in the engine room below as fireman. The boat immediately began picking up speed as it drifted momentarily downstream by the stern. "Ahead-Half!" ordered Clapp through the tube. The large red stern wheel changed directions and churned up white water as it fought the strong current of the river. The bow began to turn towards the north shore.

After thirty minutes had passed, someone on the deck yelled to Gill through the open window on the main deck. "We're going to go over the falls!" Gill ran out onto the deck and looked down river. To his shock and surprise, the boat was not making headway and instead, was slowly sliding backwards towards Celilo Falls, which dropped hundreds of feet, disappearing in a white thundering mass of water and boulders below.

"Great-Gawd-Amity!" yelled Gill, slapping his forehead. He turned and scrambled back into the engine room and yelled to Clapp through the tube.

"What do you want?" responded Clapp, obviously busy at the moment.

"GO AHEAD-FULL!" screamed Gill, "or we'll be over the falls in thirty minutes!"

"AHEAD-FULL!" screamed the voice back from the wheelhouse above. The telegraph bell clanged, ringing its urgent call. The Spokane drifted downstream for some distance, her large stern wheel cutting into the dark swift water of the river, churning up white foam and froth behind her. She seemed to be sitting still on the river, not making headway against the swift deadly current of the Columbia. It seemed an eternity for those watching the looming white mist of the falls boiling up behind them. They could hear the distant roar of the falls over the noise of the boat's engine as they drifted backwards towards certain death. Gill and his firemen cursed and sweated as they struggled, heaving blocks of wood into the firebox. The boat was fighting for steam and its life. Thick black smoke and sparks bellowed out of the black smokestack, its bright red painted band shining in the sunlight as the wheel buckets tore into the water. Suddenly, yet smoothly, everyone could feel the tough boat gripping the current. Slowly the Spokane's one hundred and fifty-foot length began to inch forward against the current and away from the thundering falls and death. A cheer rent the air as the passengers shouted relief and gratitude to the crewmen. Soon the Spokane was making headway against the Columbia's mighty current, her flags snapping in the wind. Within forty-five minutes the stern wheeler nosed to port and found itself easing into the OS&N's crudely built work docks.

Once the crew had tied the bow and stern lines, the passengers began to disembark, still shivering from their ordeal. They set up temporary housekeeping until the Army arrived. Gill flopped down onto the boat's deck, his chest heaving, trying to get his wind back from the recent struggle. He heard the familiar clicking heels of Captain Gray's shoes approaching him. "Well, Sam, that was some feat. I don't think I've ever seen the Spokane get up steam so fast. My compliments."

Gill, whose chest still heaved as he sat glaring out across the river, spoke to his captain, "I don't know how we did it, you and that damned Clapp almost got us caught in those Indian salmon traps at the bottom of the falls! Fish food! All of us!" snorted Gill, shaking his head in wonderment. "I didn't see any Indian sign at the boat works, did you?" he asked, lowering his voice.

"No, and I didn't see any before or after the alarm," said Gray thoughtfully. "They might have been peaceful local Indians. We'll post lookouts here anyway, at least until the Army gets here in the morning. I think we should keep the boilers lit, don't you, Sam?" asked Gray, almost apologetically.

"You can bet your ass on that, Gray. I don't want to ever get caught between hostile Indians and Celilo Falls again, no Sir!" Gill stood up stiffly, wiping his sweaty hands on his pants. "I'll get a crew and get up some firewood right away. No offense meant, Gray, you brought us over here in fine style." Gill shook his head smiling, as he hurried off noisily down the creaking gangplank.

Gray leaned on the top-rail outside the pilothouse, watching Gill mustering the wood crew ashore. "Good man," he thought to himself as he lit his pipe, returning his gaze across the Columbia from the pilothouse of the Spokane. He could still see the stack smoke from their recent charge upriver just minutes ago, sliding eastward up river.

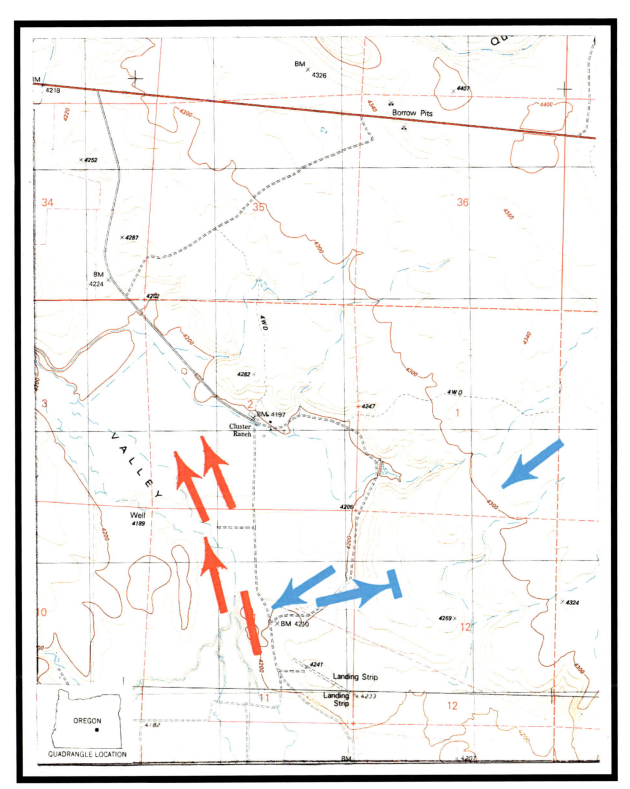

SILVER CREEK BATTLEFIELD
Oakerman Lakes Quadrangle, Harney County, Oregon, 7.5 min. USGS
(25 miles west of Burns on US Highway 20)

1" = 2,000'

NORTH

135

Silver Creek Battlefield, present day photograph showing the Indian defensive line on relatively flat terrain (arrow to the left). View is to the north where Bernard's two cavalry charges at 9:00 am on 23 June 1878, failed to overrun the Indian line, and were thrown back to the right (center arrow) and prevented from accessing the Indian Village. Bernard's tenuous overnight position and rock corral are to the right (right arrow). Oregon Highway 20 lies in the distance just out of sight. The location is approximately 12 miles west of Burns, Oregon, on private land. Photo courtesy Greg Hodgen.

Present day photograph of Long Creek log stockade site (arrow), Long Creek, Oregon. A few ranchers and their families huddled in horror as up to seven hundred Indian combatants, trailed by some thirteen hundred dependents, paraded silently in a column-of-fours to within yards of hastily prepared defenses, in June 1878. The Indians marched northward over the timbered hills, in this view of the site looking south. The intent was to make a show of force and not necessarily to kill everyone in the stockade, which they could have easily done. Oregon Highway 395 is to the right of photo. Photo courtesy Greg Hodgen.

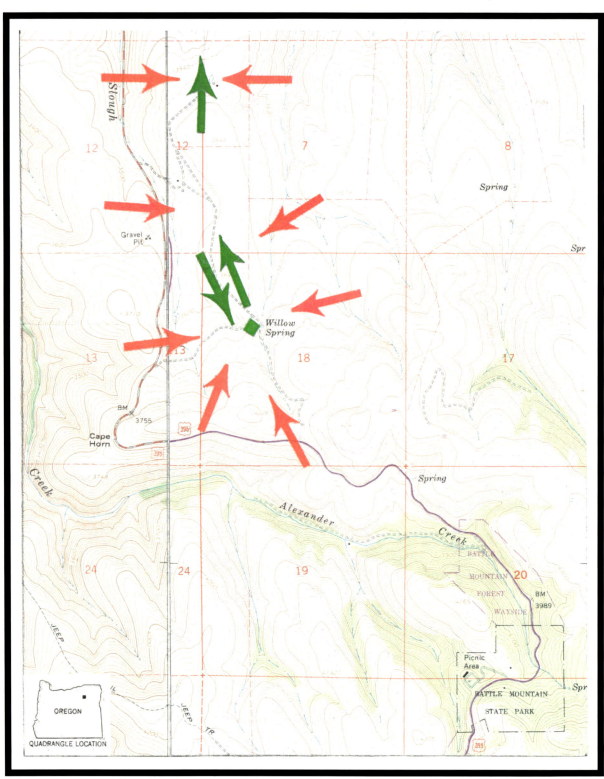

WILLOW SPRING BATTLEFIELD
Carney Butte Quadrangle, Umatilla County, Oregon, 7.5 min. USGS
(15 miles south west of Pilot Rock on highway 395)

NORTH

1" = 2,000'

OREGON

VOLUNTERS

Present day photo of Willow Spring, scene of the deadly trap sprung upon fifty-two volunteers from Pendleton, Oregon, on Saturday July 6, 1878. Left arrow points to the probable location of the sheep-shed where volunteers ran for cover and were soon surrounded. Right arrow shows the location of Willow Spring. Two people on the lower left exhibit the scale. Photo is taken from the eastern Indian firing position looking downward from the hilltop. The volunteers' escape to Pendleton during the early hours of the next morning is to the right, northward. Oregon Highway 395 runs north and south near the top of the photo. Photo courtesy Larry Purchase.

Painting of Battle of Willow Spring

Mrs. B. F. Swaggart painted the details of the 1878 battle scene in 1896, as they were pointed out to her by the men who fought the engagement. The painting was then exhibited at the Lewis and Clark Fair in Portland, Oregon, in 1906. The Portland Historical Museum housed the painting until 1948, when Mrs. Swaggart reclaimed it to be displayed in the main room above the fireplace in the old Umatilla County Library building. Today, the painting can be found hanging in the Morrow County Museum in Heppner, Oregon. The Oregon Historical Society thoughtfully photographed it before releasing it. The above rendition is digitally enlarged from their two inch by two-inch photo (ORHI 97189). The scene is shown looking east. (Reference: East Oregonian Newspaper, April 24, 1948, article "Famous Battle Between Indians and Whites Painted By Pioneer.") Courtesy Oregon Historical Society.

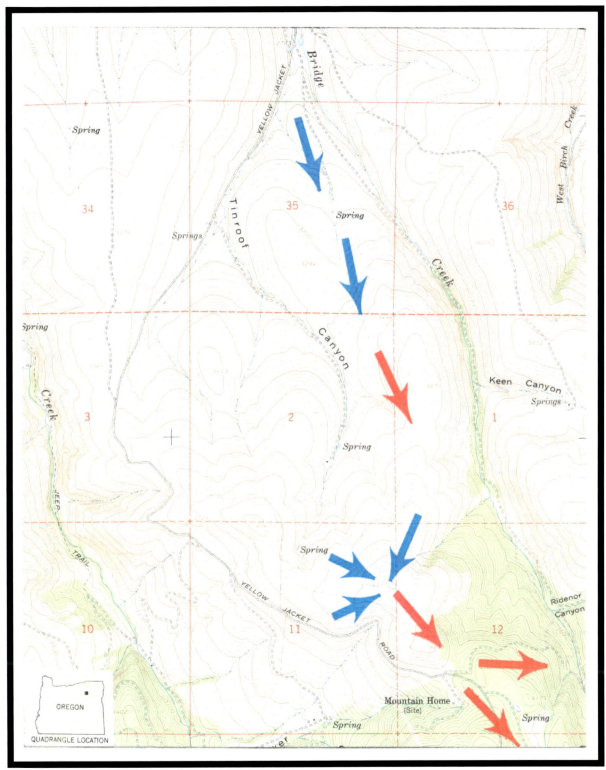

BIRCH CREEK BATTLEFIELD
Carney Butte Quadrangle, Umatilla County, Oregon, 7.5 min. USGS
(13 miles south east of Pilot Rock on Yellow Jacket Road)

1" =2,000'

NORTH

Present-day photograph of the Birch Creek Battlefield, looking southward at the lava outcrop fortification held by the Indians, as seen in the distance at upper lift-center of photo (center arrow). Photo was taken near the bridge where the Hostiles ambushed the point riders of Howard's Column, beginning the battle (right arrow). From this point, Bernard led the troops upward, systematically using the Gatling Gun and dismounted Cavalrymen as skirmishers against harassing fire from Indian warriors (left arrow) as they advanced upward in the nearly three mile assault. Location is approximately five miles south of Pilot Rock, Oregon, via Yellow Jacket Road on West Birch Creek. Photo courtesy Greg Hodgen.

Present-day photograph of Birch Creek Battlefield as seen from the Indian position looking downward (north) toward the advancing Cavalry troops. The main Cavalry assault on the Indians' fortified position came from the center of the photo by troopers formed on line, directly to the front with the Gatling Gun (arrow) probably in place to their center of line. The second Cavalry assault line was to the left of the photo to the west, with a third assault still further west. Photo courtesy Greg Hodgen.

Birch Creek Battlefield, present-day photograph of the west face of the lava Indian fortification, as viewed from the third Cavalry assault line. Note the steep incline to the top; a very difficult and deadly advance for horses and troopers under fire. Photo courtesy Greg Hodgen.

Pilot Rock in the 1880's. Named for the large bluff of basalt rock shown on the left. Bernard's Cavalry troops, reinforced from Fort Walla Walla, formed up here, numbering two hundred fifty-three Cavalrymen in seven troops (Companies A,E,F,G,H,K, and L). They, with Brigadier General Howard's presence in the field, and commanded by Captain Bernard, proceeded to the Birch Creek Battle site. Photo courtesy "Umatilla County: A Backward Glance," p. 236.

U.S. Army Rapid Fire Gatling Gun, caliber .45 used in the final approach of the Birch Creek Battle. Photo courtesy U.S. Artillery School 1886.

The "Spokane" only eight months off the stocks at Celilo, where she had been built in the record time of thirty-two days and six hours, for the Oregon Steam Navigation Company, and was commandeered by the U.S. Army. Nineteen regulars (2nd Infantry) and forty-two cowboy volunteers were armed with rifles and a Gatling gun. Sacks of flour on deck provided breastworks. This photo shows sacked wheat on her bow. She burned at the Lewiston Dock in 1922. Photo courtesy "Blow for the Landing" by Fritz Timmen, p. 149.

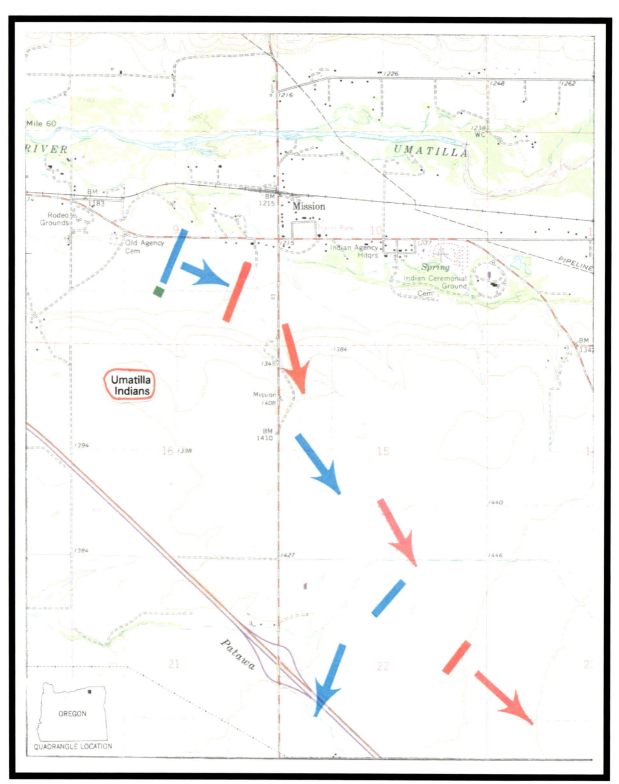

AGENCY BATTLEFIELD
Mission Quadrangle, Umatilla County, Oregon, 7.5 min. USGS
(4 miles east of Pendleton on US Highway 30)

1" =2,000'

NORTH

21

148

Present-day photograph of the Old Umatilla Agency grounds, looking southward toward the battlefield. The Infantry and Artillery lined up on the right facing the Hostiles on the hill and flat below, to the left. The Umatilla Reservation Indians waited on the hills to the right before officially deciding to swing to the U.S. Army's side. One troop of Cavalry, on the left of line of six companies of Infantry, with two companies of Artillery in the center, fired at the Indian positions most of the day. A small group of Pendleton volunteers were on the far right. Late in the day, led by the Cavalry, all units were ordered forward, dislodging and scattering the Hostiles into the Blue Mountains (seen in the distance at far left of photograph).

The present Umatilla Indian Reservation Agency is to the left and east approximately one mile, and the Mission Highway can be seen in the foreground, with a power line, running east and west. Photograph courtesy Greg Hodgen.

Old Umatilla Indian Agency grounds gathering, looking north, in approximately 1880. At least some of these buildings were defended at the Battle of the Agency. Indian Agent Cornoyer reported seeing Chief Egan and Chief Buffalo Horn recruiting warriors here prior to the outbreak of hostilities. The dark area in the upper left is a result of the photo glass plate having been broken. Photo courtesy Waible Patton and Mildred Searcy, published in "Umatilla County: A Backward Glance," p. 135.

Old Umatilla Indian Agency as it looks today, taken from the same perspective as the photo above; it is now a wheat field. The Umatilla River flows to the left at the base of the hills in the distance. Pendleton is located about three miles to the left (west) of photo and the present Agency is one mile to the right (east). Photo taken from beside the old highway from Pendleton to La Grande (Mission Road), which was built over the roadbed of the Oregon Trail. Photo courtesy Greg Hodgen.

Hotchkiss Mountain Howitzer (1.6 inch), with its accompanying Artillery pieces, being trailed along side an unidentified Calvary Troop in the field. This photo, taken in approximately 1880, shows a configuration of Cavalry as it might have looked at the Battle of the Agency. Photograph courtesy Greg Hodgen.

GEN. SHERMAN.

William T. Sherman, General, U.S. Army, is noted for his destructive "march to the sea" through Georgia during the Civil War. In 1878 he was the General of the Army. Photo courtesy Greg Hodgen.

Oliver O. Howard, Brigadier General, U.S. Army. Brady photo taken in Washington, D.C., after the surrender of the Confederacy in April 1865, when he was attending the Grand Review of Union Armies in the nation's capitol. Note the black mourning ribbon on his remaining left arm, in memoriam of recently assassinated President Abraham Lincoln. Photo shows two stars of a Major General, his rank at the end of the Civil War. Photograph courtesy Greg Hodgen.

Irvin McDowell, Major General, was Brigadier General Howard's boss at the Precedio of San Francisco. McDowell, associated with early defeats in the Civil War that were not his fault, was posted to the Department of the Pacific beginning in 1864. Photograph courtesy "Historical Times, Illustrated Encyclopedia of the Civil War," by Patricia L. Faust, p. 459.

Reuben F. Bernard, Captain First Cavalry, photographed at Walla Walla, Washington, probably in 1878. Photograph courtesy "One Hundred and Three Fights and Scrimmages," by Don Russell.

William C. Brown, Second Lieutenant, First Cavalry, photograph taken about 1880. Frank B. Abell photographer, Portland, Oregon. The young officer, having graduated from West Point only the year before the 1878 War, would participate in most of America's military adventures over the next forty years. He would see action in the Sheepeater War in Idaho (1877), the war in Cuba and in the Philippines (1898), the Mexican Border incident against Poncho Villa (1916), and finally, during World War I (1918-1919). He earned promotion to Brigadier General. His bachelor life, devoted to the Army, is well documented in one hundred forty-two linear feet of shelf space containing his maps, letters, books, etc., donated to and housed at the University of Wyoming, at Laramie. Photograph courtesy "Cavalryman Out of the West, Life of General William Carey Brown," by Francis G. Brimlow.

Dr. Jenkins (John) A. FitzGerald, Captain, a surgeon, is credited for having collected the skull and forearm (ulna and radius) of Chief Egan for the U.S. Army Museum in Washington, D.C. He died the next year of bronchial and pneumonia complications first contacted during the rigors of the 1878 War. Photograph courtesy "An Army Doctor's Life on the Frontier," by Emily FitzGerald

Captain Thomas McGregor, Commanding Officer of Company A, First Cavalry, participated in the Silver Creek and Birch Creek Battles. Photo probably taken in 1878. Photograph courtesy Greg Hodgen.

Charles Erskine Scott Wood, First Lieutenant, Twenty-first Infantry, U.S.A. He was aid-de-camp to Brigadier General O.O. Howard during the Bannock-Paiute Indian War. A West Point graduate, he later in life became famous as a Portland attorney, and Northwest poet and artist. Photograph courtesy "Life of C.E.S. Wood," by Erskine Wood, Jr., p. 15.

Buffalo Horn, Chief of the Bannocks, had served as a scout for the U.S. Army, and was Chief of Scouts for Brigadier General Howard during the Nez Perce War of 1877. He, however, masterminded the Bannock-Paiute War of 1878. He was mortally wounded during the first skirmish at South Mountain, Idaho. He, with a hand-picked raiding party of sixty warriors, was engaged by Captain Harper's small and inferior group of twenty-eight volunteers. But for Paiute Joe's action of taking aim at the lead warrior approaching the fleeing volunteer group, whom he recognized as Buffalo Horn, the volunteer group would most surely have been annihilated. The Bannock War Chief was reported to have ordered his warriors to leave him to die in the brush, and continue their fight on to the west. They promptly complied. Sarah (Winnemucca) Hopkins, in her book "Life Among the Piutes (sic): Their Wrongs and Claims," reports torn clothing, cut hair, and broken beads on the trail, signifying grief at the loss of their leader.

From this photo, it can be seen that Buffalo Horn was very good looking. Had he been born in more recent times, he may have had a successful and lucrative career in Hollywood. Photograph courtesy "Cattle Country of Peter French," by Giles French.

Sarah Winnemucca, one of the first Native American authors, published her autobiography in 1883, when she was almost forty years old. She had lost her mother, sister, and brother in the violent aftermath of the earlier Paiute War of 1860. Much is known about the Indian side of the 1878 War from her book and other well-researched books of her life, written since. She was a good orator, and championed her people's causes on the lecture circuit of her time. Typical of her people's misfortunes, she was dealt a hard life. She was married four times, and in October 1891 died of tuberculosis in Montana. Photograph courtesy of "Three American Indian Women, Pocahontas, Sacajawea, Sarah Winnemucca, of the Northern Paiutes," by Gae Whitney Canfield, p. 15.

Umapine, hereditary Chief of the Cayuse Indians, is thought to have participated with the Hostiles at the Silver Creek Battle, and to have escorted them to the Umatilla Reservation to join up with his tribesmen. After reconsultation with Chief Homily and others, he secretly agreed that the best direction for the Umatilla Reservation Indians was to divorce themselves from the Hostiles' Religious Dreamer Movement. This set the stage for War Chief Egan's secret entrapment by the Umatillas, which when sprung, he resisted. Unfortunately this resulted in the deaths of War Chief Egan and several members of his family. Photo courtesy Bradley and Rulofson, San Francisco, California; procured by Second Lieutenant William C. Brown about 1879, probably at Pendleton, Oregon. Photograph courtesy "Cavalryman Out of the West, Life of General William Carey Brown," by George F. Brimlow.

Sitting Bull was the great spiritual leader of the Sioux Indians, who in 1876 defeated Custer at the Little Bighorn River. For the succeeding two years he was hiding as a refugee in Canada. As may have been the case for Chief Joseph of the Nez Perce in 1877, who was stopped short of the Canadian border, the Bannock-Paiute alliance's goal was to join Sitting Bull if pressured by the U.S. Army. Photo courtesy U.S. Signal Corps (Brady Collection).

Quitatumps and White Owl, Umatillas, hand-signaling good by. At close inspection, you can see that their ankles are shackled. They were tried, convicted, and hung on the corner of Main Street and Dorian in Pendleton, Oregon, in 1878 for having been involved in the killing of Coggins and the wounding of Bunker. Their conviction was based on the testimony of a female Native American from the Umatilla Reservation. They were personally hung by Sheriff John L. Sperry who, as Captain of the Umatilla County Volunteers, suffered a disastrous defeat at the Battle of Willow Spring.

A heart-felt witness to the event, Nancy DeSpain, writes in "Reminiscences of Oregon Pioneers," that all were deeply touched and saddened when White Owl's wife tried to breath life back into her husband, by mouth-to-mouth resuscitation, as they were being driven in a buckboard back to the Reservation. Photo courtesy Oregon Historical Society #OHS 0341.

President Rutherford B. Hayes in 1878 continued a house-cleaning program designed to eliminate corruption in the administration he inherited from President Ulysses S. Grant. He was the nineteenth president of the United States (1877 to 1881). Photograph courtesy Greg Hodgen.

Governor Stephen Fowler Chadwick of Oregon met with Brigadier General O.O. Howard to offer assistance during the 1878 War. He was instrumental in having guns issued immediately to citizens; later armed militia from the Willamette Valley were sent by him to wherever was needed during the Indian War. Photograph courtesy "Governors of Oregon" by George Turnbull, p. 40.

Orlando (Rube) Robbins was an Indian fighter associated with the Idaho State Militia. Noted for wounding Chief Egan twice at the Silver Creek Battle. He was reported wounded at the Birch Creek Battle. Photograph courtesy Idaho Historical Society, "Indian Wars of Idaho," by Ross Arnold, p. 193.

Mr. William V. Rinehart was the last Malheur Indian Reservation agent. As a Major of Oregon Volunteers and Commanding Officer at Fort Klamath in 1868, he may have had unfortunate experiences with Indians that caused his prejudiced mindset against them. Photograph courtesy "Three American Indian Women, Pocahontas, Sacajawea, Sarah Winnemucca of the Northern Paiutes," by Gae Canfield.

Narcisse A. Cornyer, who had been a Major of Oregon Volunteers, was very skillful as a Umatilla Indian agent, and kept most of those in his charge out of the 1878 War. Perhaps part of his success was due to his closeness to the Indian community: he was married to an Indian woman. Photo courtesy "Chief Sarah," by Dorothy Morrison.

Dr. William Cameron McKay was the grandson of fur trader Alexander McKay (who was blown up with the Astor ship Tonquin at Clayoquot Sound in June 1811). His father, Thomas, fought in the Cayuse War from 1847 to 1849 on the side of the whites. His mother was a Chinook Indian. He was born in Astoria, Oregon, in 1824 and died in Pendleton in 1893.

A Pendleton physician in 1877 and 1878, he had worked on the Umatilla Reservation since 1868. He served as Field Surgeon to Major Throckmorton's Artillery Unit during the 1878 War. Dr. McLoughlin, of early Fort Vancouver prominence, assisted him in his education in the East, and was part of his family, having married McKay's grandmother. Nancy DeSpain wrote that he was known as a gentleman, kind, and courteous, sympathetic, and an able doctor. "Reminiscences of Oregon Pioneers," p. 101. Photograph courtesy "The Cayuse Indian, Imperial Tribesmen of Old Oregon" by Ruby and Brown, opposite p. 204.

McKay Creek and Dam, seven miles south of Pendleton, were named for Dr. McKay, who in 1851 and 1852 settled near its mouth. For a biography of Dr. McKay, see the January 2, 1889, issue of the East Oregonian (Pendleton) newspaper.

William Blakely served as a Lieutenant in the Umatilla County Volunteer Company and survived the disastrous Battle of Willow Spring. A stockman and wheat farmer on Wildhorse Creek, he was buried near the town named for his family, Blakely, Oregon. Photograph courtesy Bob Grant, Eastern Oregonian newspaper article, July 4, 1978, p. 13 by Virgil Rupp.

Colonel J.H. Raley wrote a detailed sixteen-page manuscript of the War. His son, James Raley, is reported to have written the script for the Pendleton Happy Canyon Pageant, with the 1878 War in mind. A successful lawyer, J.H. Raley became a State legislator. A park near the Pendleton Round-Up grounds is named for the family. His home in Pendleton, though partially burned in a recent fire, has been rebuilt to its historical stature. Photograph courtesy "An Illustrated History of Umatilla and Morrow Counties, State of Oregon," by William Parsons.

Mr. Jacob Fraser has a street in Pendleton named for his family. He was wounded in the calf at the disastrous Battle of Willow Spring on July 6, 1878. Photograph courtesy Bob Grant, Eastern Oregonian newspaper article, June 2, 1978, p. 13.

Mr. John W. Salisbury, serving as a private, was wounded twice at the Battle of Willow Spring . Photograph courtesy "An Illustrated History of Umatilla and Morrow Counties, State of Oregon," by William Parsons.

Mr. W.S. Byers' stone grain mill and warehouse became the safest place in Pendleton for women and children during the 1878 War. Mothers have been reported to have tied their children to the wooden pillars, amongst the choking grain dust, to prevent them from panicking and running out into the line of fire. The town panicked several times, but was never attacked. Some of Pendleton's phobic male defenders holed up in the stone walls with the women and children and refused to come out (pointing their guns), when ordered to defend the town's defensive outside fence perimeter with every one else. Photograph courtesy "An Illustrated History of Umatilla and Morrow Counties, State of Oregon," by William Parsons.

Egan's Scalp Wanted.

"Robie has offered a thousand dollars for Egan's scalp."

Portland Oregonian, Monday, July 1, 1878.

Preparations at Wallula.

"Wallula, (WT) July 3 – Settlers are coming in here, though not many. We have the Northwest here with steam up. In case they stray on to us, we can put what women there are aboard of her. We are pretty well fixed here; have about thirty needle guns, besides lots of others."

"A Company of 50 men under command of Col. Cornoyer, left Pendleton this morning. This force will be increased by at least 50 more at Pilot Rock."

Portland Oregonian, Thursday, July 4, 1878.

Chapter 6

Pendleton, Fear and Folly

The small town of Pendleton sits between two high bluffs that have been cut by the Umatilla River for thousands of years. The Umatilla, Cayuse, and Walla Walla tribes had inhabited the area since before recorded time. Now the peaceful Indians were watching from the Umatilla Agency east of Pendleton where they had come for protection. Not all of the Agency Indians were there, however. Some were Dreamers and were riding with the Hostiles coming from the south, having been recruited months before by Buffalo Horn and Egan. The two bluffs to the north and south of Pendleton had been carpeted with green grass during the spring and early summer, but had turned brown now with the summer heat. This was high desert country and the sun had dried out the grass and the earth quickly. Only the lazy flowing Umatilla River appeared indifferent to the summer heat as it trickled westward, where it would eventually enter the mighty Columbia River.

The Umatilla River flowed through Pendleton at the north end of town, dividing it from the northern bluffs. A sturdy wooden bridge spanned the river, allowing access north and south for the regular stagecoach lines as well as cattle herds and travelers such as miners traveling to and from the gold fields in Idaho. Farmers hauling grain to the Byers' Mill also required it. The stagecoaches passed over the bridge and through town, coming from Umatilla Landing on the Columbia River and headed south to John Day, carrying mail and passengers. Since the first defeated volunteer force had returned to the small town, it appeared that nothing could stop the advancing hordes of Indians coming down upon the defenseless town. The mostly one-story buildings were no match for the massive force coming towards them from the south. Their occupants had never imagined that so great a force of Indians could ever have gathered in such strength to destroy their town. Pendleton had the typical businesses and buildings of cow towns in the eighteen seventies. The only important government building in town was the wood framed two-story courthouse, which stood in an open plaza. Byers' Mill was also a building of prominence. The remainder of the buildings housed saloons, a hardware store, blacksmiths' shops, and livery stables. Three hotels, the Goodwin, Golden Rule, and The Pendleton, offered their services. A planing mill stood on the north bank of the river.

Pendleton was usually a quiet town that hummed with a fair amount of business. Today however, Friday, the fifth of July, was much different. Today businesses were closing. News had been coming in all day from travelers, bringing word of the approaching Indians. Small groups of men stood on street corners and sidewalks, talking in low voices. All were packing revolvers. The sight of the beat-up volunteer scouts who had returned earlier had unnerved everyone. Two large farm wagons were wheeled into Main Street, blocking the entrances at both ends. Men with rifles stood guard, scanning the bluffs with narrowed eyes. The flag hanging from the pole in front of the courthouse hung limp in the hot, dry air. A group of men attempting to recruit more volunteers for a foray against the oncoming Indians stood in the small plaza near the entrance to the courthouse as men passing by entered the structure. A town meeting was held and sweating men elected Frank Vincent, the town's past mayor and the local dentist, as captain of the volunteer company assigned to defend the town if need be.

The courthouse was filled to capacity. "Gentlemen!" shouted Vincent over the loud talking and shouting. He finally slammed the butt of his carbine on the table before him, abruptly halting the commotion. Vincent talked loudly enough so that everyone could hear him. "Gentlemen, now we can't be sure that the Indian news is all bad. First, they may not come to us and it sounds like they are heading north with a purpose. And I don't believe that we are a part of that purpose. Second," Vincent continued, "Those of you who wish to take your families to Fort Walla Walla, may do so now. To wait much longer would be folly, as the Hostiles are getting closer." Vincent withdrew his handkerchief and wiped his forehead. "Those of you who wish to stay must expect to fight for your lives if necessary. The Indians will show us no quarter, you all know that."

A low murmur traveled through the men, some nodding. Vincent poured water from a small pitcher into a cloudy glass and took a drink. He placed the glass back onto the table. "We cannot defend this town against these Indians, due to the number of warriors. But I do feel that the Army is hard on their heels, which puts the Army closer to us. I believe that the Army will do whatever it can to assist us, provided they arrive in time." He looked out the courthouse window, through the wavy glass at the businesses and his dentist office. "We all have property and holdings here. We stand to lose everything if we leave it for the Indians. They will burn what they don't take with them. I for one will not give up all the work and struggle that it took to get this far. Now, who's with me!" A roar and shouts of approval split the hot, heavy air within the room, as Vincent grabbed his carbine and worked his way through the crowd to the fresh air outside, pondering the question of how many of these men would leave on a fool's errand, leaving the town even more defenseless.

After Vincent had assigned the town's volunteers to their posts, he walked to the south end of the street and stepped onto the wooden sidewalk in front of a saloon, carbine in hand. He was suddenly drained of strength. He leaned against a lamppost, looking towards the barren bluffs to the south. "What were they hiding?" he thought. He heard boots clomping across the wooden sidewalk behind him.

"Vincent?" the familiar voice of Sheriff John Sperry addressed him as he approached.

"Hello, John," responded Vincent, not taking his gaze from the bluffs. Sperry stood beside Vincent, also looking at the bluffs. "Vincent, I've deputized two groups of men. One will follow me to Pilot Rock, where we will meet the second group of men. From there, we will attempt to meet these so-called Hostiles. After what they did to Whittmore's men, I can't let it go," said Sperry, his bushy mustache twitching.

"So I thought," said Vincent quietly. "You do realize, John, that you are leaving Pendleton with no defenses at all, don't you?"

Sperry spit into the street, wiped his mouth and turned to look at Vincent. "Vincent, yesterday we celebrated Independence Day and had a good time. Some of the boys are still hung over and some are still celebrating." Sperry turned his gaze back to the bluffs. "Whittmore got his ass whipped and that's a fact." he said quietly. Vincent turned his head, looking at Sperry, who showed sweat beads on his forehead. "I can't stop them, Vincent, they want a fight and I have to make it legal if I ever want to get elected again in this county. I can't show the white feather on this one."

Vincent looked into Sperry's eyes. There would be no change of mind for him. He was committed to go. "John, all I can say is I wish you luck. I don't know for sure what is heading for us, none of us do. But one thing is brutally clear. They have one hell of a lot of power behind them. Power like we've never seen before in this country. We could all get killed before this is over."

Sperry gently grasped Vincent's shoulder. "Vincent, I couldn't leave this town in anyone else's care but yours. I don't know what we're going to run into out there either, but I do know we have to find it and face it. We'll be back in about a week or sooner. By then the Army should be here with you. We'll see you then." Sperry turned and walked towards the mounting posse across the street and the wagon containing supplies and men.

"If you have a town to return to!" Vincent yelled after the departing man. Laughter came from the wagon, as a whiskey bottle was offered to the mounting men. The posse was ready. They could beat anything they might pitch into. Vincent and the others watched the column of men as they slowly wound their way up the bluffs and out of sight, trailing a cloud of dust. As the dust cloud drifted way to the east, Vincent thought he could hear singing drifting on a hot breeze. A cold shiver ran down his spine.

Fifty-five miles to the south, Captain Bernard was carefully leading his battalion upwards and out of the Middle Fork of the John Day River. It was rough going for the men and animals. The steep canyons and mesas above them sat like royal thrones, while below them ran cold streams and creeks. The pungent smell of pine and juniper trees hung heavily in the sunny mid-morning air. The battalion frequently dismounted, waiting for the next report from Robbins' scouts. The scouts reported the Hostiles to their front about twelve miles, moving northward. The scouts also reported smoke columns rising from the path of the moving Indians. By now, everyone knew what that meant. Yet, without reinforcements, there was nothing they could do. The thought maddened Bernard as he impatiently wiped the sweat from his forehead.

No bugles were to be blown now, just hand signals. Indians were too close, they were everywhere. Bernard had that strange feeling so common when he was getting close to an adversary and a fight. Indian sign was everywhere as they had followed the Indians' trail into the mountains. Bernard signaled his commanders to get the men up and to march forward, leading their mounts beside swiftly flowing Granite Creek. The creek was an ice cold snow runoff and refreshed men and animals, almost chilling them as they passed from warm sunlight into groves shaded by pine trees and juniper. High above them, an eagle and its mate circled the red clay rim-rocks in the warming air currents. After four hours of marching along the creek, Bernard ordered a rest, seating himself on a tree stump. The Middle Fork was far below them. He heard a commotion down the line of men, growing in intensity as he could see and hear a group of riders approaching from the south along his dismounted column. He stiffly arose, brushing off the seat of his worn sky blue trousers. He placed his beaten black campaign hat on his head, awaiting the excitement.

A cloud of red-clay dust engulfed Bernard from the approaching men. He immediately recognized the dust and sweat-streaked face of Lieutenant Wood, Howard's adjutant, as he reined in his mount, saluting through the haze. "Lieutenant Wood, Sir. General Howard sends his compliments. The General is just behind me, accompanied by Captain McGregor and his company. Glad we found you, Sir!" Wood croaked through the passing dust cloud.

Captain McGregor rode up, stopping beside Wood. A grin showed through his usual "business only" expression when he saluted Bernard. His face was grimy and his horse heaved from the forced march out of the Middle Fork below. "And a good mornin to ye, Sir!" McGregor toned.

Bernard waited for the last of the riders to arrive. He knew who it would be and felt relieved. Soon, out of the dust rode the one-armed General, Howard himself. He stopped his horse beside the other officers.

Bernard stood straight and saluted. He managed a strained smile as he spoke. "At your service, Sir, your presence is welcomed by all of us."

Howard returned the salute and dismounted with a grunt. The missing arm always upset his balance and gravity when he mounted and dismounted. "Captain Bernard, at last we meet again," Howard said as he guided Bernard out of earshot of the others, who were filling and drinking from canteens and wiping wet kerchiefs over their dust-covered faces and hair from the cold creek beside them. "Captain," Howard began, "I know you are looking for the rest of my command. It isn't here. The wagon train won't be up with us for two days, they needed the extra time to take on provisions at Dayville and the infantry was needed to protect it and the artillery from possible attack."

"I had expected, Sir...?" blurted Bernard, as he gazed from where Howard had come. Only drifting dust clouds could be seen, nothing else.

Howard spoke as he removed his hat, taking a red bandana from the inside of his blue coat. "Come," he said to Bernard as he walked to the banks of the creek, kneeling and dipping the soiled cloth into the cold water. He stood up, wiping his grimy face with the icy cloth.

After refreshing himself, Howard motioned Bernard to sit across from him on a large granite boulder. "Reuben?" Howard said as he placed his black campaign hat back on his head and looked upward towards the high canyon above them, "How are you?"

"Ready to engage these people, Sir." answered Bernard, looking directly at his commanding officer. "I had hoped that with your reinforcements I could attack the Hostiles and take the fight out of them, Sir. We could do it," Bernard said, with a hopeful tone of voice.

"Captain," Howard said wearily, "I know your record and it is indeed remarkable as well as honorable against any enemy, showing great courage and fortitude in conquering your foes in battle." He paused. "There will come a time shortly when I will call on you to take the enemy and stop its march. But right now, the trap I have planned for them is rapidly coming to a point of being sprung upon them." He stood up stiffly, unconsciously reaching for his missing arm. Howard again turned his gaze upward toward the high canyons around him. "Captain, Companies E and H of your regiment are en route to meet us at Pilot Rock. By the time we have joined up with them the wagon train with its companies of infantry and artillery will be in place south of the Hostiles." He turned to Bernard. "You and I must hold the Hostiles in place until we have formed all of our units together, forming a trap with one opening to the east."

Bernard's eyes snapped as he stood up facing his commander. "Sir, are you going to allow the Hostiles an opening to escape?" His hands began to tremble.

Howard's eyes moistened as he approached Bernard. "Captain Bernard, I know what your thoughts are about attacking and destroying these Hostiles. You are a soldier without reproach and an expert in your field." Howard took in a breath. He had nothing but respect for Bernard. "Reuben, more and more I believe we are following a group of misguided people led by devils who don't care about anything but killing and getting their way, just like Chief Joseph did last year. I think that one good defeat of these Hostiles will break their back and their desire to continue. But let us not repeat last year. Let's let General Miles take care of the few that make their way towards Sitting Bull. But we mustn't allow ourselves to destroy the women and children, the innocents who have become victims of their own people. We must allow them a way out."

Bernard sucked on a blade of grass, staring into the running creek. He pulled the blade of grass from his mouth and stood up, looking at Howard. "You're right, General. But as before I'm never clear just where the line is drawn between combatants and noncombatants. This lesson may not be learned for generations to come, and maybe not then. All I can do is follow orders and do the best that I can." He threw the blade of grass away and shoved his hat on his head, looking at Howard. "None the less, Sir, I think we are nearing the time of truth."

Having traveled nearly ten miles, the edgy battalion pulled into a flat grassy meadow with a flowing brook running through it. Troopers looked over their shoulders nervously as they unsaddled their mounts in the late afternoon sunlight. They were quieter than normal, as they gazed upward towards the surrounding hilltops and buttes around them. The uneasiness was contagious. They were getting close to the enemy. Even the large Army horses seemed spooked.

Egan sat in deep thought upon the red blanket before his crude shelter. His wounds were beginning to heal, the wounded arm was in its sling. The sound of someone approaching brought him back to the present. It was Charley, his brother-in-law. "Egan, something has happened," Charley spoke quietly. He stood before Egan, cradling his Winchester in the crook of his arm. "Umapine and a few other Umatillas have left us. It is said that he is afraid of the One-armed General that follows us and returns to his tribe."

"And what do you think, Charley?" questioned Egan, looking across the vast green meadow where shadows were beginning to fall within the groves of timber.

"Some say that Egan no longer has the heart to fight the soldiers and that Umapine goes to save his own skin." Charley lifted the rifle from the crook of his arm and sat down cross-legged before Egan. He laid the rifle across his legs and, reaching into a dirty shirt pocket with his long narrow fingers, removed a small tattered piece of newspaper found in a raided farmhouse. Egan watched as Charley withdrew a small soiled sack of tobacco. The faded imprint "Bull Durham Tobacco" still remained on it. He carefully dribbled a tiny string of the contents into the folded newspaper and rolled the contents into a tightly rolled cigarette. A sulfur match was struck on the rifle stock; the cigarette paper sputtered and flamed. Soon the smoke and smell of tobacco surrounded both men.

Egan's eyes bored into Charley's. "We must leave these people and soon, if we are to survive." His eyes darted to where Oits' shelter stood in the distance. "I need to know who is with us. When the time is right, I will lead us out." Charley's eyes followed Egan's gaze. He pinched off the burning end of the rolled cigarette and placed the stub into his shirt pocket as he stood and walked off. Egan's chest hurt but it wasn't from the bullets that had tried to kill him.

On Saturday, the sixth day of July, the fiery cap of the rising sun peeked over the dark horizon of the Blue Mountains, shooting golden rays into the dark morning sky. A long line of civilian riders and a wagon wove its way in the still semidarkness, quietly departing the small town of Pilot Rock. Sheriff Sperry and his volunteers huddled over their saddles in the cold morning air. The small group of men snaked their way southward toward the foothills in the blue-black dawn. Only an occasional cough and the sounds of horses' hooves betrayed their presence in the vast countryside.

Alarm at Celilo
Celilo, July 3, 1878.

"Fires are burning on the hills up the Columbia. A friendly Indian told me today to tell the people on the Deschutes to be on their guard, as the hostiles were going to divide in small bands and scatter, crossing the Columbia wherever they could."

McDonald
Portland Oregonian, Thursday, July 4, 1878.

Chapter 7

Governors' Boat Ride

In the pilothouse of the Spokane, the ships clock rang "Four Bells," six a.m. It was Saturday, the sixth of July. Captain William Gray was standing on the Texas deck, where he had been since daylight. He peered through his binoculars, watching for any signs of the approaching Army column along the road to the west. Suddenly two riders appeared in his view, trotting towards the quietly steaming vessel. "Attention on deck!" Gray roared to the armed guards below him on the main deck. He could hear sentries' rifles being cocked, followed by "Halt!" Gray dropped his glasses and sprinted down the portside ladder to the main deck. As he walked to the bow he saw two mounted soldiers.

"Corporal Clancy, Sir, Fourth United States Artillery," shouted one of the young soldiers. By now women and children were scampering to the bow of the vessel to see what was happening.

"Are you leading a column, Sir?" shouted Gray over the hissing boilers of the Spokane.

"Yes, Sir, Captain Kress and the two governors from Oregon and Washington are following directly behind us and should be here in about thirty minutes."

"Very well," shouted Gray. "Return to your officer and tell him that we are preparing to make way upriver upon his arrival."

The two artillerymen saluted and wheeled their mounts around, galloping westward where the dust of the column could be seen approaching. Gray shouted orders to the crew and passengers to make-way for the approaching column. Immediately the main gangway was lowered from the bow, as Gray called down orders to Gill, who manipulated the steam pressure and assisted in maneuvering the Spokane against the current of the Columbia, making for a more secure boarding of soldiers and equipment. The Spokane's clock rang "Five Bells," six-thirty, just as the Army column approached the steaming vessel, with its sternwheel slowly turning astern in the river's current. The sternwheeler's stack poured out a constant billow of thick black smoke, which slowly drifted westward down river in the morning breeze.

In his quarters, Captain Gray fumbled through his wooden sea trunk, looking for a clean set of white paper cuffs and a collar. No cuffs. His fingers felt a starched white collar down at the bottom of the weathered trunk. Quickly he buttoned it to his shirt and headed to the gangway, where the governors and military would be waiting. Sweat glistened on his forehead. Standing before him on the shore were his passengers. Gray walked down the gangplank, forcing a smile as he approached the three men standing before him. The Army captain stepped forward, offering his hand. "Captain John Kress, United States Army, Sir. I would like to introduce governors Chadwick of Oregon and Perry of Washington Territory."

Gray stepped forward and shook everyone's hand. He took in a deep breath. "Gentlemen, I am Captain William Gray of the Oregon Steam and Navigation Company and captain of the steamer Spokane. At your service, gentlemen. May I suggest that in light of the urgency of your mission, we make all possible haste in the immediate boarding of you and your compliment?"

"By all means!" spoke Chadwick, looking at Kress.

Kress turned to the officer standing behind him. "Lieutenant, prepare to load all men and equipment immediately!"

"Yes, Sir!" the lieutenant responded, saluting and walking quickly toward waiting troops. The large forward hatchway was opened and horses and mules were coaxed up the wide gangplank and led through the hatchway and were secured facing the opened side hatches. Bales of fresh straw were thrown on the deck beneath them and water barrels were filled.

As Captain Gray watched the last of the animals being brought on board, he saw ten soldiers rolling a gun carriage up into the bow of the boat. Its barrels seemed shorter than he had seen before. The strange piece was covered with gray Army canvas and had large olive drab painted wheels. Once the soldiers had secured the gun carriage to the deck, they returned ashore and proceeded to wheel aboard an artillery caisson, followed by its limber, both containing ammunition and tools for the strange looking gun. An artillery cannon was also loaded aboard. The soldiers were now climbing the gangplank, cursing and grumbling under their breath about their situation. Gray's eyes widened as he noticed some of soldiers carried musical instruments with them. A curse was heard as an infantryman was accidentally jabbed in the back with a trombone. Soon the decks were jammed with soldiers, men, women, and children. The clang of brass musical instruments striking rifles mingled with crying children and the shouting of deck hands. Gray and Captain Kress took a quick walk through the boat, making a safety inspection prior to shoving off. Kress separated the soldiers and confined them to the forward portion of the boat.

A sergeant approached Kress and saluted. "Beg yer pardon, Sir?"

Kress responded to the salute. "Yes, Sergeant Conners, what is it?"

"Well, Sir, I don't see any means to cook the men's breakfasts and they sure could use some hot coffee after marching all night."

"Not in this case, Captain." laughed Gray. "We'll be at Umatilla Landing in a few hours and I will gladly repay you for your hospitality. Now! If you and your men are ready, Captain, we'll get underway." Kress nodded with a smile.

White steam shot out of the stack whistle of the Spokane with a shrieking moan. The boat's telegraph rang "Astern-Slow" from the pilothouse down to where Gill and his two firemen, Stockham and Tom Monohan, were heaving large chunks of pine into the firebox of the boiler. Black smoke began to roll out of the stack into the clear morning air. The large, bright-red stern wheel began to turn backwards, slapping against the Columbia's current. Soon, the boat's stern had swung down river, bringing the boat's bow facing up river against the current. Gray ordered "Ahead-Half." The stern wheel reversed its direction, and the wheel buckets began to dig into the current. It seemed to slide down river for a period of time. "Ahead-Full" rang the telegraph in the boiler room. More black spark-filled smoke burst from the stack. The Spokane began to win over the current, slowly making its way upriver.

THE INDIAN REVOLT!

"The fight at Camas Prairie – One Indian and three or four Whites Reported Killed – No Hostiles in Umatilla Valley."

Umatilla, July 5, 1878.

"Four men arrived early this morning from Pendleton and report a fight with the Indians at Camas Prairie. They killed one Indian and think they wounded two others. They captured the scalp and headdress of the Indian they killed. There were forty whites fighting against 26 hostile Indians. These men from Pendleton come after arms and ammunition, and forty men will leave Pendleton as soon as they get arms, and will go after the hostiles."

Portland Oregonian, Saturday, July 6, 1878.

Chapter 8

Crimson Prairie

"Looks like another warm one today," Vey said as he threw the remaining coffee in his cup into the campfire at their sheep camp in the Blue Mountains. The fire erupted with a whoosh and hissing of gray steam and ashes as he looked into the early morning sky around him. His partner, Crisp, stopped rolling up his bedroll for a second to glance at the sky and also toward the herd of five hundred sheep and lambs surrounding them. Their sheep dogs were already out, trotting around the large herd, occasionally stopping to sniff the ground and chase a stray sheep back into the herd.

"I reckon so," answered Crisp as he continued to roll his bedroll. When finished, he and Vey started carrying the folded tent and camp utensils to the spring wagon. The two sheep men had been grazing sheep on the Little Camas Prairie for a week. They had an abundance of grass and water. The camp was approximately forty-five miles south of the town of Pendleton, high in the Blue Mountains. The two sheep herders were planning on moving the herd today, further across the prairie to newer grass. Both men grunted as they lifted the heavy folded canvas tent onto the tailgate of the wagon.

"Dogs sure went out early," Crisp said as they walked back for more equipment to load. "You don't suppose Whittmore might have been right about hostile Indians bein around, do you?" he mumbled.

"Na, Whittmore's a good man, but I'd guess he isn't up to snuff when it comes to knowing Indians like we do up here on the mountain. Leave them alone and they will leave you alone," Vey said as he glanced toward the herd, noticing that the dogs had stopped trotting and sniffing. The three sheep dogs were standing rock still, with their eyes looking toward the timber to the south of camp. Their shiny wet black noses twitched, trying to identify something out of sight in the timber. One of the dogs at the far edge of the herd raised his head upward and gave a low pitched wail, startling the sheep, who by now were all on their feet and beginning to bunch in a circle. The other dogs stood frozen.

Crisp carried the still warm frying pan and coffeepot to the wagon, setting them down on the wooden tailgate as Vey shoveled earth onto the smoldering fire, then threw the shovel into the wagon bed. He too wondered what the dogs were so curious about. Neither man wanted to show uneasiness to the other, but it was beginning to show. "Let's get the team hitched and saddle the horses," Vey said with an unnatural nervousness in his voice as he stared at the dark trees. "I wonder if the Campbells are going to move their band today?"

"Might be a few days early for them, but maybe one of us should ride over there today and ask," Crisp said nervously, as he picked up his saddle and bridle from the wagon and began walking to where the horses were picketed a short distance from the wagon. His eyes glanced alternately from the herd to the timber as he walked through the wet, dewy grass. Vey climbed onto the wagon seat and stood for a better view. He shaded his eyes with his hand, trying to see what was bothering the dogs from the higher vantage point as he gazed into the slowly disappearing shadows at the timberline. Nothing. Yet he felt something ominous was near. A cold shiver ran down his spine as he began to climb down from the wagon. As his boot touched the ground he heard a low whimper below him. At his feet sat Maggie, the oldest of the three sheep dogs. As Vey looked at the dog he could see an arrow dangling loosely in the top of her back. He also saw the other dogs sitting on the other side of the wagon growling and looking into the high grass. Vey froze, trying to sort out what he was seeing. His eyes darted to the leather scabbard that contained his Winchester carbine. As he quickly darted upward upon the wagon wheel, reaching for the carbine, a hail of arrows fell upon him. Some arrows struck the side of the wagon, some glanced off, others struck metal hardware ringing, as they glanced off in every direction. Vey hunched his back as if warding off the deadly rain of death. He couldn't believe it, he hadn't felt anything hit him. With another burst of energy he climbed up to the wagon seat and reached down for the carbine. "Ssssssmack!" an arrow sliced into his neck between his shoulders. Another hissed into his right buttock. The pain was instant and overpowering, as he lost his grip on the wagon seat and toppled to the ground, landing on the arrow stuck in his buttock, snapping the shaft off and driving the head in deeper. He heard someone running towards him yelling "Vey!" It was Crisp.

He felt Crisp lifting him and dragging him from the camp toward a small rocky rise on the prairie. Arrows whizzed and whirred around them as they struggled onto the rise, where they lay down amongst the rocks. Up until now, they hadn't seen anyone. Vey's neck wound was bleeding profusely and he lay in a pool of sticky blood from the hip wound. His breathing was rapid and weak. He was dying. The arrows had stopped momentarily. Crisp checked his old shotgun. It was loaded. His fingers groped the insides of all of his pockets for ammunition. He came up with three shells. His mouth tasted like copper and he was already thirsty. The water barrel was in the wagon. So was the extra ammunition and Vey's carbine. No good to him now. Crisp slowly stuck his head above the lava rocks.

He could see and hear movement in the tall grass surrounding them. The grass would sway at various times in different locations. He knew he was surrounded. Vey began to gurgle and choke in his own blood. Every time Crisp tried to make him more comfortable, Vey would emit a wet scream and spray blood everywhere. The arrow had clipped his windpipe. A high whistle came from his throat each time he struggled for a breath.

Crisp turned over onto his back, looking at the white puffy morning clouds drifting across the bright blue sky. "This is it," he thought. "No more tomorrow." He heard more sounds of Indians crawling around him in the grass, getting closer. He raised his head and shotgun over the rocks, trying to get a clean shot at them. He closed his eyes and pulled the trigger. It roared and bucked against his shoulder. He could hear the shot spray through the grass. In wild frustration, he again reloaded and fired into the grass. Nothing. He rolled over to check Vey. Vey's eyes had rolled back into his head and he was beginning the death rattle. He would be dead soon.

Crisp rolled over onto his back again. He fingered his last shell in his hand, studying it. Suddenly another shower of arrows rained down upon him. This time he was struck three times in various places. Even though the arrows had lost most of their velocity, having been shot upwards, the three that did hit him stuck. He easily pulled them away, leaving bleeding wounds. Routinely more arrow assaults were made against him. Most missed him, breaking their obsidian points on the rocks, but others found their mark. Crisp now had multiple lacerations and puncture wounds from the arrows. He was dehydrating from the sun and loss of blood. Vey had died. Crisp clutched the shotgun shell in his shaking, slick bloody fingers. His vision was becoming cloudy and he was very weak. It was painfully difficult to move, and he had to make a choice. With shaking hands, he managed to remove an empty shell case from a chamber of the shotgun. With trembling fingers he dropped in the last shell and closed the breech. Crisp closed his eyes and quietly recited the Lord's Prayer through his dry, bloody lips. He said good-bye to loved ones and opened his eyes again. He looked up into the bright blue sky and took a breath. He cocked the hammer of the shotgun. In one desperate attempt to gain his feet, he found that he didn't have the strength and slipping, rolled down the side of the rocky rise. He mustered all of his strength and managed to raise himself halfway up into a seated position, raising the shotgun. "Come and get it! You sons of bitches!" he screamed. The shotgun hammer dropped again, firing its charge harmlessly into the seemingly empty grass. Immediately, five warriors stood up from the grass not twenty feet from him. Crisp lay back on the rocks, panting and bleeding. Seconds later a long agonizing scream drifted across the prairie.

Five miles to the north of Little Camas Prairie on Snipe Creek, another large band of sheep was grazing on the rich meadow grass. The sheep dogs lazily sat or trotted in circles, scolding the sheep that had started to venture away from the band. The two Campbell brothers had finished packing their wagon with camp equipment and were preparing to move their herd of sheep further north a few miles, towards better grass and water. The wagon team was hitched. The horses were saddled and were gently pulling at the grass around them, reins laying loose at their feet. It was a peaceful scene. "Spose ol Vey will venture over here today?" asked the younger of the brothers, sitting on the tailgate of the wagon.

The elder brother stood up and poured another cup of coffee from the pot, then returned it to the dying coals of the breakfast fire. "I doubt it, at least not today. Ol Vey still has good grass and water where they are right now. No reason to move so soon," answered the brother as he dropped a finger full of sugar into the hot metal cup, stirring it. They had worked hard through the bitter winters and drought of recent years and this year finally promised to pay off. The spring lambs had come in strong and plentiful. The wool alone would tide them over until next year, if the price were right. And it looked like it might be even better next year, weather permitting.

Worn out shoe soles hurt the traveler with every step he took on the rocky mountain stage road. The drifter had been walking since he had left Pilot Rock a day ago. No one there was traveling over the mountain to John Day, so he'd pulled up his britches and started walking with directions from the few town folks left in the abandoned town. The two biscuits and the piece of bacon in his pocket would have to support him until he found a ranch to work a meal off. He'd seen no one along the road. He felt perhaps he'd made the wrong decision by heading out on his own in strange territory, but he needed work. The morning was sunny and bright and that lifted his spirits some. He'd been walking along the road where the large prairie opened up on both sides of him, without even one head of sheep to be seen of those which had had been reported to him in Pilot Rock. He'd hoped at least to be able to share a cup of coffee with a herder. The thought made him hungry, but he had to save the food in his coat pocket. In the distance to the south he saw a small group of riders coming towards him on the road. Their presence relaxed him. It was good to find fellow travelers in such a barren landscape. As the riders came closer, their clothing seemed odd to the traveler. He couldn't remember ever seeing cowboys riding shirtless and wearing feathers in their hats. His heart stopped as the riders came closer. Indians! His first thought was to run. But where? He decided to talk to them and try to reason with them, if possible. Besides, these might be friendly Indians. He stopped, waiting for them to greet him. As the Indians rode up to the traveler, he could hear them laughing and talking in their guttural tones. They reined up and around the traveler. "Gentlemen," greeted the traveler, looking around at the Indians now surrounding him in the road. "I'm looking for work, do any of you know where a ranch might be found?" he asked, looking at the riders. He noticed two bloody scraps of hair and flesh hanging from the bridles of two of the horses. "Scalps!" he thought to himself. The riders just laughed and jeered in their own language as they played with him. "Look!" blurted the traveler, reaching into his coat pocket. "I have food!" A rifle roared in the morning air. The traveler stumbled backwards, losing his footing and fell onto the road in a cloud of dust. He raised up on his elbows and looked down at the rapidly spreading crimson stain across his chest. He looked up into the quickly fading faces of the men who had shot him, then fell backwards with a thud, his sightless eyes staring upwards with a questioning expression, his hand still in his coat pocket. A red hand pulled the dead man's hand from the pocket and removed the biscuits and bacon, hungrily wolfing them down with mutters of satisfaction. The riders rode away to the north, leaving the dead traveler lying naked in the dusty road. His nose and ears had been cut off and his head smashed in with rocks. A lone eye lay in the dust, attached to what remained of the head.

"What was that!" asked the younger Campbell boy of his older brother as he dropped from the wagon bed, looking toward the south.

"I'd say it was Vey dropping a fat buck for meat, but it was pretty close," answered his brother as he walked to his saddled mare and smoothly slid the Winchester out of its scabbard. He levered a cartridge into the chamber. Without speaking, the younger brother took his gun belt and holster off the wagon seat and buckled it on. "Do you reckon Whittmore's warning was true, brother?" asked the younger man.

"That's why we keep our guns handy, ain't it?"

The band of sheep didn't seem alarmed by the distant sound of the gunshot. The dogs, however, were on their feet and pacing back and forth nervously, tails between their legs. "We got problems, I think!" said the older brother as he mounted the chestnut mare. He swung the horse around, rifle in hand, and trotted toward from where the shot had come. The younger brother drew his 44-40 Colt's six-shooter from its holster and, checking its six chambers, loaded all six. He re-holstered it as he watched his brother ride south along the stage road. After what seemed an eternity he heard a shot, two followed by two more in the direction where his brother had ridden.

He looked around at the sheep, which were beginning to mill around with the dogs yapping and barking at their heels. At least they weren't afraid, thought the younger brother. Suddenly, the sheep dogs began to bark and raise a commotion towards the treeline. He could see his brother riding back to camp. He sighed a breath of relief. His brother's horse would stop mysteriously for a moment, then ride on. When the horse and rider came close enough, the younger brother looked in horror. The little mare was covered with blood from its rider. The older brother's body hung limp, with its arms tied around the mare's neck. Quickly, he removed the body from the horse and laid it on the grass. The younger brother sobbed as he tried to clean the blood and grass from his brother's face, but it was of no use. He was dead.

Suddenly, the young herder regained his senses and pulled his revolver from its holster as he stood up. It was too late. A Bannock warrior stood to the side of him, three others to his rear. There was no way out. "Why!" he screamed at the three warriors, his fingers flexing around the pistol. Then in a rage, he brought the revolver up. A shot rang out and a bullet smacked into his jaw, passing out the other side and stricking the wagon with a splintering thud. He spun, falling against the wagon as an arrow thudded into his chest, driving through into the wagon bed. He hung momentarily, then his weight snapped the arrowhead loose from the shaft, allowing him to fall to the ground in a convulsive death rattle. Another long scream drifted across the wide meadow.

An hour later found another raiding band of warriors at the Connell ranch and dairy, to the east of the murdered herders. Its owners, in the wake of the spreading alarm, had abandoned the ranch, fleeing northward to the small town of Pendleton. The sounds of crashing furniture and breaking glass came from within the ranch house, as the warriors vented their anger at the white man's lodge. High pitched screams came from inside the hog pen adjacent to the log barn, distracting the warriors inside the house. They came out onto the porch and walked quickly toward the hog pen, eating scraps of food found inside the kitchen. As they approached the pen they observed five of their band sprayed with blood, their bodies glistening with it. Their eyes burned brightly through their wet crimson masks. Laughter erupted from the corral as the Indians caught Connell's prized hogs and slit their throats. A whoop came from the large springhouse across the way. Some warriors had laid their weapons down and were exited the springhouse, arms laden with large rounds of cheese.

A warrior shouted from the grisly corral. "Come! Bring the white man's cheese and give the white man's hogs something to rest their heads on! They are very tired!" The Bannock laughed through glistening white teeth, which contrasted with his blood-splattered face and war paint. His chest heaved with excitement. The fiendish devilment went on as the dead and dying hogs were dragged into a line through the blood-soaked manure and mud of the pen. Beneath each bloody head was placed a round of cheese. Soon, the sounds of destruction resumed inside the house and buildings.

Far to the south, Scout Robbins and his point riders had dismounted at the southern edge of the prairie. They were peering through their field glasses at the mysterious objects several hundred yards in front of them. "I don't like it," Robbins said in a whisper. His scouts said nothing. They already knew what Robbins was thinking. Robbins took his field

200

glasses from his eyes and turned to one of the scouts. "Sam, ride back to the column and tell General Howard that we are facing something ahead of us and I think that he should come up."

"You got it, Rube!" replied the scout as he mounted his horse, wheeled it around and cantered into the timber to the south.

Within the hour, Howard was also glassing the mysterious objects across the priarie. "Strange, but it appears to be a white stone pyramid or marker. I can't say what the two poles are." He brought the glasses down with his one hand. "Rube, let's find out, shall we?" Howard turned to Captain Bernard at his side. "Captain, put your battalion on the flat and form a line. We will approach the objects guiding to the center at a walk." Bernard nodded, saluting, and issued orders to the trumpeters and company commanders. Soon the battalion was approaching the objects in line at a walk. Troopers and officers were anxiously looking in all directions for any signs of a trap. Mounts wanting to chomp at the sweet-green meadow grass were kept at a tight rein. In the distance one of Robbins' scouts was galloping toward the center of the line to where Howard rode at the front of the column. The General reined in his mount. Commands were shouted behind him as the line came to halt.

The scout reined in before Howard and Bernard. "Colonel Robbins sends his respects, Sir, and says to come up. Two dead men, Sir!" reported the excited scout.

Howard turned to Bernard. "Forward, Captain. When will this death and destruction stop?" he spoke quietly and sadly to himself.

"When we catch them, Sir," answered Bernard, then turned and shouted orders. The line advanced forward again at the walk. As the battalion crossed the meadow, the objects in the distance became clear. The smell reached them first. Mounts became jittery as the familiar scent of blood and death reached their noses. "Halt!" and "Dismount" were sounded. Troopers quickly dismounted, removing their carbines from the carbine boots. Sergeants moved down the line, inspecting the troopers and closing files. They didn't need as much inspecting these days.

Howard and Bernard rode to where Robbins and his men were standing near the upright poles. The scouts appeared visibly shaken. Two crudely built upright pine poles were stuck into the ground. At the top of each pole rested the decapitated heads of Vey and Crisp. The sun had blackened and swollen them. Birds had apparently fed on them for some time. No eyes remained in the sockets. Noses and ears had been cut off. Beneath the poles lay the outstretched, headless bodies, stripped of clothing and cut to pieces. The charred evidence of a small fire made from dried grass and parts of their clothing was found on each man's chest.

A short distance from the dead men stood a large blood-clotted pyramid of dead sheep stacked nearly seven feet high. Nearly five hundred dead and dying sheep were scattered about the meadow like so many stuffed toys, their throats cut or legs hamstrung. The whine and buzzing of flies and yellow jackets was the only sound at the deadly place, save for the noisy "cawing" of crows, pleading for the intruders to leave so that they might continue their feast. Magpies scolded the soldiers from the pine trees in the distance as a burial detail set to work.

Bernard walked out onto the meadow a short way and stood gazing across the grassy prairie. He was more tired than usual after seeing the carnage. He didn't know why, he'd seen much of death and the human body blown to bits, but somehow this intentional, grisly scene had imprinted on his brain. So close to death and with the stench of rotting flesh in his nostrils, he oddly thought of Alice and the children. Strangely, all he wanted to do at the moment was to hold them very close to him, if nothing more than to assure himself that they did indeed exist and were not just a figment of his imagination. He needed to know that they were real. The clanking sounds of shovels digging the two graves brought him back to reality.

"Reuben?" Howard's voice alerted him gently. "Are you not feeling well, Sir?" He addressed Bernard more like a father than a commanding officer.

Bernard slowly placed his hat on his head and turned to Howard. "Yes, Sir, I had a strange lonely feeling just now."

"Have you heard from your family? Are they well?" asked Howard thoughtfully.

"The letters you brought helped immensely, Sir. Yes, I'm sure that they are all right. It's just that...?"

"Alice, isn't that your wife's name?" questioned Howard.

"Yes Sir, she is a lovely, devoted woman. She's been my constant support since the war. I'd thought that perhaps our age difference might make the marriage suffer, but the fifteen years difference hasn't even been addressed. If anything, her youth and strength has been a tonic for me as a soldier."

Howard noticed the other man's eyes begin to water slightly. He gently gripped Bernard's shoulder. "I too know the heavenly gift of a good wife and children, Reuben. At times I don't believe I could have stood up to the strain Army life places on us. When I lost the arm at Fair Oaks, I thought my life as a soldier was over and I became very depressed over it. But my Lizzie healed me body and soul. She just would not let me quit. They certainly are a blessing. We owe them much." Bernard nodded. The two officers walked back to the bloody ground and the Army. Jack trotted behind them.

Officer's Call was sounded. The company commanders grouped around Howard. "Gentlemen, my compliments to the discipline of your men. They are well seasoned for what we are soon going to ask of them." The officers eyed one another. "We are very close to the Hostiles. This work we've found is quite fresh. As early as this morning, the scouts tell me. It sends a clear message to us. Dispatches tell me that captains Parnell and Winters, with Companies H and E, will arrive at the town of Pilot Rock, just to the north of us, early tomorrow. Captain Throckmorton's battalion, consisting of two batteries of the Fourth Artillery and one company of the Twenty-First Infantry, will also arrive there. Once we meet them, our combined strength will consist of seven companies of cavalry, two batteries of artillery, and one company of infantry. According to Scout Robbins, it appears that the enemy has abruptly stopped and may be preparing to engage us several miles from our present location."

A murmur traveled amongst the officers. "Robbins also reports finding three more bodies to the north of us, just across the prairie." The officer's eyes shifted to the north. Howard continued, "Tomorrow, we will break camp and travel to the northwest of the Indians, trying not to alarm them. I'm hoping they will think we have lost them, or do not wish to engage them. If we are successful in this attempt, we will have succeeded in blocking them and will attack them in force on our own terms, preventing them from crossing the Columbia. I've issued orders to Captain Miles to have the wagon train with the mounted infantry and artillery to be in position on this meadow on Monday morning, the eighth, the day after tomorrow, the same day that I plan to engage the enemy from the north. Captain Miles will form a blocking force should the Hostiles attempt to break through to the south."

Howard looked each officer in the eye. "Gentlemen, the next two days will tell us if we have been successful and I believe that we will be. Have your sergeants and corporals re-check every trooper and his equipment, especially ammunition and water. Our intelligence from Robbins tells me that this entire country is full of Indians. Some are peaceful, most are not." Howard eyed Rube Robbins. "Robbins also reports an Hostile campsite abandoned early this morning northeast of our present position. It appears that it was the largest one yet." The officers began to shift. "We must stop them now, or we may never have another chance. If the Indians should be allowed to cross the river and join the Yakimas, there will not be enough military to stop them, so we must do it now." Howard concluded, "Keep your men and mounts close and do not allow the horses to graze outside of your pickets. Thank you, Gentlemen, you may return to your companies." The officers saluted Howard and walked slowly to their companies, speaking in low tones. Some laughed and joked with excitement.

Bernard approached Howard. "Well, Sir, it appears that things are warming up quickly," he said, smiling.

"Yes, it does look that way, Captain. But remember the main reason that we are getting this chance is because the enemy has apparently decided to stop and swat at the bee that has been buzzing his flanks for the last month or more. I cannot think of any other reason why they would stop here and now, unless they feel that we need to be stopped for good and have no fear of us. We must proceed with caution," Howard said as he wiped his sweating face with a white kerchief, looking to the north across the sprawling green meadow. Heat waves shimmered from its green carpet.

Sarah and Mattie quietly approached the two officers. Mattie looked genuinely shaken. "General?" Sarah said. Little Mattie stood shyly near her.

"Yes, what is it, Sarah?" asked Howard, continuing to wipe his face.

"I sense the presence of great danger, General, may Mattie or I be of some service to you now? Perhaps you would have us go to the Numa ahead of us and try to talk to them. Mattie believes that Egan and his people are in great danger from those they travel with."

Howard turned and faced the two women, smiling. "Not quite yet Sarah, but as I've said before, it will be soon."

Sarah gave Howard a blank look and spoke to Mattie in Paiute. The two turned and walked back to their horses, talking in hushed tones. Howard placed his worn campaign hat back onto his head, staring at the departing women. They sensed something that Howard couldn't understand. And they would never open up to him. He exchanged concerned looks with Bernard. "I think those two women have known all along that Egan wasn't totally convinced to go along with the Bannocks. But we now know that he and Buffalo Horn were seen at the Umatilla Agency just a few months ago, probably recruiting Umatillas. A very confusing situation, Sir."

The two Paiute women made no eye contact with the soldiers as they walked through them to their horses. There were bad looks coming from troopers as the two graves were being closed and marked. The familiar sound of clanking spades again rang amongst the troops. It chilled more than one of them. No one spoke much now. The battalion was soon posting picket guards, watering mounts, and preparing to make camp. The men felt the tenseness of their officers. The enemy was close and wanted blood. The buzzing insects feeding on the bloodstained poles and grass proved that.

Twenty-two miles to the northeast of the encamped battalion, the grassy green meadows and thick lodgepole pine trees gave way to the high craggy hills of the northwestern Blue Mountains. The grass had already burned to a golden straw color, contrasting with the brownish red of the lava rocks high above on the hilltops. Since the beginning of creation, rivers had cut deep canyons and ravines downward to the north. Now only small creeks remained, sending narrow gurgling ribbons of water downward onto the floor of the barren landscape, soon disappearing into the rocky creek bottoms. Occasionally, a small green patch of brush or willows could be seen in the dry vastness of the barren country, betraying the location of a small spring that refused to dry up in the rocky earth of a side hill or in a deep canyon below.

On one of the hilltops stood a group of Bannock and Paiute Warriors, holding their war ponies while looking northward into the vastness. Oits and War Jack silently peered through their binoculars. At their sides stood Beads, Surger, Boss, Big John and Bannock Joe, also peering into the distance with their eagle-like eyes. Behind them on war ponies sat over seventy-five warriors. Three times that many were well hidden in ravines to the rear. "WO!" blurted War Jack, pointing his arm to the north. "There is the big river and the land of our Yakima brothers!" Indeed, sixty miles to the north lay the land of the Yakima. Washington Territory.

A wisp of warm air brushed the feather in Oits' tattered hat. "The time is quickly coming when we shall see the great Sitting Bull. The time is coming soon when there will be no whites upon this earth! Smohalla told me this!" Oits said. War Jack and the warriors grunted their approval.

Suddenly something flashed in Boss's eyes. "Hey!" he hissed quietly to the others. His warning wasn't necessary; all of the warriors had immediately dropped, looking to where Boss had pointed to the right of them. There wasn't a warrior silhouetted against the sky. War Jack peered through his glasses. Big John was pointing the barrel of his rifle to their left and below from where he lay prone. He returned the broken piece of mirror to his pocket. War Jack immediately swung his glasses downward toward the foothills below them. In the far distance, approaching them from the north, was a thin line of dust winding

205

itself across the foothills to the northwest of them. Through his glasses Oits could just make out the tiny dots riding ahead of the line of dust. "Soldiers!" he spat at War Jack.

"No!" uttered War Jack. "There are too few of them. They ride like white farmers. They are returning to show us their power. And we shall again show them ours!" He rolled to his side and waved his arm. Warriors rose from the ground and mounted their horses. Within minutes all had disappeared, riding westward in the direction of the horsemen far below them.

Indian Excitement:

"Pendleton is at present pretty lively; some 700 families help count its population; families from down the river – Meadows and Happy Canyon, Butter Creek, Willow Creek and in fact all through this North-west and West country they have all cleared out, leaving their cattle and sheep to the mercy of the Indian and wolf. The excitement is great. Teams arrived at all hours during the night and up to a late hour Wednesday morning. Campers on every street; the schoolhouses are filled and the rest take shelter where opportunity offers. A Company was organized to guard the town and another of 10, which took their departure for the scene of war"

The (Pendleton) East Oregonian, Saturday, July 6, 1878.

Chapter 9

Willow Spring Nightmare

"What time's it getin to be, Sheriff?" asked William Blakely as he rode beside Umatilla County Sheriff John Sperry.

"Why, Bill, you gettin hungry already?" grinned Sperry, as he looked at the large canyons and hogbacks facing the group of fifty-two volunteers as they approached the foothills of the Blue Mountains. The wagon and horses kicked up powdered alkali dust as they plodded along. There was little or no breeze in the hot midday air.

"Matter of fact I am, John. That was hard traveling across the foot of these mountains looking for that shot up sheepherder. Lucky we found his cabin," answered Blakley.

Volunteer Sergeant William Lamar reached into his pants pocket and retrieved his gold pocket watch. "John, it looks to me like it's near on to one o'clock. Willow Spring is just a few miles from here up that canyon. We could get a fresh drink of water and a rest there. Damn, but that water is cold," Lamar said to Sperry. Lamar had served in Her Royal Majesty's Army in England and had immigrated to the United States recently. He'd betrayed his vow to never serve under a volunteer group again. But since they'd fought these Indians just a few days before, he'd agreed to again volunteer. But this was the last time, he'd promised himself. He needed to re-assure himself to the others that his reputation was above reproach, because he was a school teacher in Pendleton, and more importantly, he was asking for the hand of the local doctor's daughter in marriage as well.

"Willow Spring is a good one, Billy" answered Sperry, as he looked into the oncoming canyons and hills before him. He gently reined his horse to the left toward Willow Spring, the wagon and riders following him. "It's getting hotter and the horses could use the rest." Sperry cautiously eyed the mouth of the canyon. "Damned if it ain't in the deepest hole around. It worries me to stop there, with all these reports of Indians, but it's the closest water around."

"Aw, hell, John," said Ellis. "There ain't no reds anywhere near here and those that are will soon be taken care of by the Army, so let's eat!"

The column of volunteers rode up the creek bottom until they reached the greenery of Willow Spring. The water flowed from a natural spring in the hillside, allowing the volunteers a chance to stop and water thirsty men and horses. Fires were kindled and coffee was soon boiling. Picket guards were stationed further out on the high bluffs to the east. Within thirty minutes a picket rider had reported that he'd seen six or seven Indians to the east watching him. Sperry responded, "Hell, it's probably the damned Umatillas watching us to see where they can steal from next. Just keep an eye on them." Sperry concentrated on building his small cooking fire. He could smell the delicious aroma from the fire-blackened coffeepot.

The picket mounted his horse and climbed the high hill, returning to his post on the bluff. Questioning eyes followed the rider as those from below watched. They knew this man and he wasn't prone to alarm. As the men unsaddled their horses in turn, Sheriff Sperry and Billy Lamar looked for a place to settle down and eat their lunch with the others. William Blakely's men were to water first, then Sperry's. Some yards from the springs stood a long, log-framed lambing shed, with a door at one end. It allowed Sperry's men the only shade for miles. Soon Sperry and his men were opening their lunch sacks, prepared for them at Pilot Rock. They had tied their horses to the sheep shed's rafter poles until the others had finished watering their mounts. When they had finished eating their lunch, Sperry planned to untie their mounts and lead them down to the springs in turn.

"I'll bet there was one hell of a lot of Indians up there, a few days ago." Lamar said, as he unwrapped the newspaper from his bean sandwich, his eyes darting across the high bluffs above them.

"Hand me that jug, Blanchard," said Ferguson, reaching his hand out, while chewing a mouthful of sandwich.

"Damned if that ain't genuine busthead!" choked another volunteer, as he swallowed a drink of whisky from the gray stone crock.

"Do you think that we'll run across Indians, John?" asked Volunteer Sergeant William Ellis, as he took a large bite from his sandwich, wiping his mustache with the back of a sleeve. His blue eyes narrowed as they scanned the high canyons encircling them. The bright sun bore down upon the hills, making them resemble browned biscuit tops just taken from the oven.

"Might!" responded Sperry, as he pushed himself further inside the shed, trying to avoid the hot creeping sunlight. He handed the jug to Ellis as he moved. The second group of volunteers were beginning to talk about how the column should continue to climb the hills and scout the high prairies to the south of them, hopefully to engage the Indians in combat. Sperry had voted no. He'd pleaded with his opponents that his primary concern was with the safety of Pendleton's citizens and to alert them if they should see Indians. The vote taken was in favor of continuing south and attacking the enemy on sight. Sperry winced at the outcome.

"You! At the spring," yelled Sperry. "Hurry up and saddle your horses so the others can water!" He didn't know why he'd given the order between sips of freshly brewed coffee. It had just come to him. He wasn't in any particular hurry.

Leisurely, the men threw saddles over the backs of the freshly watered horses and began to tighten cinch straps as they chatted amongst themselves. Others began to untie their horses from the shed's rafters and began leading them to the spring. A peaceful silence reigned over the volunteers as they quietly munched their noon meal. Picket guards sat or stood on the high bluffs around them.

"I don't like it," thought Lamar, as he plucked a large dill pickle from the green Mason jar handed to him. The high hills surrounding them closed in on him as he gazed at them. Something was wrong. He could feel it. Even the idle chatter around him in the shed didn't calm his anxiety. The smell of dried sheep dung hung in the hot air. Thirteen mounts had been unsaddled and were being watered at the spring by fifteen to twenty men, who sat or lay around the spring laughing and joking amongst themselves. The whisky jug was being passed amongst them. Soon they would be allowed the pleasure of eating their own lunches, while the others watered their mounts. Jacob Frazer was concentrating on opening a can of sardines. As he twisted the small screw, the rich fishy smell met his nose, making him yearn for its contents. Suddenly a shout came from the pickets on the hillside above them. He could see men running down the steep side hill, stumbling and sliding as they came, all the while shouting and screaming something he could not yet understand. Something was wrong.

Gunfire erupted from the canyon between them and the spring as well as from the south. Men who had managed to mount their horses at the spring galloped by the seated group, shouting "Indians!" Their eyes were white with terror and fear. "What the...!" blurted Sperry, as he watched the other men at the spring trying to throw saddles upon their wide-eyed horses. At least thirteen men turned their horses around and spurred them northward down the creek bed. The "Crack!" and "Zip!" of bullets striking the walls of the shed

211

caused him to duck his head instinctively. His coffee cup clanged onto the rocks as he dropped it reaching for his rifle.

Coming down on them, galloping and shooting, were over seventy-five warriors screaming like demons. Confusion and bullets rent the air as volunteers who were on foot chased their mounted fleeing comrades. "Wait, stop!" Their pleadings fell on deaf ears as the riders spurred their horses on, engulfing the terrified runners in their dust from which erupted slim narrow shafts of gunfire from the Indians, who had closed the circle between the runners and their escape. Silvery sardines spilled onto the sheep-dung covered floor of the shed as Frazer scrambled for his Winchester, dropping the forgotten sardine can at his feet. Bullets struck the logs and boards of the shed, splintering wood and driving leaden missiles into the logs and through the boarded rooftop into its interior.

The horses that were still tied to the roof supports outside the shed were screaming as they frantically pulled at the reins holding them to the shed. One had been hit in the flanks and was down on its rear, blood streaming from the bullet wound. To their horror, the men watched as two struggling horses began to pull the shed supports apart. "Gawd damn it!" shouted Sperry as he pushed the muzzle of his rifle through a crack in the logs, firing at the nearest horse. Through the thick choking dust of the shed's interior, Sperry could hear his bullet strike the horse. It dropped heavily to the ground, still tied to the shed. Sperry bent over and ran through the men to the other end of the shed where the other horse was attempting to pull away from the shed. He took aim and fired. The wounded animal fell completely flat from its sitting position, dying. Soon the attacking Indians had encircled the small group like an invisible giant wrapping its arms around them. The volunteers were trapped. Quickly they regrouped, and began to throw out a strong defensive fire from within the confines of the sheep shed, slowing the Indians' attack.

Within the shed there were cries of fear. "Let's get the hell out of here or we'll all be butchered!" Their faces shone with fear and sweat. Others yelled, "Let em surround us and be damned. We'll kick the hell out of them!" They shoved fresh cartridges into their rifles, indifferent to the leaden missiles driving through the boards inches above their heads. Gunfire rattled from all sides of the shed now, as Bannock and Paiute "Wolves" quickly surrounded it, driving off and dividing the mounted riders from those on foot seeking protection from the shed. The clouds of dust from the fleeing volunteers stung the noses of those left behind. As the last of the panicked riders galloped away from the foot of the canyon, disappearing into their own dust, a veil hung in the still hot air like a deadly fog, separating the two foes for the moment.

War Jack signaled across the canyon from where his warriors had dismounted in a natural trench just two hundred yards from the sheep shed. He waved his carbine back and forth. No shots had come from the shed to his front. Across the gulch, Oits waved his rifle back in return as Beads, Bannock Joe, and others quickly settled into firing positions. The sheep shed was between them now, and Boss and War Jack's warriors had settled down behind rocks to the east of the shed. They had the shed and the men inside surrounded in a crossfire. The dust left by the retreating volunteers was slowly dissipating, making the weatherworn building a better target for the warriors looking down upon it. Fish in a barrel. High above the scene on a hilltop stood Egan, Charley, and the chiefs of Egan's three bands. Egan peered through his looking glass at the surrounded volunteers jammed into the defenseless shed, frantic with fear. They were as stupid as the sheep for which the shed had been made. But he would not take a part in it.

Inside the thirty by fifteen-foot log structure lay nearly forty men rapidly checking their weapons, choking in the hot, dusty interior. So far no one had been hit. However, the thin bright rays of sunlight streaking into the interior of the shed showed where bullets had struck the roof, then plowed into the earth of the shed's floor. Only the sharp ratchet sound of Winchester levers driving cartridges into chambers could be heard within the shed. "I knew it! Just as sure as hell!" spat Bill Lamar, as he slapped his Winchester in frustration. He struggled, looking for a target through the logs of the shed.

"I know, Bill," said Frank Hannah calmly at Lamar's side. "Listen," continued Hannah as he patted his pockets for ammunition, "I know you vowed to never fight with volunteers again after your hitch with the British Army, but this is different. We ain't like them!" spoke Hannah, as he continued to fumble through his pockets, nervously counting his cartridges.

"The hell it isn't!" blurted Lamar as he looked along the barrel of his rifle for a target. "I've got a nice girl waiting for me back in Pendleton. We're getting married as soon as I get back from this groundhog chase. I volunteered to go along this time, because I thought Sperry knew how to lead this group. I was wrong." Lamar continued staring out into the gulch, filled with unseen Indians. "I'm not coming back from this one, Frank. I know that I'll never see her again. I also know that my students at school will never have an opportunity to learn from me again. It's funny, but I will miss that as much as losing her." His eyes watered as Hannah looked at him.

A volley of shots erupted the silence coming from the gulch. Bullets struck the shed, splintering the rooftop and log walls. "Fire!" yelled Sperry. A volley roared from within the shed, sending lead upward toward the gulch where the Hostiles were entrenched, kicking up dust and rocks.

Lamar studied his fingertips where he'd wiped his stinging cheek. They were bright red with blood. He levered another cartridge into his Winchester and stood up, his shoulders scraping the ceiling of the low shed. "I'll get that bloody bloke!" he shouted as he went to the door at the far end of the shed. He kicked it open with his boot and stepped out. "There, that's better!" he shouted as he brought his rifle to his shoulder. "K-Pow!" a rifle cracked from the gulch. "Thud." "Ugh!" Lamar muttered as he staggered backward on rubbery legs. Falling, he crashed against the outside wall of the shed with a heavy thud. He looked downward slowly to the crimson stain quickly spreading across his belly and smiled weakly. "So this is how it is to be?" he thought to himself, panting as he began to feel cold and very thirsty. He managed to raise his head up weakly, facing the deadly gulch; in doing so he painfully raised his right hand upward in a sign of peaceful surrender toward his unseen enemy. Another shot cracked from the gulch, the bullet striking him in the chest, and shoulder simultaneously. Lamar's body bounced from the impact. His lifeless body slid downward, resting against the end of the shed, the limp right hand stiffening in the upheld position toward his killers.

"Gawd damn!" yelled Hannah as he ducked, pushing his face into the sheep-dung covered floor. He screamed as another bullet struck him in the back. Immediately his friends turned him over to give aid. As he was laid back he muttered through trembling lips, "I'm OK, boys, just let me lay a minute." Sperry and the others flinched every time Hannah's chest rose and fell, whistling air through a gunshot lung.

Outside the shed, gunfire rose in intensity as three volunteers who had attempted to escape on foot with the retreating riders were shooting their way back through the Indian fire towards the sheep shed. Salisbury, who was first to have his horse shot from beneath him; Sam Rothchild, who had lost his horse; and Tom Ogle, who hadn't been able to jump behind an escaping rider, were desperately shooting their way through the Indian cross-fire. Shouts of encouragement came from the sheep shed as cover fire was turned against the Indians to the east and south. Indian 50-70 Sharps and 44-40 rim fire bullets cracked around the three men as they stopped to fire, then hobbled toward the shed. Foot by foot they fought onward. If one stumbled, the others picked him up as they continued firing toward the Indians gaining on them with each step. Ogle winced at the pain in his thumb; its nail was growing black from being struck by a spent bullet. Salisbury trailed the other two, using his rifle as a crutch due to a bloody wound to his right thigh and a gunshot wound to the toes of his left foot. Miraculously, the three men made it to the shed. They crashed through the door and fell to the ground, exhausted. A thunderous splintering of bullets into the shed followed them as they were dragged inside. Rothchild looked at his leg and at the spreading red stain soaking his pants. He dropped to the dirt floor of the shed painfully and thrust the barrel of his Springfield rifle through a hole in the log wall as he thrust a fresh cartridge into the rifle's breech, snapping the trapdoor closed. He whispered, "Sweet Jesus" as he cocked the hammer of the rifle and waited in silence.

Throughout the rest of the day the men fired at available targets through the logs of the shed. Some fired while on their knees, others lay prone, while some stood erect within the confines of the shed. Most had been wounded. Rothchild kept at his post, his leg swollen with the .50 caliber bullet still inside it. The interior of the log shed was thick with dust and gun smoke. Coughing and hacking combined with the deafening firing of rifles. The sounds of incoming bullets crashing into the shed added to the clamor of battle. The groans of the wounded grew in intensity. Bullets continually hit the structure throughout the afternoon and into the evening. The screams of the gunshot horses outside added to the misery of the men. As the burning sun began to set in the west, the firing from outside began to slacken somewhat. The burning thirst of the men was beginning to turn them to madness. After nightfall, a few men managed to creep out and bring a little water from the spring. All settled in for the waiting game. Sperry whispered a plan to the men in the darkness of the shed. "Men, I think the only way out of here is straight down the canyon. I don't think we all will make it, but some might." No one made a sound or remark. "The moon should be down around eleven o'clock, as I figure it, then we might stand a chance of getting out of here. But we must stay together!" he whispered loudly. The men listened quietly. "No one will be left behind, that is certain," Sperry continued. A low sigh of relief could be heard within the dark enclosure.

In the deadly darkness outside, the men could hear movement on the hills surrounding them. Occasionally a wailing animal call could be heard. No one believed that it was truly a four- legged creature that made the sound. From the quiet darkness of the shed, someone whispered just loud enough so all could hear. "Say, boys, did you hear about the baby that was born in Pendleton yesterday? Damned if didn't have a mustache!" A few snickers ran amongst the men. "That ain't all," continued the low voice. "Old Doc here says that the mother was quite tickled!" A welcome murmur of quiet guffaws and chuckles filled the miserable shed. It was just what they needed.

The moon had long since disappeared from the night sky above the sheep shed. A sharp creak broke the stillness as the door of the sheep shed was carefully opened and its occupants slipped out quietly, making their way to where the wagon and a few surviving horses stood in the inky night. They had been somewhat protected by a small shed located below the hill in front of the Indians' eastern position. A team was quietly hitched to the wagon and blankets were thrown in its bed, where the more seriously wounded were gently placed. No groans were heard. Those unable to walk were helped aboard horses. They bit their lips, stifling their screams. Soon all were ready. No gunfire came from the surrounding darkness.

They started out. Sperry guided them as best as he could over the rocky ground and down the ravine. Only the low crunch and clatter of hoofs stepping on rocks could be heard. To the volunteers, they sounded like a brass band as they felt their way through the darkness. The group traveled in a column of twos, slowly making its way down the canyon. After they had traveled nearly four hundred yards, a blast of gunfire ripped through the darkness, spitting lead through the black night into the volunteers. Harrison Hale felt the bullet slam into his chest like a horse kick. He stumbled sideways, then his legs were cut from beneath him as two more bullets struck him in the thigh. He fell heavily onto the side hill, sliding along the rocky ground. He was dead before he had time to wonder what had happened.

The volunteers dropped to the ground and fired two volleys into the darkness. All was silent. In the dark deadly silence that followed, the only sound was that of Hale's short death rattle that quickly stopped in the black night engulfing them. "Hale!" someone yelled.

"He's dead, Gawd-damnit!" someone blurted in the dark.

"Shut up, damnit, or we'll all be killed!" hissed Sperry. They rose again and proceeded down the canyon. On two more occasions they were fired upon and returned fire but made it out of the deadly canyon. The Indians had again lost interest.

As Sperry led the wounded column down the canyon, the first blue-pink light of dawn began to show across the eastern skyline. He turned his head backward towards the deadly canyon of Willow Spring, still covered in a dark haze in the early morning light. He shivered and tightly grasped the reins of the horse he was leading. His jaw muscles tightened and a drop of sweat ran down the middle of his back in the cold morning air as he stumbled and led the survivors towards safety and salvation. It was Sunday, the seventh day of July.

"Where are all our fine looking Indians who were inhabiting our street corners some two weeks ago?"

The East Oregonian, Saturday, June 29, 1878.

A Dispatch from Washington, says:

"In view of the urgent demand of troops for service on the plains, orders have been issued to the various recruiting officers to hasten, as far as practical, enlistments, in order to bring up the numerical force of the Army to 25,000 men, the maximum number authorized by law."

Army Navy Journal, July 6, 1878.

Chapter 10

Seeds of Assassination

To the north, the steamer Spokane was plying the waters of the Columbia River, attempting to make an awkward docking at the river town of Umatilla. To the few spectators watching the docking of the vessel, the boat appeared damaged as she had a list and not just from her overcrowded decks. The boat's wheel was broken and splintered in several places, making navigation cumbersome. Soon the large boat's hull scraped along the wooden dock and lines were quickly thrown out and secured. Governor Chadwick and his party thanked Gray and departed the boat. The town was awakened by the activity at the docks. Everyone scrambled out of bed to greet the Governor. Their fearful faces showed what they had been going through during the past few days. Some were terrified at the thought of everyone being killed by Indians. Chadwick was escorted to the Umatilla House Hotel. As the Governor passed into the hotel, the Star Restaurant next door came to life and the smells of frying bacon and flapjacks drifted out into the street. The Cherry Saloon, which hadn't closed in over a week, finally closed its doors, as everyone rushed next door to the hotel to hear the latest news from Governor Chadwick.

Down at the docks, Captain Gray was shouting orders to his small crew as they and the soldiers helped remove the broken and splintered paddleboards from the ship's wheel. Gray scowled from the dockside as the broken wheel arms were removed, anxious to see what damage had been done. Soon fuel wood had been brought from the town and a large fire was built near the boat, where Sam Gill went to work forging bolts and ironwork on a forge borrowed from the local blacksmith. Gray opened his silver pocket watch. It read five a.m. It had taken them twenty-two hours instead of the usual twelve to make the trip to Umatilla Landing. He snapped the case shut and returned the watch to his pocket. Gray recounted in his mind the happenings of the previous day. After picking up the governors and Major Kress' battalion, they'd made good time steaming east up the Columbia, stopping now and then to destroy boats that the Yakima Indians had hidden along the river for the approaching Hostiles. The weather had been sunny with just a light tail wind at their stern.

At eight a.m. the day before, Major Kress had stepped into the engine room where Sam Gill was studying the gauges and dials of his engines. "Mr. Gill?" Kress said loudly over the engine noise. Gill turned and nodded to the major. "You mentioned an interest in weapons, did you not?" questioned Kress.

Gill grinned, "Yes, Sir! What have you got?" he shouted.

Kress returned the grin. "Follow me, Sir, and I will introduce you to Mr. Gatling's gun."

Gill shouted to Fireman Monohan, "Take over, I will be back in a minute, Tom!" and chased after Kress, who was already on the bow where a gun crew was setting up the piece. Gill's eyes widened as the gun crew removed the canvas tarp covering the gun. He stared at the six lead-gray barrels, each with a large caliber hole at its muzzle. The gun rested upon a wooden and metal gun carriage. The many coats of bright olive green paint from the wooden gun carriage and spoked wheels shone in the bright sunlight. The smell of gun grease met Gill's nostrils.

"It will fire one hundred shots a minute nearly a mile in distance. However, we keep it down to fifty shots for safety's sake," explained Kress.

Gill's eyes darted back and forth as he looked at the fine machine work. It was a well oiled machine every bit as good as his boat's engines.

Kress continued, "The piece itself weighs just under fifteen hundred pounds and the caisson weighs just over two thousand pounds. We carry just under twelve thousand rounds of ammunition with us. Would you like to see it fire, Mr. Gill?" asked Kress. Immediately Kress shouted up to the mate in the wheelhouse. "Hey, Dave! Bring her closer to Long Island over there and let us shoot some jack rabbits!" The boat's bow swung to port and was soon approaching offshore of the island. Jack rabbits could be seen hopping about on the sand and in the sagebrush of the island in the late afternoon sunlight.

Sergeant Conners stood to the rear of the Gatling Gun and began to shout orders to the gun crew. Like disciplined robots, the men placed a long metal magazine into the top of the gun with a snap and stood back. "Fire!" shouted Kress. The gunner turned the crank at the side of the gun. Instantly the gun roared, spitting out fire from its six barrels. The bullets raised a line of high froth and spouts of water across the river, eventually striking the island, kicking up a great cloud of dust. Gill was brought back to reality when he heard crashing and clanging coming from the stern wheel of the boat. Pieces of the large paddleboard splintered and flew through the air as the wheel arms and eccentric rods were bent or broken. The navigator, while watching the firing of the gun, had taken his eyes off the boat's course and had struck the underwater rocks near shore.

Passengers covered their heads and faces, running for cover as wooden splinters rained down upon them. Captain Gray sprang up the ladder to the wheelhouse, where he proceeded to scream and shout at the poor navigator, who was almost of a mind to jump overboard to escape Gray's wrath. They were able to make way across to the Oregon side where there was ample firewood to build a fire to straighten the bent rods. With the help of cursing soldiers, the rods were carried ashore and straightened. Hours later, the Spokane had limped into Umatilla Landing. The shouts of soldiers going ashore brought Gray back to the present. Having reflected on the events of the day before, he climbed down the ladder and proceeded to the hotel.

To the north in the dense Blue Mountains, the excited sounds of women and children setting up lodges and teepees reverberated against the sides of the deeply timbered canyon south of West Birch Creek. More than two thousand Indian souls filled the canyon. Dogs barked and snapped at the heels of horses that began wandering from the now immense horse herds. Campfire smoke began to rise from both within and outside of lodges as the women began to cook. Armed warriors rode slowly and solemnly at the village's perimeter, looking for signs of the enemy. There was plenty of water and grass here and firewood was in abundance.

High above the village on the north slope of the great canyon, the timber stopped and gave way to a steep-sided mesa-like, pie-shaped lava outcrop that rose over four thousand feet above sea level into the mountain air. Its steep sides were covered with dried yellow grass and scattered red lava rocks of various sizes. The hilltop was flat and was ringed by large brown-red lava rocks, ideally suited for defensive fighting positions, as all sides were protected from an enemy, who could be seen approaching from miles away. Surely this was a sign from the prophets announcing to the Dreamers that this was the time and place to rest. Also, the time had come to kill the pony soldiers dogging their heels. War Jack had nodded his approval to Oits. It was time to slap the unwanted soldiers.

The chiefs had gathered upon the high hilltop, amongst the lava rocks. They could gaze miles northward far into Washington Territory from the position. A breeze cooled them from the morning sun. Oits, his face freshly painted, spoke first. "Smohalla's teachings are true, we will be with Uncle Bull in the Queen Mother's land within the changing of two moons." The small bones braided in his hair gleamed in the morning sunlight. His eyes glared into the eyes of those standing around him. "But first, we must kill this yapping dog who bites at our heels! We will do it here at this place!" he spat as he reached down and threw a handful of the brown-red earth into the air. Grunts of agreement ran among some of the leaders.

War Jack looked around the group with a scowl on his painted, greasy face. His blood was up. His eyes shone brightly, piercing anyone he looked at. He stopped staring out into the vast distance to the north and suddenly turned to face Egan, who had been watching the two leaders with interest and caution. Egan shifted his revolver around closer to his hand. Leaders behind Egan stepped back and Oits stepped closer to War Jack. War Jack moved closer to Egan, his eyes glaring, thirsting for Egan's blood. "There are Paiute cowards within us. They do not share in the fighting. They are women. Egan is a coward!" shouted War Jack as he drew his knife from its beaded sheath and threw it downward, where it stuck in the hard earth at Egan's feet.

Below them, warriors who had been resting while their leaders talked were now on their feet, holding their rifles as others swiftly withdrew theirs from saddle scabbards. Allies one second, potential enemies the next, they began to draw apart into their own groups. Cat-like eyes darted back and forth nervously as they watched each other. The air was tense. Fingers rested on triggers.

Egan didn't flinch as he glared at War Jack. "I am no coward. We have talked of this before." Egan spoke calmly, staring at War Jack with a serious expression. "We didn't want this war, but neither did we want to go to the soldier prison after you had killed whites and then came to us for warriors. I will fight you here and now if that is what you want. I am not afraid of you. But I cannot tell you what my warriors would do to you if you should kill me." Oits and War Jack traded quick glances. A murmur of discontent rumbled through the alerted leaders.

War Jack was uneasy now. He could sense the nervousness coming from Oits. This is not what he'd expected. Egan turned his look to Oits. "You have never been strong for my people until now, after the agent was bad to us. Only then did the Numa look at you. I looked at you and perhaps I was wrong. I do not know. The white Soldier Chief Howard is coming after me and will hang me for the white settlers you have killed. I have looked into my sad heart and have seen you and the Bannocks take our precious time to kill and destroy the white settlers and their animals for only the blood in it. This is not good. This is not why I came with you."

War Jack broke his glare and slowly reached down and picked up the knife, wiping the blade on his leggings before returning it to its sheath. He looked at Egan. "Egan, you are a powerful leader amongst the Paiute. My heart sees that you are with us, it also sees that you are weak in spirit and are still wounded. Stay with us and watch us kill the pony soldiers when they come; then you will feel the spirit of the Dreamers again." Grunts of agreement came from the leaders on the hilltop.

Egan realized that he had already said too much and decided to calm his approach toward the two spiritual leaders before him. "My people and I will stay as long as you can defeat the soldiers and then let us go to the Queen Mother's land," Egan said. The tension lessened. Warriors returned rifles to scabbards on the side hill below.

Egan and Charley returned to Egan's lodge in deep thought and silence. "Egan!" a voice called from outside the lodge. Charley reached over and threw the entrance cover open. It was Umapine. Umapine's presence startled both Egan and Charley, since he'd left the group days ago, presumably to return to the Umatillas.

"Enter, Umapine," called Egan. Umapine came into the lodge and sat down before Egan and Charley. A set of fearful eyes stared from the shadows at the rear of the dwelling. "I can take you and your people from here and to the Soldier Chief Howard," Umapine said in a near whisper, his crafty eyes darting at the two men seated before him. "I have talked with them. They are not angry with you. They know that you and your people are prisoners. I will do this so that the soldiers are not unhappy with me. This is what they told me," he finished.

Egan and Charley sat dumbfounded. Egan rubbed his slung arm slowly. "How will all of my three bands escape without a fight?" he asked.

"Only you and your family will come out. You may work with the soldiers to get the others out when I take you to them," Umapine said.

Egan pondered the offer a long time before answering. He looked to the rear of the lodge where in the darkness the Old Woman and Evening Star and the two girls sat in silence. "I will go," said Egan.

"Good, then it is done!" said Umapine confidently as he stood up and exited the lodge.

Egan and Charley sat and looked at each other for a long while, ultimately shaking their heads in disbelief and wonder. Charley spoke. "Why would Umapine do this, and why now?" Egan shrugged his shoulders, not taking his eyes off Charley. The Old Woman's eyes showed fear at seeing Umapine, as did Evening Star's. She came from the shadows of the wikiup and sat close to her husband. The lodge was silent except for the buzzing of flies.

High on the lava hilltop, warriors and young boys were preparing their defense against the approaching troops. Stones were piled and fighting positions were fortified. Oits and War Jack were supervising the preparations when Umapine approached them. "Ho! Umapine!" greeted War Jack with a sly grin. He motioned Umapine out of earshot of the others. "Did you catch our lamb?" he questioned the dismounting Umatilla.

Umapine smiled. "It is done. I will talk with Homily and the other Dreamer Prophets at Thornhollow on the Umatilla River to the north. Egan has left the faith and they want revenge. I don't care of such things. They want Egan's scalp, as I do. Perhaps his blood soaking the earth will avenge my dead father's spirit," Umapine pronounced through clinched teeth. His eyes blazed. "I will arrange to have Egan and his group killed without suspicion being placed upon either of you. Then perhaps his warriors will stay and follow you."

"It is good," said Oits. "The Dreamer Prophets will look on you with favor for having killed him who has turned against us." Umapine nodded to the two chiefs and mounted his Cayuse pony; turning it eastwards towards the blue timber, he trotted into the dense forest.

War Jack ground his teeth as he watched Umapine ride away. He wanted to cut Egan's throat as much as Oits did, but they had to leave the act to Umapine, Homily, and the Dreamers at Thornhollow. He and Oits needed Egan's warriors badly. If the Paiute ever suspected that Egan had been sacrificed to promote their cause, the Paiute would be a formable enemy to deal with. That was trouble they could not afford.

"I can defeat all my enemies! No bullet can hurt me. I have the power to kill any of you! It is wrong to dig up the face of the earth - the earth is our mother; we must live upon what grows of itself."

Oits, Northern Paiute Dreamer–Prophet.

Died:

"McCormmach – In Pendleton, June 21, 1878, of malignant diphtheria, daughter of J.W. and M.J. McCormmach, aged 9 years and 6 months."

The East Oregonian, Saturday, June 29, 1878.

ARIZONA TROOPS FOR THE WAR
San Francisco, June 26.

"Two companies of the Eighth Infantry – one from Tucson, and the other from Camp Verde, Arizona – arrived today by the Southern Pacific, and marched to the Presidio, where they will await orders. They will probably be sent to Idaho with but little delay."

The East Oregonian, Saturday, July 6, 1878.

Chapter 11

The Eagles Gather

Captain Bernard raised his arm skyward, halting the forward march of the cavalrymen as he watched three riders approaching the column, riding through the stirrup-high green marsh grass of Camas Prairie. It was Robbins' scouts. The lead rider rode directly to Bernard, reining his large quarter horse in to a slippery stop. "Cap'n, they have stopped about ten miles from here and it looks like they mean to stay there. Pitching tents and everything, like they <u>want</u> us to come visitin!" The volunteer spoke through tobacco stained whiskers. His horse twisted and blew its nose nervously beneath him.

Bernard's face took on a sober expression as he looked to the northeast into the blue-green timber. "Very well, Mr. Beagle, thank you for the report," Bernard said to the sweaty rider. The volunteer wheeled his fidgety horse around and rode to where Rube Robbins was riding flank with the other volunteers. General Howard raised his head from the map he'd been reading while in the saddle. He knew what the volunteer +had to say to Bernard. Bernard cantered toward him as he folded the map and returned it to the leather case on his saddle.

Bernard approached Howard and turned his mount so that he was riding alongside his commander. "They've stopped!" was all he had to say to Howard.

Howard raised his arm, stopping the long column. As the dust from the column passed by the two officers, they talked about the next plan of operation.

"Praise God they've stopped," whispered Howard to himself, lifting his dusty hat from his head and wiping the headband with his soiled handkerchief. Howard's eyes bored into Bernard's, as he spoke to him. "Captain, are your men ready to take on this band of Hostiles that you've been following for the last two months?"

"Let me have them, Sir!" responded Bernard, leaning forward in his saddle, white knuckles grasping his reins.

Howard removed his silver-rimmed glasses, returning them to the inside pocket of his tunic. He turned his glance toward the northeast, away from Bernard. "Not quite yet, Sir, but soon. We'll divert around them to the west. Possibly they will think we've lost their trail, but I doubt it. They want a fight now," Howard said calmly.

"But what about Miles and his infantry and artillery following us, Sir? Won't we be needing them?" asked Bernard with shock.

Howard raised his arm directing the column forward. The column jerked itself from its static position and began to rumble forward across the grassy prairie. He made a clicking sound with his tongue. His mount stepped out with the others.

"Captain," Howard said, "Miles won't be on this prairie until late tomorrow afternoon and the Indians know that. But, if they stand still for a few more hours we can fight them on ground of our own choosing. We can then drive them eastward and back where most of this nonsense started, hopefully with a minimal loss of life. Don't you agree, Captain? asked Howard, his sharp eyes scanning the meadow and hills before them.

Bernard rode for some time beside Howard, not answering. He finally turned to Howard. "General, I do not believe that the citizens of this country want us to <u>save</u> lives but to take them if they pose a threat to them. And these people are a threat, General!" Silence reigned for a moment between the two officers. "You, Sir, are my commanding officer and I am at your service. Now what would you have me do?" questioned Bernard.

Howard swallowed. "Follow me, Captain. I will have great use of your fighting abilities quite soon. You may return to the point, Sir. We travel to the town of Pilot Rock and I believe that we will see action very soon. And it will be hot." Howard's eyes again bored into Bernard's. "Captain, we are the <u>only</u> force existing between the Hostiles and what is left of Sitting Bull's band in Canada. Do you understand what I am saying, Reuben?"

Bernard startled at the familiarity of Howard's calling him by his first name. After thinking for a minute, he took in a breath of the warm morning air. The only sounds were the clomping of horse's hooves in the meadow. Slowly a knowing smile crossed Bernard's face. "Yes, Sir, I believe I do," he answered to the one-armed general, and snapping a quick salute, spurred his mount. The large Morgan shot to life beneath him as they cantered towards the point of the column, kicking up clods of dark earth and grass behind them as they crossed the meadow to the northwest. Howard watched Bernard ride to the front of the column. He removed his hat again and wiped its band, then his forehead. "I am indeed fortunate to have him," he thought to himself.

A meadowlark chirped from its observation point, resting on an abandoned red-digger squirrel mound. The procession it was watching was like nothing it had ever seen before. It looked on with wonder at so many horses and men, yet there weren't nearly as many as the thousands of people that had passed by this place a day earlier. What could bring so many strangers to this place now? The meadowlark watched as the long column worked its way northward, marching towards the small town of Pilot Rock.

Pilot Rock sweltered in the late afternoon heat. Only the buzzing of blow flies around the stagecoach barns were active at this time of day. Everything else was in any available shade. The high lava rock butte that gave the town its name loomed over the town to the northwest. The town was deserted. Nearly everyone had rushed north to Pendleton in panic following the news of the approaching Hostiles. But it was not entirely a ghost town. In the shade of the tree-lined road entering the small town, a red-over-white Guidon moved slightly with each puff of a drifting hot breeze. A red "1" stood over a white "E," identifying the flag as belonging to E Company of the First U.S. Cavalry. One hundred yards to the east of the Guidon stood another. This one carried a white "H" beneath its red "1." Behind the guidons over seventy off-white tents stood in a row. Before each tent lay two black McClellan saddles and tack. Groups of troopers sat or stood in small groups, chatting quietly, as if not wishing to contribute to the sweltering heat. They were waiting for the arrival of their commanding general coming from the south. Sentries were posted about the town, sweating in the hot sun as they walked their posts. They gripped their carbines tightly as they gazed outwards for any signs of the approaching battalion.

This was the rendezvous point for the regiment and all were anxious to hear first hand the news about the battalion's campaign. Most had close friends riding with Howard. Only the sounds of buzzing flies and the snapping of grasshoppers in the dry weeds and grass disturbed the still, hot air. By late afternoon, as the sun was beginning to give up trying to fry the town's existing occupants and was casting small shadows as it slid towards the western horizon, the sharp barking of the town's abandoned dog population broke the silence. The troopers stopped talking and rose to their feet. Horses at the picket lines jerked their heads up from feed bags, ears pointing to the west. Something was coming. "Corporal of the guard!" shouted a sentry on the stagecoach road at the west end of town.

Captain William Winters shot up from the small field table where he and First Lieutenant William Parnell had been playing cards. "Bugler! Sound 'Assembly.' First Sergeant, detail the guard on the road west of town!" shouted Winters as he buttoned his dark blue blouse. "Move, Lieutenant, and form your company," ordered Winters as he drew his revolver, re-checking it before returning it to its holster.

229

Parnell didn't need the order; he was already trotting towards H Company, shouting "Lieutenant Knox!" Second Lieutenant Thomas Knox didn't need the order either; he was already forming the company. Captain Winters mounted his horse and cantered to where the sentry had given the alarm.

E Company's first sergeant, George Webber, was standing, revolver in hand, barrel downward, talking to the sentry as they watched the stage road. Winters dismounted quickly in the dusty road. "Cap'n," acknowledged the sergeant, throwing a quick salute, savoring the fresh cut of tobacco in his cheek. His eyes glared at the barking dogs, which apparently wished to bond with him in the excitement. His thumb twitched, wanting to draw the revolver's hammer back as he listened to their racket. Winters began to speak over the clamor of the barking dogs and the cussing of the sergeant who, forgetting the Army for the present, was preoccupied in jabbing his spurred boot at the circling mongrels. "Gawd damit! You sons o bitches! Shut up!" he shouted at the dogs, who were happy that they had finally found a friend who would play with them. The dogs and the sergeant danced around in a dusty circle, oblivious of their surroundings. "This is delightful!" thought the dogs.

"Sergeant!" snapped Winters.

The sergeant turned back, reholstering his revolver and raised his carbine, as did the young sentry at his side. Winters slowly unbuttoned the flap on his holster, not taking his eyes off the three riders approaching them. The dogs, apparently sensing trouble, surrendered the contest to the sergeant and trotted to the rear.

The three riders came to a halt before the Army sentries. The soldiers could smell the riders twenty feet away as their dust cloud engulfed them, passing eastward down the main street of Pilot Rock. To Winters they resembled cavemen dressed in homespun shirts and buckskin trousers. Horses and riders were caked with dust and sweat. Their faces were as dark as Indians and they wore scraggly beards. Their hair was long and shaggy and their clothing was tattered and torn. The man in the center carried a shotgun across the pommel of his saddle and was smiling. "Howdy, Captain," he greeted Winters. "I'm Rube Robbins and these are my scouts. We're ridin point for General Howard's battalion, which is about two hours back. I spek we look a mite dry. Would you have water for me and my boys?" asked Robbins hoarsely, as he glanced around the empty town.

"Of course, Sir," answered Winters. "Sergeant, take them to water. And, Mr. Robbins, I would welcome a briefing from you about our situation here." The riders dismounted with a tired, dusty thud as they took their horses' reins and stiffly led them to the stable for water and grain. They had a story to tell. After the scouts had walked and watered their horses, they watered themselves.

"Whoosh!" spat Robbins as he thrust his head out of the cold watering trough, spraying droplets of water in all directions. His crusty whiskers shone brightly in the light of the late afternoon sun. Later, he sat in the shade of one of the trees, slowly drawing a long Cuban cigar beneath his still wet nostrils. His eyes closed to slits as he drew in the rich pungent odor of the tobacco. He'd finished briefing Captain Winters and Lieutenant Parnell.

Parnell nervously eyed Winters after receiving the news of Howard's difficult campaign and the death and destruction witnessed by the command. Robbins opened his bright gray eyes and looked directly at Winters. "Yessir, Cap'n, it looks like you and the rest of Howard's command are going to open the ball with the Hostiles real soon now." He grinned slightly, his eyes drifting across the creek and upward towards high Pilot Rock.

Captain Winters turned to Lieutenant Parnell. "Lieutenant, take a detail and go meet the general and escort him to this place. Take a trumpeter and sound Ruffles and Flourishes once you identify the command." Parnell saluted and briskly walked to his company's area, shouting orders. Troopers jumped and began to saddle horses. Soon the detail had departed the town and had disappeared westward into the setting sun. Immediately, cooking fires were started and preparations were hastily made to provide accommodations for the approaching command.

"Corporal of the guard!" shouted a sentry as he brought his carbine up. "Riders approaching," he shouted over his shoulder. Immediately a corporal trotted to his side.

"Sergeant of the guard!" shouted the corporal, as a bugle call drifted in from the closing darkness to the west. Captain Winters buckled on his belt and holster and mounted his horse, spurring it toward the west end of town. After what seemed an eternity, Winters could make out the approaching column through the closing daylight. He turned slightly, looking to his rear to insure that his troops were formed up properly to greet the general. They had formed into ranks at attention. The dust of the approaching column greeted Winters first, followed by the rest of Robbins' scouts, whose grimy faces contained little or no expression except fatigue as they passed by him. Following the scouts rode Company G.

In the dim light Winters could make out the faint glimmer of a captain's shoulder straps on the first rider, who abruptly came to a halt before Winters, saluting. "Captain Bernard's battalion, Sir. How are you, Bill?" Bernard asked Winters through a dry, dusty mouth.

Winters could see a grin through the dark beard. "Ready and willing as usual, Sir!" responded Winters with an answering grin and a salute. Winters turned, shouting to First Sergeant George Webber. "First Sergeant, direct the column to water and forage and to the bivouac area."

"Yessir!" snapped the sergeant, barking orders to his corporals. The column followed the bivouac detail. Winters stood in place, greeting each company as it proceeded past him. Friendly, sincere greetings were exchanged as troop commanders passed by him, turning toward the bivouac area in turn.

Soon, General Howard's adjutant, Lieutenant Erskine Wood, passed Winters with a quick salute. Behind Wood followed Howard, who drew up before Winters and saluted with his left hand. Winters had seen Howard many times in his career, but he had never seen the general looking so thin and haggard. His usually spotless uniform was worn thin but his warm smile wasn't. "Captain Winters, it is good to see you and your command. I'd hoped and prayed that you would be at this place at this important time. God has been merciful."

"Yes, Sir," answered Winters, as he dropped his hand in salute. "If it would please the General, I have prepared a private tent area and cooking fire for you, Sir," Winters said as he tried to identify the two Indian women riding behind Howard.

"Excellent, Captain," answered Howard as Winters mounted his horse and led the way. Sarah and Mattie followed behind, silently eyeing the abandoned town's buildings and the looks of hatred coming from the few citizens standing in the shadows. The two women also noticed the Gatling gun as they rode passed E Company's tents. Even in the fading light, the two Paiute women could see the ominous black holes at the muzzle of each blue-black barrel. It made them shudder.

Another welcome sight greeted Howard's eyes as he led his tired and dusty column into Pilot Rock. Secured to their picket lines were the mounts of companies E and H, which had now enlarged his strength considerably. The two company guidons hung in the warm evening air, truly a welcome sight to Howard and his men.

As Winters led the General and the two women, he thought to himself, "These people have been through hell. What kind of enemy could wear these troops down so badly and still keep going?" He knew that he was going to find out very soon. The yellow-orange light of the cooking fires and lanterns began to glow through the trees and wooden buildings of the growing Army camp. Smoke columns trailed lazily upward through the trees, into the darkening sky. The smell of coffee and bacon drifted amongst the rows of tents. The sounds of quiet voices and laughter drifted from the troops standing or sitting around the cooking fires. Excited news was exchanged between soldiers who had been on the trail of the Hostiles for over two months and those who were just joining. Some groups of men became hushed at the news of the dead and wounded. Others couldn't comprehend northwest Indians being so powerful and destructive. New recruits stood wide-eyed, hearing of the death and destruction that had proceeded them. Some recruits walked to their tents and began to write hurried letters home, suddenly having lost their appetite.

Less than thirty minutes later "riders approaching!" was called from the sentry at the north end of town. A battalion under the command of a dust-covered, sweaty captain of the Fourth Artillery entered the town. Howard stepped from his tent, buttoning his blue blouse as he watched the activity coming towards the bivouac area past the sentries. "Captain Throckmorton, Sir," Wood said, as the general walked closer to get a better look at the arriving troops.

In the growing darkness, the dusty captain stiffly dismounted his worn-out horse, handing the reins to an orderly. The captain slapped his shoulders and sleeves, creating small clouds of dust and exposing red shoulder straps instead of the yellow or blue cavalry and infantry colors. He was an artilleryman. He shook his head with tired frustration. Behind him, his battalion of fifty-eight soldiers passed, heading to the bivouac area. They consisted of mounted Twenty-First Infantrymen and two batteries of the Fourth Artillery. The wheels of the heavy caissons and the long rifled cannons crunched loudly as they were pulled along the rocky street by lathered horse teams. The officer's blood-shot eyes darted back and forth, searching for the headquarters tent. His eyes showed white against his grimy face, showing where he'd been wiping them clear of the dust that coating everything. "Sound 'Officer's Call,' Mr. Wood," Howard ordered, buttoning his top button. His eyes followed the last of the artillery battalion as it passed into the bivouac area.

It was Sunday, July seventh, and away from the main bivouac area a field table had been set up and sentries had been posted. Lanterns were hung from low tree branches near the table, casting yellow light upon the scene. Moths fluttered and fell around them. Once "Officer's Call" had been sounded, thirteen officers arrived. Wood sounded "Aten-Hut!" Immediately the officers came to attention, cigars dropping to the ground. Behind Wood walked Howard, carrying a map and papers beneath his arm. Wood took the large map from the general and began to attach it to a rigged map stand he'd been carrying.

"At ease, Gentlemen," Howard said, returning their salutes. The officers relaxed as much as possible. There was an air of excitement around them as a new energy recharged their fatigued bodies. Backs straightened. Howard looked at the officers standing before him. Most wore ragged pants and blouses and scraggly beards. A few had found time to groom themselves. He looked at the newly arrived officers and could see that while not so tattered, they too were seasoned men ready to follow him wherever he ordered. Very soon he would demand every ounce of energy from them and their troopers.

Howard cleared his voice and spoke. "Gentlemen, through the Grace of God we have come to this place at this critical time and I bid welcome to our newly arrived units. As you all know, for nearly two months we have been attempting to contain this group of Indian Hostiles now numbering nearly twenty-five hundred. Of those, nearly one thousand are reported as warriors. We now know that they consist of Fort Hall Bannock, Shoshoni, Northern Paiute, Warm Spring, Umatilla, and Yakimas, to name a few. It appears that they are moving to Canada to join Chief Sitting Bull of the Sioux, who, it is believed, is desperately in need of support since his own confederates have left him and have surrendered to the War Department. Most of you recall our campaign last summer against Chief Joseph began in the same way as this one has, and I believe for the same purpose. It is also believed that a Ghost religion or Dreamer faith has sprung amongst the Indians and has given them new energy and purpose. Recent dispatches from high command support this." A murmur ran through the officers before him. "Captain Throckmorton reports that an advance band of these same Hostiles attacked and defeated more than fifty civilian volunteers under their local sheriff yesterday and that he had escorted them back to the town of Pendleton south of here this morning. Captain Throckmorton?"

Throckmorton cleared his dry throat. "Thank you, Sir. My battalion having left Fort Walla Walla en route to this location arrived at Pendleton last evening. We had not been there but an hour when survivors of the civilian skirmish entered town. They earnestly asked for my services in relieving their comrades from the Hostiles, who would surely kill all of them by morning. I consented. At first dawn I met them just south of this location and escorted them back to Pendleton and safety. Many were wounded, most in hips and legs. Two of their number had been killed and left behind. They reported that at least one hundred warriors had struck them as they were eating lunch by a spring at the foot of a draw eight miles from here. They were encircled quickly and driven into a shed from where they fought a defensive engagement, ultimately making their escape late last night. The Hostiles are reported to have repeating rifles and Army breechloaders. It is also reported that they seem well schooled in their use."

Another murmur drifted through the officers. "Thank you, Captain," Howard said, stepping toward the map. "Gentlemen, here we are," pointing to a small dot on the map. "I had to pen this dot on the map, as this village is too small to rank a government one." He smiled. A chuckle ran amongst the officers. Howard moved the pointer again. "This is the trail we have been following the Hostiles on for the past weeks. To the south of us comes the wagon train accompanied by the Twenty-First Infantry and Fourth Artillery units under

Captain Miles. By the Grace of God, Robbins' scouts report that the Hostiles have stopped momentarily just south of us and have encamped. This finally places us in a position to fight them on ground of our own choosing. Now we are finally to their front and blocking their direction of advance. Since no Indian had dared to previously scout for us, I have been carefully listening to my two companions, Sarah and her sister-in-law, Mattie. They tell me that there is very strong dissension within the Hostiles' leadership." Thirteen sets of suspicious eyes stared at the two women, standing just inside the circle of yellow light. "It seems that one of the Paiute leaders, Egan, may no longer share the same beliefs as he did at the beginning of the outbreak. He leads three bands within the group. Perhaps this is the reason for their stopping at this time. I don't know. But this may be the one and only opportunity we will have to block the Hostiles from their line of march." His eyes narrowed.

The pointer dropped as Howard took a breath and spoke again to the officers who were paying strict attention to his every word, most of their faces tense and drawn, dead serious. "Gentlemen, we now have the combined strength of seven companies of cavalry and Throckmorton's battery, consisting of over three hundred and forty-five men, not including Rube Robbins' scouts and the Gatling Gun. From what little intelligence information I have at my disposal, I believe it is safe to say that we are facing an enemy of much greater numerical strength and we have no immediate support forces. Gentlemen, with the exception of several gunboats on the Columbia River to our north, there are little or no military reserves available to us in our area of operation."

Howard drew his handkerchief from his coat pocket and blew into it, returning it to its pocket. His eyes seemed to freeze each commander's eyes like a bird dog transfixing its winged prey. "We _must_ and _will_ attack the Hostiles here and now! Should we lose them without striking a severe blow, they will continue marching north, growing more powerful each day as others join them, spreading untold death and destruction in their path." He took a breath, picked up the pointer and tapped it against the map. "If we strike them hard at the earliest opportunity here and now, I believe that we can break them up and turn them southward with a minimum of loss to both sides. But it must be done now." Howard sat the pointer on the field table. "Robbins' scouts are in the field as we speak, attempting to locate their exact campsite to the south of us. When they report the Hostile's position to us, the command will proceed immediately to that location and engage them."

The general continued, "Captain Miles' wagon train will be on Camas Prairie tomorrow morning and will provide a blocking force to the south, and as a rally and supply point if necessary." All eyes were on Howard. "Gentlemen, see to your men and horses. I want double rations and issues of grain placed in the wagons as well as water. Inspect your ammunition, insure as to its reliability and clean it if necessary. Issue extra ammunition for cartridge belts and saddlebags. Surgeon Fitzgerald will accompany me with the Headquarters Company." Howard looked at Captain Winters of E Company. "Captain Winters, please see that your Gatling gun battery is well prepared to go into action at a moment's notice, once we are on the field." He cast Winters a knowing glance. Winters nodded his assurance. Howard knew he was ready. "Now, are there any questions, Gentlemen?" asked Howard.

"Sir?" spoke Captain McGregor.

"Captain?" acknowledged Howard.

"Sir, am I to understand that once the Hostiles are within our grasp on the battlefield, that we are going to purposefully leave a door open for them to escape to the east? Respectfully speaking, Sir." McGregor asked.

"That is a good question, Captain," answered Howard, again pointing toward the map. "My intentions are to neutralize the Hostile's pilgrimage and morale with one solid blow, thus creating confusion and hopelessness within their ranks. I believe that they are already beginning to fragment at the command level and we will hasten that fragmentation with the least amount of death to those who wish to surrender, and destruction to those that do not. If backed into a wall, they will all die to a soul and be glad for it. I do not wish to give them that satisfaction. Any further questions, Gentlemen?" There was no response from the dust-covered officers standing before Howard, save a few nodding or shaking heads. Nervous, anxious eyes darted amongst the younger officers. This was to be their baptism of fire. Once Howard had looked into each set of eyes and felt satisfied, he concluded. "Good then. See to your commands, and thank you, Gentlemen."

"Ten-Hut!" called Wood. The thirteen officers braced to attention, watching the general stiffly walk to his tent, grasping the maps beneath his one arm and managing a smile towards the officers whom he knew so well.

A dim half-moon slowly rose into the night sky. It was in its first quarter and rested pale against the inky darkness, allowing stars to twinkle and shine in all of their glory. They looked as if a person could reach out and pluck them from the darkness. Far beneath the glistening heavens stood a Paiute wikiup, hidden in the darkness amongst the forest of lodgepole pines. Hundreds of lodges and teepees also lay hidden in the darkness of the night. The moon's chalky light gave the treetops and the rocks on the high bluffs above a frosty appearance in the warm night. Inside the wikiup, the glowing coals of a small fire gave the interior a reddish light.

The Old Woman was quietly talking to herself or to long dead loved ones, as she rocked back and forth sitting cross-legged at the rear of the lodge. Through closed eyes she spoke. Her creaky voice resembled the sound of wind sighing through broken boards of an old cabin. The two teenaged girls lay quietly beneath their blankets. Egan lay propped against his saddle, cushioned by his red blanket. Fresh bright red stains showed through his bandages. The angry wounds refused to heal. His face glistened with a new fever sweat in the firelight. Mattie and Sarah had left them an hour before, after treating his wounds and consoling him as best as they could. If caught, the two women would be killed. Friendly Paiute had managed again to get them in and out of the vast village undetected.

"Will tomorrow bring the white soldiers?" whispered Evening Star as she lay beside Egan, her eyes transfixed, staring into the glowing embers of the wikiup's small fire. The Old Woman stopped her rocking and began to hum softly. Egan awoke from a fevered sleep, focusing on the Old Woman, whose ancient eyes burned a deep path into his.

"Yes, they will come. And they are very angry for what we have done," Egan said quietly. The Old Woman's eyes burned, shining in her dark aged face, which contrasted with her snow-white hair. Evening Star squeezed Egan's arm gently, as she turned her gaze to the Old Woman. The tiny lines and wrinkles of the Old One's face resembled those she had seen drawn on the white soldier's war maps that she had seen as a small girl so many years ago.

"Then tomorrow it will be over?" creaked the old soul, as she slowly rocked back and forth.

Egan turned his eyes upward, following the wisps of smoke drifting out through the open smoke hole of the wikiup into the starlit sky above them. He wondered if Evening Star and his daughters knew what lay ahead for them in the next few hours. He fought back a tremor. He nodded to the Old Woman, "Yes, the beginning of the end." The Old Woman wrapped a blanket tightly around herself and continued her low mournful song that told of happier times, when the only worries were that of the berry and rabbit harvests, and the crying of newborn Paiute babies sending their first sounds wafting across moonlit sagebrush prairies.

Outside of the wikiup, the hundreds of lodges and tents were nearly all empty because of the great "Nanigu'kwa" Ghost Dance being performed upon the high lava outcropped ridge above them. A large bonfire lit the hilltop, resembling a Roman candle in the black night. The deep booming sound of the drums echoed downward, bringing with it the sounds of loud singing and shouting. Silhouettes of the dancers cast long dark shadows down between the rock pillars that surrounded the hilltop, as they danced in the great "Ba

237

wa" circle. The pony soldiers would be stopped tomorrow; their bullets could not hurt the Numa.

Within the circle Oits threw a handful of red lava dust upward, spraying the dancers with dirt and pebbles as he shouted, "The dust shall become gunpowder for our weapons!" The entranced dancers responded with a resounding shout that shattered the dark night surrounding them. They danced within the large circle, moving right to left, feet barely lifting from the earth. Left foot, right foot, left foot, right foot. Bright sparks and burning embers shot skyward from the large roaring fire. The drums boomed, joining the high-pitched nasal voices of the singers.

Several hundred yards below the dancers, Egan stood weakly outside his wikiup, staring up at those on the hilltop. Beside Egan stood Charley. The burning tip of a rolled cigarette made from torn newspaper glowed against Charley's bronzed cheeks in the darkness. Numerous other men from Egan's bands stood or sat upon the ground in the darkness, watching the scene on the hilltop. "The 'Kotso-tika'ra' Buffalo Eaters are looking for strength to kill the white soldiers that come tomorrow," Charley said, referring to the Bannock dancers above them.

"Oits has them where he wants them. The 'Nanigu'kwa' Ghost Dance gives them false bravery, as we shall see tomorrow," Egan uttered in the darkness. He could hear and feel his men shift ever so quietly. Some of them still believed. He was aware that rifles surrounded him in the darkness. "I believe that we may see many Numa walk the road of Gosipa when the soldiers come," Egan said quietly.

Outside, Charley exhaled smoke in the shadows. The smoke's strong smell reached everyone's nostrils in the clear night air. The sounds of horses whinnying to each other in the darkness met their ears. The drumming from above echoed against the deep surrounding canyons, resembling gunfire in the ears of Egan's small group of Paiute, watching and listening from the darkness below. Cutting through the drumming and singing, came Otis' high pitched voice, singing "Nuva'ri'pa Noyo'a! The Snowy Earth comes gliding."

To General Sherman:

*The following despatch was received from General Howard, dated Head of Birch Creek, July 8:
"The different sides of the hill were steeper than Missionary Ridge, (Battle of Gettsyburg, PA.,
author)) still the troops, though encountering a severe fire that emptied some saddles and killed many
horses, did not waver, but skirmished to the very top, the enemy abandoning his position and running
to the next height in defences of lava rock. In twenty minutes the height was charged from different
sides and taken. [Captain Bernard is entitled to special credit for this engagement, as indeed for the
entire campaign, and his officers and men did as well as brave and true men only can do. Could you
know the difficulties of this wilderness you would then appreciate their loyal services."]*

McDowell, Major–General
Army Navy Journal, July 13, 1878.

*"No baseball pitcher is now considered an expert unless he can curve the ball into the batter's
stomach three times out of every possible five."*

East Oregonian. Saturday, July 6, 1878.

Eighty Nevada Rovers.

*"Capt. Scamthonda, with 80 Nevada volunteers, arrived this afternoon, and will report to Major
Egbert. They have a roving commission from the Governor of Nevada who supplies them with arms
and ammunition."*

East Oregonian, Saturday, July 6, 1878.

Chapter 12

Gatling Guns and Ghosts

From outside General Howard's tent, Richard Barrett the sergeant of the guard cleared his deep voice in the early morning darkness. "Sir, First Sergeant Barrett! The scouts are back, Sir, and they have located the Hostile's camp." It was four a.m., Monday, the eighth of July. From inside the darkness of the tent, lit only by a small, nearly consumed candle, two eyelids popped open from a deep sleep.

"Sergeant?" asked Howard.

"Yes, Sir?" responded Barrett.

"Get them up, sound 'Officer's Call' and 'Assembly'!" he ordered, throwing off his blanket.

"Yes, Sir!" responded the sergeant as he called for the trumpeter, who was already trotting towards the general's tent, wiping his mouth on his sleeve. As the sergeant's form disappeared into the inky morning darkness, the sounds of shouted commands and curses mingling with the shrill sound of the "General Call," followed by "Officer's Call" broke the morning stillness. Soon troopers were up, tents were down and packed into the wagons, and cooking fires were kindled. Within minutes the smell of wood smoke, boiling coffee, and bacon drifted throughout the camp. Those cooking had been the first to feed water and groom their mounts.

A small section of troopers from E Company stood or squatted around their cooking fire, sipping what they called coffee and munching on their hard tack and recently acquired sowbelly. Without changing his gaze from the fire or lowering his tin Army cup, Private Bill Schaffer spoke to his bunkmate, Private Joe Howard, who sat across the fire from him. "Joe, I swear, you are going to lose your eyesight trying to pick out all the weevils from them worm castles you eat in the dark!" A chuckle drifted around the ring of men.

Private Howard seemed preoccupied as usual, carefully picking anything resembling off-white out of his hard tack biscuit, seemingly unaware of Schaffer's comment. He slowly turned the biscuit against the firelight, examining the hard cracker. "Bill," said Joe, as he intensely studied the hard tack biscuit, "if you didn't eat so much of that 'embalmed beef' you swallow down whole, you wouldn't spend as much time running to the privy as you do groomin that crockhead mount of yours. I swear, the two of you do suit each other." Schaffer choked on his coffee as laughter mingled with the coffee. The two troopers didn't know that within hours they would be bleeding and fighting for their very lives.

Other recruits were cursing their clumsy fingers and hands as they struggled to adjust bridles and saddles in the darkness, their heads still foggy with sleep. The low grumbling of corporals and sergeants lashed and challenged their pride and abilities as cavalrymen. They would leave with empty bellies. That was the cavalry.

In a semi-circle outside of General Howard's tent stood the officers of his command, including Rube Robbins, Sarah, and Mattie. Some were still buttoning shirts. The two women seemed asleep on their feet. Howard scanned the group before speaking, then began, "Gentlemen, our scouts have located the position of the Hostile's camp south of here. Scouts Beagle and Morton will brief you."

Howard directed the two sweaty, dust-cloaked men to report on what they had found. Beagle stepped forward, his face glistening with sweat even in the cool morning air. It shone in the lantern light. Beagle cleared his dusty throat and began nervously, "Well, Sir, Cal and I headed south on the stage road nearly thirteen miles and we seen a large fire in the mountains, high up. At first we thought it were a forest fire. Well, we slowed down some and walked our horses until we seen it was a big bonfire way up on a high mesa. We dismounted then and walked the rest of the way until we could hear singin and dancin like we never heard before. It were somethin awful, like thousands of banshees was wailin from hell itself. They weren't worried about nobody findin em, either. So we come back here real quick like!" Finished, he stepped back alongside scout Cal Morton. Officers and scouts exchanged worried glances. Some concentrated on moving pebbles with the toes of their boots, while others hastily scribbled in their small notebooks before returning them to their blouse pockets.

Howard stepped forward. "Gentlemen, this is the plan of attack." All eyes were on him. "At six a.m., we will move southward on the stagecoach road and will proceed southward to engage the enemy. Captain Throckmorton will take his battalion to the west, guided by a scout from Heppner to block any attempts of the enemy of breaking free to the west and crossing the Columbia River. I will take the battalion southward on the stagecoach road to locate and engage the enemy where he stands. The battalion, consisting of companies E, F, G, H, K, and L, will be placed under the immediate command of Captain Bernard. Company A, commanded by Captain McGregor, will remain with me and the supply wagons and will be the rally point and headquarters. The Gatling Gun Battery will accompany E Company, under the command of Captain Winters and in turn will be directed by Captain Bernard. Rube Robbins and his scouts will take the point, reporting anything they see. They will, in all probability, run into the Hostiles first. They will report to headquarters upon any contact with them. Is that clear, Mr. Robbins?" Robbins nodded gruffly, spitting tobacco. He liked to ruffle the general. Howard stepped closer in the lantern and firelight of the camp. "Gentlemen, let us pray." He removed his hat, as the others removed theirs. Mattie and Sarah bowed their heads and clasped their hands. Howard began, "Oh, Heavenly Father, grant that we may approach our enemy with compassion, yet with Thy staff and Thy rod in order to show them our purpose. And in Your almighty wisdom and judgment, show them the light. We commend to you our spirit, Dear Lord. In God's name we pray. Amen." Howard placed his worn campaign hat back on his head and saluted. "Posts, Gentlemen." The officers returned the salute and quickly walked to their companies.

As the first blue-gray tints of color lightened the eastern sky, the cavalry companies formed into line, standing to horse and ready for the command to mount. Howard mounted with Sarah and Mattie to his rear and stood before the long lines of dismounted troopers to his front. The Color Guard stood behind them, the colors cased in the cool dark air. Bernard trotted to where Howard stood with the Color Guard and saluted. The two men exchanged quiet words. Howard returned the salute and wheeled onto the road, the guard and women following him.

Bernard turned his mount about, facing the formed companies. He spoke so that his trumpeter could hear him clearly and gave the commands. Sitting upright in the saddle, he ordered, "Battalion, prepare to mount!" The trumpeter sounded the call, as voice commands came from company commanders. As one, every other trooper walked his mount forward and placed his left foot into the stirrup, grasping the saddle and horse's mane. "Mount!" shouted Bernard. Again as one trooper, they swung their right legs over their mounts as the rear mounted rank rode forward, forming one single mounted rank. Bernard ordered, "Battalion fours right, march!" The trumpeter followed suit, with other trumpeters repeating the call down the line. Soon the entire command was marching westward along the stage road. The town's mongrels stopped at the edge of town and continued to bark at the departing troops, wanting to play more games with them. From a few dwellings stepped sleepy citizens, looping suspenders over their shoulders as they watched the command leave their abandoned town. They scratched themselves, yawning in the darkness, as the dust settled in their street. They felt secure with so many troopers about.

The column marched about a mile out of town, then turned abruptly to the south on the stage road. As the end of the column reached the turnoff point, Captain Throckmorton signaled to his short battalion, which continued onward to the west departing from the main column. The wheels of the cannons and caissons kicked up dust amongst the men and horses of company M and A, Fourth Artillery, and the mounted infantrymen of Company C, Twenty-first Infantry. The battalion's strength consisted of fifty-eight mounted troops. The departing men glanced nervously at the main column as they rode onward. The main column consisted of two hundred and eighty-seven men and officers. Soon, the younger, friskier mounts had settled down in the ranks, leaving only the sounds of an occasional horse's whinny, mixed with the tinkling and clanking of cups and other metal gear secured to saddles. There was little talking or chatter, as everyone fully expected to see action soon. It was what they'd been waiting weeks for. The older, seasoned horses marched with heads up, ears pointed forward. They sensed the excitement also. Far to the column's front, Howard and Bernard could see tiny wisps of dust in the gathering daylight. It was Robbins' scouts, out sniffing for Indian sign. At either side of the column rode cavalry flank riders, combing the hilltops for Indian sign. They had entered the valley of Birch Creek.

Bernard turned to Lieutenant Ward riding behind him. "Lieutenant, order 'Guidons Out,' pass the word."

"Yes, Sir," responded Ward. Soon covers were removed from the troop flags and the slight breeze picked up seven red-over-white Guidons. Their colors shone brightly as the first rays of yellow sunlight struck them.

"Well, Captain, it was good to get mail, was it not?" Howard said to Bernard, his head constantly moving left to right. "I trust that good tidings greeted you from Mrs. Bernard."

Bernard's eyes glowed. "Yes, Sir, it was comforting to know that Alice and the children are well. I'm looking forward to greeting them when this is over. It's hard on them, you know."

"Oh, yes, Captain," Howard said, laying the reins loose on his favorite Morgan. The pace was automatic for the large horse and he had a comfortable gait that Howard treasured. "My Lizzie, you know, writes letters even when there is nothing for her to say. She is such a dear. She knows that even a brief line is so very comforting to me, when I'm in the field. They are Godsends, are they not?"

"Yes, Sir, they are that," responded Bernard.

Howard cleared his throat. "Reuben, when combat is imminent I want you to do what you think is best. I know that placing a captain in command of seven companies of cavalry is rare, to say the least. However, it is my professional belief that you and your men have earned the privilege and duty to bring these people to their knees and I have full confidence that you will succeed."

Bernard's eyes continued to glow, looking to the front, concentrating on the flankers and scouts. Slowly, he turned his head. His eyes softened briefly as he looked at Howard. "Thank you, Sir. We'll do our very best." Bernard's eyes blazed again as he turned in the saddle, inspecting the troops following him.

As the column rode onward, corporals and sergeants rode alongside the ranks, eyeballing equipment and men, making corrections where necessary. At the rear of the column rode A Company. Captain McGregor was speaking with Second Lieutenant Edwards. "Lieutenant, when the ball opens, be ready to find the rally point with the General quickly and get those packs off pronto. And be sure that a detail is posted to assist Surgeon FitzGerald in setting up the aid station. Got that?"

"Yes, Sir," responded Edwards, rapidly penciling in his small notebook.

McGregor smiled briefly. He wondered how this action would go. "We're outnumbered certainly," he thought to himself, his eyes constantly scanning the landscape. His thoughts wandered briefly to his wife, Jennie, and their three children. "What she doesn't know today won't hurt her," he thought, as the dust began to boil upward into the troop.

Riding beside Lieutenant Edwards was Captain (Surgeon) John FitzGerald. FitzGerald's mind was not with the present as much as those of the others were. His medical career had turned out less advantageously than he'd desired. Since attending Jefferson Medical College at the beginning of the Civil War, he'd risen through the ranks from private to captain, practicing medicine. He was a fine doctor. He had found himself dragging his wife, Emily, and their small children from post to post; most recently from Sitka, Alaska, then to Fort Lapwai, Idaho Territory, to Fort Boise, also in Idaho Territory. Emily had a weak constitution and had no desire to continue raising their children in such harsh conditions. John had decided to leave the Army at the end of this campaign. He was worried about Emily and the children and felt helpless. He'd written her recently, telling her to put their affairs in order and to leave Fort Boise and return to her family in Pennsylvania. FitzGerald had one thought on his mind now, riding towards the enemy.

Fighting a bad cold, he thought to himself, "I hope Emily sends me that new pair of Army trousers I asked for." He fingered the tattered hole in his pants leg. The rising dust caused him to cough convulsively.

Ahead in the column rode Company E under the command of Captain William Winters. At the rear of the company the Gatling Gun was drawn. Its wheels rolled smoothly, its axle recently greased and serviced. Ahead of the Gatling gun, riding in the ranks, rode Private Philip Murphy. His eyes scanned the surrounding hills. He was a veteran serving his second enlistment. He'd won the Medal of Honor while serving with the Eighth Cavalry, fighting Apaches in Arizona. He was a Company Saddler. His thoughts, too, were on his wife, Bridget. As his bright blue eyes studied the terrain, he remembered how pretty she had been at their wedding, held in the large St. Cannis Cathedral in Kilkenny, Ireland. It seemed like only yesterday. He knew that Bridget and the children were in good hands at Fort Lapwai. They'd followed him from post to post, for nearly ten years. They were a true Army family. (Note: as a saddler Phil Murphy had the same pay as a corporal, but could not direct troops, as a corporal would have).

Then something jolted him back to reality. That old feeling that came when a little voice told him to be alert. It had always been true, that little voice. And Murphy was listening.

The command's marching order was changed as Bernard ordered, "By Twos, March." Quickly, the line of fours pulled back, leaving only two long lines of troopers. Bernard had narrowed the width of the command since the road and canyon were narrowing. By now they had marched nearly eleven miles and by Howard's pocket watch, it was 7:45 a.m.

Riding a half mile ahead of the column were scouts Bud Beagle and Cal Morton, who had brought the news about the location of the Hostiles' camp earlier that morning. Bud had been recruited for scout duty from Pendleton, as he was familiar with the area. While other scouts were spread outward, Beagle and Morton were riding on the stage road itself. Earlier, before dawn, they had seen the remainder of the fire from the night before still glowing on top of the high ridge. Nothing appeared on the ridge now where it rose in the far distance three miles away. As the two scouts rode around a sharp bend in the road they noticed a wooden bridge straddling Bridge Creek. Both riders brought their horses to a stop. Morton removed his hat, brushing the hair out of his eyes. Beagle unbuttoned a shirt pocket and brought out a white packet of tobacco by its string. As he prepared to lick the cigarette paper while holding his reins, he paused. He heard no bird or insect. He turned to Morton, who sat frozen in his saddle. A gunshot cracked from the hill on their left. Immediately, heads popped up from behind the hill and a volley of gunfire roared, sending leaden missiles snapping past the two scouts. "Whoa!" blurted Morton, as he wheeled his horse around, drawing his revolver at the same time. Beagle was already galloping ahead of him, cigarette papers flying in the breeze. The firing stopped as suddenly as it had begun.

Back at the column, hearing the shooting, Howard grinned at Bernard as he threw him a salute. "Good hunting, Sir!" Bernard spurred his horse and was gone, shouting to his trumpeter. Immediately the call "Battalion at the Trot, Forward!" rang down the canyon as the command sprang to life. Beagle and Morton rode up to the command, trotting alongside Bernard. The two gave an excited report and galloped toward the flanks. When within five hundred yards of the ambush site, Bernard brought the command to a halt and ordered, "First Three Sets of Fours, Forward!" Immediately the first twelve troopers led out, following Bernard at the trot. Once they arrived at the bridge no Indians were to be seen, just Beagle's cigarette papers strewn along the road. "There they are, Sir!" barked a trooper, pointing towards a lava-encrusted ridgeline in the distance and slightly a mile to the left. Bernard was already looking at the dust trails raised by the group of Indians as they rode toward the top of the ridge. He also noticed other dust trails that covered the entire top of the long hogback that climbed upward towards the summit, ending at another high lava outcropped ridge that shot out of the earth at four thousand, two hundred feet in elevation. The advance would be over two and three-quarter miles uphill. The Indians would be able to see nearly every move the Army made.

Bernard lowered his field glasses and turned to First Sergeant Miles Chaffee. "Sergeant, go to the General with my compliments, and ask that he join me here with an 'Officer's Call'." He pulled out his pocket watch. It showed 8 a.m.

"Yessir!" responded the sergeant, saluting as he wheeled his mount about. He was soon lost in a cloud of dust as he spurred his horse back along the column to Howard.

Bernard again brought up his binoculars. He could see movement on the lava ridge directly in front of him. The Indians were digging in. He heard the bugles sounding "Officer's Call" behind him. Howard had gotten the message. Within minutes Bernard was looking into the eyes and faces of his officers. They had dismounted and were facing him in a semi-circle with the high slope to their front. They watched as the dust trails streaked upwards like fingers along the top and sides of the hogback behind Bernard. He had the officers' full attention. Howard sat mounted on his horse, peering through his field glasses, seemingly detached from the others. Bernard's eyes glistened as brightly as the buttons of his blouse. The July morning's sun brought the yellow metal buttons to life against his dark blue blouse and those of the officers standing before him.

At Bernard's side stood Rube Robbins. His cheek swelled outward, filled with a fresh cut of plug tobacco. Robbins' eyes were affixed on the closest lava ridge behind Bernard, where a large group of Hostiles were now fully dug in and awaiting the first move of the troops. There was only one way to reach the main position of the Indians and that was over the position directly before them, a half a mile up the hogback. "They sure as hell chose the best damn position within thirty miles," thought Robbins to himself, as he spit into the dirt at his feet, wiping his mouth, his eyes not veering from the rocks to Bernard's rear. He snapped his eyes toward Howard for an instant. "That old man knows it too," he thought, returning his eyes to the Indians' position to the front. The fact that no gunfire had come from the position worried him. His attention returned to Bernard.

"Gentlemen!" Bernard said, his eyes boring into the eyes and souls of the officers before him. "We've been fired upon by the Hostiles at this position and will mount a combined attack upon their works. The battalion will attack by companies in line in the following order. Company E with the Gatling Gun will form the front rank, followed in order by companies G, H, L, F, and K. Captain McGregor's Company A will remain with the pack train and will be Battalion Headquarters and rally point as needed. Surgeon FitzGerald will remain with A Company and will supervise the aid station for the wounded." Bernard took in a quick breath, his forehead beginning to shine with perspiration beneath his dusty campaign hat. "Gentlemen, this is our situation. We are outnumbered and outgunned at close range with their repeaters. However, at long range, we can defeat them with the careful use of carbines and the firepower of the Gatling gun, using it in the frontal assault of their positions." Bernard turned, facing the Indians' nearest position to the front. He removed a red bandana from his hip pocket and tied it around his neck; his eyes locked onto the position. He turned back to the officers and finished tying the knot of the bandana. "I want your companies to dismount and attack as skirmishers until we gain the advantage of the hogback. As we dislodge their defenses, remount and attack until they stop. When they stop, we stop and dismount, until we reach their main position. No one fires from horseback unless ordered, and by all means <u>do</u> <u>not</u> go down into either of the two canyons saddling the hogback. And keep your trumpeters close. Is that clear, Gentlemen?" The officers nodded their heads.

Bernard cleared his voice. Howard had dropped his field glasses and was carefully studying him. Sarah and Mattie had quietly ridden up beside Howard. They wore frightened expressions upon their faces. "Gentlemen," Bernard continued, "return to your companies and prepare to advance in five minutes. Captain Winters, prepare the Gatling gun for immediate service, Sir." Winters gave Bernard a knowing grin. "Posts, Gentlemen!" ordered Bernard, saluting the officers. They returned the salute and mounting, cantered back to their companies. Almost immediately, the sounds of barking orders broke the morning's stillness along the long line of the column as it prepared for action. Howard's stern gaze caught Bernard's eyes for an instant. As their eyes met, Howard nodded slowly and his eyes softened. Bernard drew in a breath of relief. Suddenly

Bernard's concentration was broken by a sharp "Yip!" Beneath him stood Jack, the company mascot. His dark, moist eyes sparked at Bernard then, instantly, he ran back to the company. He'd wished his commander luck. After all, that was his job. Bernard watched as Jack ran down the line towards G Company. A cheer broke from the ranks of the men as the dog ran up the line.

Nearly three miles to the south of the Army troops, high up on the lava ridge fortress, bands of warriors were busily settling into their fighting positions. An appointed chief or leader led each band. The ridge consisted of red lava outcroppings that seemed to have been made millions of years ago just for this fight. There were rocks that a man could climb into unseen from any direction, complete with firing ports for rifles. The rocks formed a short wall that surrounded the hilltop like a walled perimeter of a fort. Anyone dominating the hilltop commanded three hundred and sixty degrees of observation for miles. The nearest cover consisted of pine trees that lay three hundred yards to the east of the hilltop. It would be the closest route of retreat should the Indians need it. This morning, it held nearly two thousand women and children, as well as other non-combatants. Shouts erupted from the Indians on the hilltop, as the slim line of blue stopped on the bridge three miles below them. The Indians could even see the dissipating haze from the Army's morning campfires at Pilot Rock, miles to the north. It was clear enough today to see Washington Territory and the land of the awaiting Yakima Indians. It was a good sign.

Egan had said good bye to the Old Woman, before she had taken down the wikiup and gone with his family into the cover of trees to the east. She had placed a piece of dried elk meat in his hand and had given him a wide, toothless grin. She cackled something to no one in particular as she limped, following the others riding into the dark trees. The three bands of Paiute under Egan placed themselves on the east end of the hilltop, closer to the trees and escape. This hadn't gone unnoticed by Oits and Eagle Eye, who were staying their distance from Egan. It gave Egan an uneasy feeling as he laid the barrel of his Winchester against a rock for aiming purposes, since he couldn't use his left arm well. He checked the rifle's action, lowering the lever, opening the breech just enough to see that a shiny brass case lay in the barrel. He closed the action with a "snap!" He was ready. He wore no war paint today.

Along the ridge of the hilltop bands of Shoshoni, Bannock, Umatilla, Cayuse, Yakima, Otis' Paiute Band, and the remainder, consisting of various smaller tribes, lined the ridge top, checking ammunition, pouches, arrows, rifles, and other weapons. Some sat looking downward, fascinated by the troops in the far distance. They carefully applied war paint to their bodies and faces. Drumming and singing were beginning.

Oits and Eagle Eye stood looking downward at the scene below them. They watched as their point warriors dismounted on a smaller, but wider, ridge of lava rock approximately three-quarters of a mile from where they had fired on the scouts at the bridge. It would be their work to decoy the troops upward, over and along the high hogback foothills, leading them directly to the steep approach to the high ridge, where the Indians waited to cut them to pieces. "The point riders are in position now, waiting to draw the soldiers to them," Eagle Eye said, studying the shaky images through the first heat waves of the day. "Once the soldiers have attacked them they will lead them to us. Are the warriors hiding in the draws ready?" Eagle Eye asked Oits.

Oits turned his field glasses downward into the two deep canyons on either side of their position. Nothing stirred there. "Yes," he said through his freshly applied war paint. His eagle feather shone white in the early morning sunlight. He lowered the glasses and gripping his rifle, proudly walked to where his men were sitting or lying behind their positions. He reached down and grasped a handful of dried grass and lava dust, throwing it skyward with a "Whoosh!" raining pebbles as the wind pulled the dust eastward. He let out a shout "EeAaaa!" Others joined him along the line. It was a good day to kill the snapping dogs below them. Oits could see the point warriors' horses being led back from the hidden firing line far below him. They would fight well.

Old Bull had directed his twenty point warriors to their positions on the first lava ridge directly in front of the maneuvering troops. Approximately seven hundred yards separated them. Boss knelt, shoving fresh cartridges into the tube of his Spencer carbine. The fresh smell of burnt gunpowder reeked in his nostrils; it thrilled him. He and the others had fired at the scouts on the bridge. Now that they'd brought the soldiers, their aim would be dead center on their targets. Their job was to bring the rabbit into the snare. And it was sniffing at them. Old Bull and Race Horse swung aboard their painted horses and trotted down the sides of the position, gesturing back and forth in front of the Army troops, waving their blankets and rifles as they shouted taunts and challenges to them.

Captain Bernard stood at the front of E Company, his bugler beside him to his left rear. Behind E Company, the other five companies waited, formed up in line by ranks. Race Horse fired a shot over the battalion, trying to draw fire. Army horses whinnied and strained at their reins as the bullet whined over their heads. Race Horse shouted to the patiently waiting troopers in broken English. "Come on! Why do you wait! Are you standing there because you are afraid of Race Horse?"

He wheeled his Cayuse back and forth in front of the Indian position, trying to draw the troops into a charge. Suddenly, the roar of gunfire ripped across the small ridge as the Indians opened fire on the battalion. Fortunately, the shots were high and wild. The

Indians watched and waited as their gun smoke slowly drifted eastward. Only the shouts of the two Indian riders far in the distance could be heard, save for the whinnies of the Army mounts standing nervously in ranks.

Bernard thought to himself as he slowly raised his right arm, "I've waited a long time for this, now let's give them a surprise." He turned in his saddle, looking at Captain Winters where he sat to the far right of E Company. At Winters' right stood the Gatling Gun Section. The gun's canvas cover had been removed, exposing its six .45 caliber dark blue barrels; the muzzles resembled deadly snouts searching for prey. The gun's brass breech casing gleamed in the morning sunlight. The ominous hand crank stood ready. The men of the gun's section waited patiently. The section sergeant sat straight in his saddle. The battery's horse teams and riders stood at attention. They were ready.

Bernard shouted his order to Winters, his eyes blazing, face shiny with sweat, "Battery to the front!" at the same time that he pointed his arm to the right front of the battalion.

Captain Winters in turn raised his arm, looking at the Gun Section's first sergeant. "On Right Into Battery, Trot!"

The first sergeant bellowed, "In Battery, Trot!" The horse teams threw themselves against their harnesses as if they had been struck by a lightening bolt. Immediately, the section moved forward out of line, speeding toward the Indians' position to the right of the battalion. The section kicked up boiling dust clouds as it sped four hundred yards ahead of the battalion.

The Indians on the ridge looked on in amazement at the riders racing toward them, away from their comrades and straight into their waiting rifles. "Crazy white soldiers!" Race Horse shouted as he levered a fresh cartridge into his rifle. The spent, ejected empty case rattled upon the rocks beneath his horse.

The section sergeant shouted, "In Battery, March! - Action Front! - Dismount!" The horse team drawing the Gatling gun and its limber suddenly turned about and stopped, the gun's barrels pointing at the ridge. The caisson containing ammunition also turned about and continued to the rear until the first sergeant shouted the same orders to the crew. Riders from each team quickly took the riderless mounts and moved them to the rear.

"Action Front!" ordered the first sergeant as he looked at the ridge before them through sweat stung eyes. Before the teams had stopped, section members had dismounted and had begun to service the gun, dragging its trail around so that it pointed directly at the ridge. A bullet struck the ground in front of the busy crew, whining off in the distance. They didn't notice. The section crew were busily opening the limber chest and removing the long magazines containing the ammunition for the gun. A soldier on each wheel moved them alternately, freeing them up in order to traverse the gun left or right as required once the firing had begun.

Old Bull and Race Horse stopped their antics on horseback momentarily, to see why the soldiers would drive their wagons so close to them without the protection of the troops some distance to the rear. Everyone on the ridge was curious. What were the small blue figures doing, as they busily moved on and around the wagon-like objects?

The first sergeant looked through his field glasses at the lava ridge to the gun's front. He could see the ridge's defenders raising up, some kneeling or standing as their curiosity caused them to throw caution to the wind. He smiled as he peered through sweating eyes at the targets presenting themselves in the distance. The sergeant lowered his field glasses and turned to the awaiting section crew at their stations. "Load!" he barked.

"Load!" shouted the gunner, as he stepped to the breech of the gun and adjusted the rear sight to the required elevation of the ridge by turning the elevating screw. He then stepped over the trail piece and sat upon a small metal seat attached to the gun. He had set the gun sight just over the forms of the Indians looking down upon them.

"Ready!" ordered the sergeant. The number one man released the hand crank from its stop and seized the handle with his right hand, ready to turn the handle. The number two man had received a full feed case from the number four man and had inserted the case into the hopper with a metallic "Clack!" The number three man was ready to assist in pointing the gun if necessary. The number five man drew five filled feed cases and waited for the number four man to shout for them. The number six and number seven men stood ready to assist in the service of the gun.

A cool refreshing breeze passed through the gun section as they waited at their stations, prepared to send death onto the ridge to their front. Most were sweating by now, dark stains showing beneath armpits and down chests and backs against their suspenders and gray shirts. It seemed that both sides were waiting for the other to make the next move.

The first sergeant brought his field glasses up for a last look. Simultaneously, Old Bull and Race Horse began their whooping and challenging shouts as they walked their war ponies back and forth, trying to incite their warriors, who stood watching the scene below. Suddenly, a warrior who had been lying on the far side of the ridge remembered what the strange objects below were. He had seen them as an Army scout while fighting the soldiers in 1877. He shouted, as he jumped to his feet and ran, shouting to the others to get down. It was too late. "Commence! Firing!" shouted the first sergeant. The number one man turned the crank with a moderate uniform motion, allowing ample time for the cartridges to drop from the feed cases into the carrier block. A roaring staccato erupted from the barrels of the gun as smoke and sharp flames sent leaden missiles across the space between them and the Indians. Almost instantly, bullets struck the rocks and earth along the ridge. Several bullets struck Race Horse's war horse. It fell beneath him with a screaming thud, sending him sprawling and his rifle flying through the air and rattling down the ridge.

The Indians caught standing were instantly thrown backwards as bullets struck them. Screams of agony rent the air across the ridge as leaden splinters and rock particles sliced into flesh. Old Bull jabbed his heels into the flanks of his warhorse and galloped toward Race Horse, who was wandering around in shock from his fall. The hail of bullets stopped momentarily, as he swooped Race Horse up behind him and galloped up the side of the ridge. Below, a new feed case had been snapped into place in the Gatling gun. The crank turned again as rolling death struck upon the ridge before them, .45 caliber bullets slapping along the sides of the ridge and over it, striking horse and human flesh. The warriors never returned fire. Demoralized, they managed to mount their horses and ride up the hogback toward the main body of Indians on the large flat-topped ridge over a mile in the distance.

"Cease fire!" ordered the first sergeant. The gun stopped.

"Battalion, Forward March!" shouted Bernard. The trumpeter sounded the call; the companies to his rear responded with trumpets and shouted orders. The battalion moved forward, sending up clouds of dust. The sounds of over three hundred troopers and horses created a low rumbling in the morning air. The echoes of the Gatling gun having drifted away, its section was ready to move again.

"We've moved them," thought Howard, looking through his field glasses. Mattie and Sarah sat on their horses beside him, worried looks on their faces. As the battalion reached the re-hitched Gatling Gun Section, it took up its position alongside E Company and moved toward the small ridge. The smell of gun smoke and cordite hung in the air. Several hundred yards from the ridge, Bernard ordered the first three companies to dismount and take position as foragers. Three long lines of troopers carrying carbines marched up the hillside to the ridge, leading their mounts by throwing the reins over their right arms. Only the snapping of grasshoppers and the whinnying of Army horses rent the clear morning air, as the troopers slowly worked their way upward, occasionally stumbling or tripping on rocks.

High above them, the sounds of drumming and singing drifted downward from the high ridge. Suddenly a scream and war whoop broke the silence, as a wounded Dreamer jumped up and ran at a trooper, raising his rifle to fire as he ran, war paint glistening through his blood-streaked face. A rattle of carbine fire tore the charging Indian to pieces, dead before he tumbled forward on his face.

The line continued upward, not stopping. "Watch it!" a sergeant shouted as an Indian and his warhorse burst from the ground where they had lain. The Indian, his useless, blood-clotted right arm hanging limply at his side, straddled the horse as it gained full footing. Heels jabbed the warhorse's flanks as its rider fumbled with his rifle, trying to level it at a trooper. The horse and rider jumped over the high lava rocked ridge and charged directly through Company E and into the troopers of Company G, who quickly dropped both rider and horse in a flash of carbines. In smoke and dust the two, somersaulting head over heels before crashing, came to a stop in front of H Company's line. The recruits stood dumbfounded at the scene, until a hard shove from a corporal known as a file closer pushed them upward.

Bernard moved the battalion upwards for two miles, returning fire time and again as the Indians broke from the canyons on either side of them, firing into the troopers. Return fire always broke the Indians off and away from the command as the troopers moved slowly upward towards the high ridge to their front. Clouds of gun smoke drifted across the ridge and hung over the canyons at either side of the battalion. So far, no causalities had been reported except for a few horses, struck by bullets fired from the ridge to their front. As the battalion slowly approached the high, flat-topped ridge, it became brutally apparent that the assault against the Indian position would have to be made up at least two steep sides of the pie-shaped hilltop. The third side assault would have to be made up a blind side, out of sight of Bernard and the command. He wouldn't risk that. Howard rode up beside Bernard, Mattie and Sarah behind him. Howard had allowed a newspaper correspondent to join him at this point. He remained to the rear of the general, obviously having been told his place by Howard. The sweating correspondent's pencil scratched into a notebook furiously, his head bobbing up and down.

Bernard raised his arm and ordered "Battalion, Halt!" Within minutes the battalion had caught up and had formed up behind him. Bernard didn't like having them exposed this way, especially with the hundreds of warriors hidden in the rocks four hundred yards to his front. The drumming and singing was louder now. No serious firing had come from the high lava fortress before them.

Mattie suddenly blurted, hand over her mouth, "General, it is Oits!" pointing to the far left side of the ridge with her other hand.

Howard shot his field glasses to the top of the ridge before them. A tall man slowly stood up on the top of the outcrop and calmly looked downward at Howard and the two women. Howard could not believe his eyes. Then, as mysteriously as he had appeared, the man returned to his fighting position. Howard could see the hatred and fanaticism emitting through the Black Death mask Oits wore. Howard scanned across the ridge again, looking for Oits, but couldn't see him amongst so many Indians. Howard rode up to Bernard. He spoke calmly, "Captain, may I suggest the possibility of a frontal assault on the works before us and a flanking charge from our right?" Bernard scanned the ridge top through his field glasses.

"You took the words from my mouth, Sir," answered Bernard, continuing to study the terrain before them. He slowly lowered his glass, looking at Howard with a smile. "It does remind one of the War, doesn't it, Sir? Howard nodded. A rifle cracked on the hilltop, the bullet whizzing past overhead. "It's time," Bernard said, looking upwards to where hundreds of hidden rifle barrels pointed down at him.

"Trumpeter, sound 'Officer's Call,'"ordered Bernard. Immediately the call echoed down the sides of the canyons and up to the hilltop before them. As the troop commanders quickly rode to Bernard, more stray, harassing shots arched downward from the hilltop, flying overhead. Bernard raced back along the formed troops to meet his officers. Once they had formed, he began, "My compliments, Gentlemen. So far we seem to be in very good shape, as I expected." The officers nervously glanced between Bernard and the Indian activity on the hilltop. "Here is the plan of attack," Bernard continued. "Companies H, K, and L on my command will form right oblique from the battalion and proceed quickly to the west of that hill, our objective, and form up in three lines by company. The Gatling Section will provide cover fire while you are getting into position, but will cease fire once you are there." Captains Trimble, Bendire, and Whipple paid complete attention to Bernard's words. They would have to move for hundreds of yards directly beneath the rifles of the Indians without returning fire. It didn't look like a picnic to them.

Bernard continued, "Rube Robbins has volunteered to take his scouts with the right flanking companies and to continue past them, encircling the third side of the hill. Rube, you'll be hanging out in the wind, so keep in touch with the flanking companies." Rube nodded and spat as he carefully placed his tattered hat on his shaggy head. Robbins looked up at the hilltop bristling with Indians, turned his horse and rode back to where his scouts stood dismounted. Rube seemed strangely detached.

Bernard cautioned the officers, "Once the three companies are in position, the Gatling Section will commence firing, raking the rocks and the hill top. On command, we will mount a combined assault against both sides of the hilltop, driving the Hostiles from their position and pushing them southward off the top. I wish all of you good luck and I'll see you at the top. Any questions?" The officers saluted and wheeling their mounts, galloped back to their companies.

The Cavalry Battalion was formed up at attention. They sat in silence as the red over white guidons fluttered slowly in the morning breeze. A deep-blue, cloudless sky looked down upon the scene. Even the Indians on the hilltop had stopped singing and drumming for the moment. Silence reigned. One could even hear the wind as it softly moaned through the pine trees at the summit on the east side of the high hill.

Bernard sat straight in his saddle. He turned to Captain Winters. "Captain, Gun Section Forward!" Winters gave the command and instantly, as before, the Section charged forward for one hundred yards when the first sergeant shouted, "In Battery, March!" The teams immediately turned right about, the gun facing the ridge. Once the section had dismounted, they went through their drill of aiming and loading. The sergeant raised his arm and quickly lowered it, his command to fire lost in the bedlam, as the gun ripped and tore across the ridge above. Immediately, bugle calls and shouted commands rent the air across the hills below the flat-topped ridge, as the three companies galloped out of formation and burst across the bottom of the high hill. No gunfire came from the hilltop as they reached the west side of the hill and formed up in line for the charge. Robbins' scouts galloped around them, whooping and yelling like Indians themselves. The Gatling continued to rake the lava rocks, sending leaden splinters and rock fragments into Indians faces and bodies as they tried to lay flat and back away from the edge of the hill and certain death. They had never experienced anything like this. Even Oits lay flat, with his cheek pressed into the red dust, his chest heaving.

A bugle call stopped the Gun Section as the crew ran to the caissons for more ammunition. Bernard's arm raised slowly as the bugler again brought the bugle to his lips. "Battalion, Forward March!" Bernard shouted. The bugler followed with the call. The three companies moved forward at a walk, uphill. They passed the Gun Section, who gave them a cheer. Suddenly, the entire top of the ridge erupted in gunfire, this time the bullets striking men and horses. Bernard screamed "Charge!" The three companies put spurs to horses' flanks. The companies shot forward, troopers screaming and shouting at the top of their lungs. Everywhere, the sound of bullets striking horses with sickening, slapping sounds could be heard within the clamor. The Indians were shooting low. Troopers went down with their mounts beneath them, their wounded horses struggling, kicking at the air as they screamed in pain. "Dismount!" Bernard shouted to his bugler, as he raised his arm and swung down from his saddle. He looked to the west and saw clouds of dust and heard heavy firing coming from that area. "Good. Trimble and Whipple have found their game!" As the troopers dismounted, some had mounts hit and were carried downhill, unable to pull their boots from their stirrups. Cussing and swearing rent the air. Bernard had jerked his carbine from its socket when he'd dismounted. A Bannock suddenly stood above him, having jumped from the rocks above. He raised his bow quickly, drawing its string back. Bernard wheeled around toward the Indian, but an Army bullet had struck the warrior, jerking him backwards, the arrow flying skyward harmlessly.

Private Schaffer was moving up the hillside, leading his horse while firing and loading his carbine in the front line with Company E. The firing from the top was general now, as the Indians were returning a heavy fire. The bullets snapped and cracked over the troopers' heads and also amongst them. Arrows whipped passed them, some striking mounts, followed by screams. The sound unnerved the men. "Hey, Bill!" shouted Private Howard to his bunkmate Private Schaffer as they moved up the hill together. "Don't this beat all, damned if it ain't hazardous!" He took aim at a rock that an Indian had just fired from. "Crack!" His carbine bucked against his shoulder. He immediately lowered the carbine and flipped up the trap door. The empty copper case ejected over his arm. He fumbled for a fresh cartridge in his belt.

"Damn right!" shouted Schaffer. "Whoa, damnit!" he yelled to his mount as it pulled back from him, requiring him to turn and pull on the reins. "Smack!" A bullet struck him in the back, breaking his left arm, throwing him downward against the struggling horse. He fell backward into the sharp rocks and rolled downhill, only a large rock breaking his fall. His mount galloped off, blood streaming from two bullet holes in its flanks. Bullets zipped everywhere.

"Bill!" shouted Howard, seeing Schaffer take the bullet and lying on the sidehill. He started to run after him, pulling his mount with him, leaving the line. Gun smoke filled the air.

"Get your ass back in line, Gawd-damnit!" shouted a corporal to Howard. Howard stopped and turned away from where Schaffer lay motionless. As he was pulling his mount back up the hill, moving to the line, a Bannock warrior knelt on one knee and took aim. It was Pit Viper. He squeezed the trigger of his carbine and saw the bullet strike the trooper. Howard jumped from the impact of the bullet striking his right thigh, knocking the leg from beneath him. He fell, crashing onto the rocky side hill. It didn't hurt yet, but the bullet had torn his thigh to ribbons. The large hole in his pants quickly spouted bright red. Darkness overtook him as he lost consciousness.

Slowly, agonizingly, the troopers fought up the sides of the high ridge. The hillsides were littered with dead and dying horses. Private Richard Smith was one of the first troopers from E Company to reach the top. The Indians were now leaving their positions and fleeing across the open space to the east of the hill and into the timber. Smith ran after the retreating warriors, hoping for a shot. His chest heaved, winded. Seeing a wounded warrior limping away from him and then falling, he raised his carbine and took careful aim. "Crack!" a revolver fired not over ten feet from where he stood. He hadn't seen Whisker the Paiute. The slug plowed into Smith's abdomen, cracking his pelvis. He dropped to his knees, falling over sideways. He would die the next morning at five.

As H Company reached the crest of the ridge, privates Unger and Harris remounted their horses and spurred them after the Indians, most of whom had disappeared into the timber. "Slow down, damnit!" roared a sergeant as they approached the timber. It didn't look right.

Captain Charles Bendire raised his gauntleted hand, shouting "Halt! Dismount As Skirmishers!" His trumpeter sounded the call. With difficulty, the company slowed down and began to dismount approximately one hundred and fifty yards from the timber. It was too late. Instantly, gunfire roared from the timber, ripping along the Army line, which was nearly two hundred yards wide. Army mounts were struck, as troopers dismounted, pulling and dragging their riders along with them. Others raised up on their hind feet, falling backwards, their feet clawing at the blue morning sky in death throes. Screaming and shouting non-coms attempted to restore order and managed to assemble the company into a skirmish line.

Bendire took his place on the right of the line, shouting orders, his trumpeter standing close to him. The company's Guidon was to his left. The bullet-torn red over white colors shone in the morning sunlight. "Ready!" shouted Bendire to the company. Immediately, sergeants repeated the order to the men. Carbines were brought up, breeches opened, snapping sharply along the line as shiny copper cartridges were pushed into chambers. As one, the breeches were snapped closed with a "Clack!" The sound rattled along the line. "Aim!" shouted Bendire. Carbines were brought up to shoulders. Bullets cracked and snapped through the ranks. The gunfire continued from the unseen Indians in the trees to the front. "FIRE!" screamed Bendire.

H Company's firing line roared, belching flame and lead into the trees. At the tree line, the impact of bullets could be seen splintering trees and striking the ground, ricocheting heavy bullets into the unseen defenders. Gun smoke hung in the air as bullets cut through it. Bendire repeated the firing orders.

Private Unger threw the "trapdoor" of his carbine upward, ejecting a hot case. As his fingers found a fresh cartridge in his belt he began to withdraw it. "THUD!" a bullet smacked him in the upper thigh, sending him backwards into a file closer, who caught him.

The corporal grasped him by the collar of his gray Army shirt and roughly dragged him to the rear of the line. "That's it, laddie, keep yer hand on the wound, ye'll be fine now," croaked the corporal, trying to smile through his grimy, sweating face as he dropped Unger and quickly returned to the company line.

As the skirmish line returned fire against the withering fire coming from the trees, Sergeant William Harris stood behind the corporal line closers, watching every step the troopers made. His revolver was held at high port, barrel upward. His head moved alternately from right to left, looking for wounded. "They are doing all right!" he thought to himself, proud of them. His walrus mustache twitched upon his sweaty face. "SMACK!" Harris felt his leg give way as he fell to the rocky ground. He'd been hit in the upper part of his right leg. Blood began to pump out of the ragged hole. He quickly tore his garrison belt off and looped it above the wound, stopping the flow of blood somewhat. "Damn!" he grimaced through clenched teeth. He knew the pain would soon come. He'd felt it before. Hands grabbed him and helped him to the rear. His revolver was quickly tucked into his waistband.

All companies had formed up now as K Company joined H to the right of its line. The Gatling Section was on its way. As Private Clarence Coon was taking aim, waiting for the order to fire, a bullet struck his left hand, shattering it, passing through and striking a K Company's mount in its front shoulder. The horse screamed and backing into another horse to its rear, it fell, spilling its rider. Coon dropped his carbine and quickly wrapped his kerchief around what was left of his hand. He could see that two fingers were missing and splinters from the carbine's stock protruded from the wound. A file closer pulled him back from the firing line, stumbling. After what seemed like hours, the Gatling Section arrived in a cloud of dust and was wheeled into position. Within minutes, a terrible hail of gunfire emitted from the piece. The .45 caliber bullets cut through small branches, splintering trees and flesh as it cut its deadly swath from right to left, then back again.

The gun stopped firing. Silence hung in the smoke-clouded trees. The Indians were gone. Far back into the forest shouts and cries could be heard as they retreated. It was a sound that some troopers would remember for the rest of their lives. The companies gave chase, but very carefully. They followed the Indian trail for nearly four miles before they decided to return to the base camp. They found themselves surrounded by a giant, unmapped forest and there were still two thousand Indians in there with them. And the Indians knew the land. The trail they followed was littered with pots and pans, dead and dying horses, and blood-clot smeared trees and brush.

Bernard holstered his revolver and removed his pocket watch. It showed twelve-thirty p.m. Once the wounded and dead had been treated or accounted for, Howard ordered "Officer's

Call." He looked at the tired, sweaty, dust-covered officers with admiration. His instructions were clear. They were to divide the battalion. Bernard was to go to Fort Walla Walla for refitting, then return to the field. The rest would go around the retreating Indians and stop them from traveling to the east. Howard dismissed his officers with his thanks and gratitude. He couldn't find the words to brief them completely. His inner emotions were overpowering at the moment. Propriety and discipline were needed now.

As the companies made haste to be on their way, Howard asked Bernard to join him. The two walked together out to the edge of the lava ledge. Below them, amongst the dead horses and litter of battle, small pockets of gun smoke hung in the air, slowly drifting through the timber and downward into the deep canyons. Bernard took off his dust-covered hat. His face was streaked with sweat and grime. His eyes were bloodshot. "Captain," Howard said quietly. Bernard looked out into the open spaces to the north. "I want you to know how grateful I am for your service during this campaign. I don't think anyone else could have done it. That's why I selected you for the assignment. I will see that your achievements will go into your record."

Bernard looked at Howard with a tired smile. "Thank you, Sir."

Howard continued, as he glanced to where the Indians had disappeared. "They are finished now. Broken and I for the sake of me, cannot tell you why. They could have beaten us but for the Grace of God couldn't find it within themselves to do it. They collapsed from within, I believe."

Bernard nodded slowly. His dry voice creaked as he said, "I believe a good dose of the Gatling gun had something to do with it."

Howard nodded in agreement. He tenderly offered his single hand. Bernard took it. "Good luck, Captain, I pray you and your family will see better days and have good health and fortune." Howard's grip surprised Bernard; it was as strong as hardened steel. The two officers walked back to the assembling companies together. It had been a long day, one that would remain in their memories forever. Jack trotted wearily behind them, wishing for a cool drink of water from a trooper's canteen.

At the east end of the rock fortress stood Sarah and Mattie. Soldiers were picking up souvenirs dropped by the retreating Indians, chuckling like children. Mattie held a small piece of beaded buckskin she'd found on the ground. It had fresh blood on it. She turned and fondled it in her little hand. Tears streaked down her dusty cheeks as, she silently cried. Sarah looked across the open stretch of ground leading into the dark timber and the long dark blood trails leading into it. She thought to herself, "The Road of Gosipa will have many travelers this night." High above the hilltop, two eagles circled lazily, taking advantage of pockets of warm air as they arose from the warming earth far below.

Indian Affairs.

The following despatch from Gov. Chadwick has been received via San Francisco: Umatilla, July 8, 10:30 A.M.

"At two o'clock this morning Major Kress went down the river on the steamer Spokane to Coyote Station, fifteen miles below this place. Two miles this side of the station he found hostile Indians crossing with a large number of horses. He ran upon them, and some of the horses returned to the Oregon side while others crossed the river. The Major then made an attack upon the Indian camp, and destroyed it and every thing about it, including canoes."

An unofficial despatch, dated Wallula, July 8, says:

"The steamer Northwest left here this afternoon. She will be used a patrol boat between here and Umatilla."

Army Navy Journal, July 13, 1878.

Chapter 13

Steamboat Warfare

At dawn earlier that same day, the Spokane had left its moorage at Umatilla Landing and was plying down the Columbia. The boat was "wooded up" and had plenty of fuel. Captain Gray had received telegraphic orders from General Howard, ordering him to patrol the river and to prevent any hostile Indians from crossing the river to join the anxious Yakimas. The steamer Northwest was patrolling the upper river between Wallula and Umatilla Landing and had aboard a detachment of volunteers and troops under the command of Captain M.C. Wilkinson, U.S. Army. The Spokane had on board fifty-three volunteers from Walla Walla, Washington Territory, and, of course, the same twenty soldiers that they'd picked up several days ago. Major Kress was still commanding the detachment, with the Gatling Gun manned and ready. They would patrol the river below Umatilla Landing. They had made their earlier repairs and had dropped off Governor Ferry at Wallula.

Captain Gray stood in the pilothouse of the Spokane, watching for shifting sandbars through his telescope. Beside him stood Major Kress, glassing the hills and shoreline for any signs of Indian crossings. Sam Gill was busily stoking the firebox full of wood while keeping a close eye on the pressure gauges. He could give Gray full power anytime he wanted it. Gill stopped working for a moment in the hot engine room and walked to a large open hatchway. The cool morning river breeze chilled his face. It was going to be a beautiful day. The morning sun glistened off of the ripples of the strong river. Gill wiped his face with a greasy rag and walked back to the firebox. Black smoke billowed from the Spokane's stack. The boat was approaching Long Island on its starboard side. The island was nearly eighteen miles long and had a slough that ran up its lower end for several miles.

"There!" shouted Kress to Gray, pointing to the passing shore. Running from the shoreline up the side hills ran fresh dark wet trails. Indians! Gray ordered "Ahead-Slow." The telegraph bell rang, a clanging acknowledgment from Gill below deck. The sternwheel slowed down against the current. Gray took the helm and turned the boat sharply to starboard as he ordered, "Dead-Slow!" The telegraph answered as the large boat slowed, landing head onto the shore with a hissing sound followed by a "Bump!" The gang plank was immediately pushed out. Kress had already slid down the ladder and was shouting orders to the Gatling Gun Section and his Infantrymen, who were scrambling over the deck, getting into formation to the sharp barking orders of Sergeant Conners. Soon the canvas cover had been removed from the Gatling and the crew was standing by, ammunition clips in hand. The Infantrymen were standing in squad formation. Volunteers found protected shooting positions behind sacks of grain. All eyes were on the shore and looking at the northern direction of the trails, nearly invisible now.

The Infantrymen went ashore first, under the protective barrels of the Gatling Gun Section. The now-meek volunteers went ashore next. Kress watched the landing with Gray and Army Surgeon Dr. Boyd, who had joined them. "Captain," Kress said to Gray, "this part of the island is close to one mile across, is it not?" Gray nodded, already thinking with Kress. "If I scout to the other side of this island, would you be able to meet us there?" Kress asked.

Gray pulled his briar pipe from his pocket, placing the chewed stem in the corner of his mouth. He looked at Kress "Well, Major, the water is lower than when we normally run the main chute and there are bad rapids part way up, but I'll try anything once!" He grinned at Kress, who smiled back. "Good hunting, Major!" shouted Gray as Kress's hands disappeared down the ladder.

From the deck below, Gray heard a commotion. He walked out of the pilothouse. Sam Gill had also stuck his head out of the open hatch to investigate. Major Kress was in the process of kicking and shoving a volunteer whom he'd noticed hiding behind a stack of wheat sacks. The volunteer was doing his best to stay ahead of the roaring Army major and dodge his boot as he ran down the plank to join the others, who were laughing. Kress turned and saluted Gray, then turned and led his men up the hill and over to who knew what.

"A man of conviction," Gray said to Boyd, smiling as he went to the voice tube. "Full-Astern!" he shouted. The bell answered as the boat slowly backed into the Columbia. Soon it was steaming down river and once the end of the island was reached, it turned to starboard and began its passage up the slough between the island and the Washington shore. The soldiers would be waiting and the Spokane would meet them.

As the Spokane made its way up the slough, Gray saw the troops waving their hats from the island shore. It would be necessary to land where there were a number of rocks projecting out into the river, where no boat had been before. The rocks rose nearly one hundred feet in height. Gray nosed the Spokane gently onto the shore as if he'd done it all of his life. Gill had the steam built up for any emergency and the engine huffed and puffed as the great sternwheel slowly turned. The troops and volunteers were nearly aboard when Gray remarked to Dr. Boyd and a sweating Kress, who'd just joined them in the pilothouse, "I've never seen so many fish jumping!" He was staring toward the stern of the boat.

"Fish, my ass!" shouted Kress, "we're taking fire from the rocks! Get us out of here, Gray, this is no place to be!" A bullet struck the pilothouse, shattering the glass and smacking into the wooden bulkhead. Splinters flew. Kress scrambled down the ladder as the last of the volunteers ran up the plank and drew it in. The riflemen were returning fire now and the Gatling Section was raking the rocks and adjoining hills with its fire.

"Full Astern!" screamed Gray down the tube. He didn't need to give the order; Gill had already thrown the levers, reversing the wheel. The water churned up a white froth, as the boat backed onto the slough. "Ahead Full!" shouted Gray in the pilothouse. He peered over the bridge, keeping out of sight. Below on the main deck, bullets had struck sacks of wool, throwing small white-lint like tufts around the deck. A bullet zipped through the forward gangway, striking the main deck and ricocheted, lodging in the engine room bench, a mere two feet behind Gill. A volunteer yelled for more cartridges. A fellow volunteer carefully reached his cartridge-filled hand over the his friend. A bullet cracked between them and struck a stanchion a foot away. The cartridges spilled to the deck as both men ducked for cover.

Once the Spokane had passed down the slough, she entered the Columbia once again. Gray turned her bow upriver, heading eastward now to meet with the Northwest. Once they found each other, the two boats would return to the island and resume action against the Hostiles. Gray and Kress stood in the pilothouse. Gray lit his pipe, sending blue puffs of smoke into the air. The fragrant smoke was immediately blown outward through the open hatch as the wind whistled and moaned through the shattered window of the pilothouse. The sun sparkled on the river. Below in the engine room, Gill had moved the splintered bench out into an open passageway. He smelled the clean, pungent odors of the river as they mingled with the sweet, rich smell of burning wood in the boat's firebox. He was right with the world.

Three Bodies Found.
Boise City (Idaho), July 13 –

"Mr. John Harley, superintendent of the Northwestern Stage Company, this evening received the following dispatch from one of his division agents, now at Meacham's on the Blue Mountains. 'A courier has arrived and reports that Captain Creighton's company found three bodies six miles from here supposed to be freighters.' "

The East Oregonian, Saturday, July 27, 1878.

"There was more fuss made over the one worthless cuss of an Indian that was killed than over all the whites killed in the county. [The Umatilla Agency Indians have been in the main our worst enemies. It was those that piloted the hostiles in on us and no one doubts that the Snakes were counseled continually.]

"Gen. Howard is no doubt a brave soldier, but he is always behind; and as stated above, we believe this slow policy of the army is intentional. The Government would like to protect settlers, but does not want to kill Indians."

Columbia Chronicle, (no date).

Chapter 14

Agency Solid Shot

In the five days following the battle at Birch Creek, the Indians had headed eastward, eventually running into roadblocks and troops. Most leaders in the same predicament would have merely ridden northward, going around the small number of troops. These people were different. After milling around near the Immigrant Road in the mountains southeast of the city of Pendleton, they had run into an infantry roadblock at Starkey. Prior to that they had attacked a team of wagons west of Meacham, killing the drivers and ransacking the wagons. They seemed disorientated and confused. A decision was made to travel to the Umatilla Indian Agency a few miles east of Pendleton, to rescue and recruit the Umatilla and Cayuse tribes to go with them. The chiefs knew that these Indians had gone in to the Agency for protection and would need some convincing. Unknown to the Hostiles, however, the Army was much closer than they knew and was slowly closing its trap.

Before dawn on Saturday, the thirteenth of July, three hundred and twenty-four soldiers and civilian volunteer scouts were starting to taste their first fresh cup of coffee in hours, having force-marched over the Immigrant Road from the east during the night. Word had been spread that the Hostiles might try to attack the Agency. Captain Evan Miles commanded the battalion consisting of Company K, First Cavalry, and Companies K and D, of the Fourth U.S. Artillery, each consisting of four batteries of three-inch Ordnance Rifles and Light Artillery. Mounted troops of the Twenty-First U.S. Infantry, Companies B, E, H, K, and I were also present. Twenty curious volunteers from Pendleton sat around their own cooking fires, enjoying the welcomed break. It had been a long night's march. Everyone was relaxing in the pre-dawn darkness. Sentries had been posted around the eight large artillery pieces. They guns sat still in the darkness, ominous and deadly.

Darkness blanketed the large war party of over six hundred warriors as they rode quietly towards the Agency buildings, winding downwards through draws and canyons that no white man could in the dark. They had Umatilla scouts with them. There was hope that the Umatilla Tribe would join them in their march north, since there was growing discontent amongst their own group, especially from Egan, who would take his three bands of Paiute if he should leave the Hostile band. Oits and War Jack needed those warriors badly, but Egan had to go. He had refused to accompany this raid and had remained in the large camp. Egan's destiny had already been determined. Umapine and Homily the Dreamer Prophet would strike soon.

The warriors stopped at the top of a high ridge above the Umatilla River, just south of where the Agency buildings stood in the darkness below. Oits and War Jack were startled to see so many open campfires below them. The Agency Indians would be inside teepees, not outside in the open. The campfires concerned the two chiefs. Whose were they? As the morning sun broke over the Blue Mountains to the east, orange then yellow sunlight bathed the countryside in its glory. War Jack and Oits carefully watched the Agency buildings through their field glasses. As War Jack scanned the Agency grounds, his sharp eyes caught something that brought his blood up. "Army Wagon Guns!" he blurted to Oits, lying beside him on the hilltop. Oits had seen them also and stiffened. It didn't matter; they had to show the Umatillas their power. Now was the time. They both stood up and walked quickly to their horses.

"Indians!" shouted a sentry. Immediately, coffee was thrown away and men ran to their posts. "Bugler! Sound 'Assembly'!" shouted Miles as he ran to his horse, buttoning his tunic. He quickly mounted and galloped toward the sentry. Sure enough, a long line of Indians stretched along the dim horizon on the hilltop to the south of their position. The line stretched for hundreds of yards. Through his field glasses, Miles watched the advancing Hostiles over a half a mile away. They had started to ride down the hill and onto the grassy flat. He glanced towards his eight artillery pieces. The men were at their posts and ready. The Infantrymen were in their assigned positions. Their shiny bayonets gleamed at the ends of the Springfield rifles. Captain Bendire's K Company Cavalrymen sat mounted behind the artillery batteries. The Pendleton Volunteers were nervously eyeing the activity around them. There was a long wait as the defenders watched the line of Indians parade down the hillside in the distance, where they stopped. The defenders had never seen so many Indians in all of their lives. Some shivered at the sight, as painted horses and warriors, bright feathers and war paint, shone across the large flat separating them. Suddenly, a large group of warriors broke away from the rest and galloped straight at the Agency and its defenders, whooping and screaming. They drew up their horses halfway across the flat and began firing at the Agency's defenders.

"Steady men!" shouted Captain Miles. He turned to the artillery batteries. "Battery D! Load solid shot. Fire over their heads. One volley. At will!"

"Battery, Action Front. Solid shot-Load!" bellowed the battery sergeant to his gunners, who immediately sprang into action, withdrawing the solid steel projectile from the limber.

The projectile weighed ten pounds. A powder charge was placed into each long, 72.7-inch barrel. The bore size was three inches in diameter. The four barrels were quickly raised high enough to send their missiles over the heads of the Indians shooting at them. "Ready-Fire!" bellowed the battery sergeant. The lanyards were pulled, firing the cannons with a "K-BOOM!" which sent the solid shot flying over the heads of the firing Indians. The projectiles screeched over the Indians, sending some to the ground from their bucking horses. The Indians charged toward the batteries again, this time close enough that their bullets zipped and snapped through the guns and soldiers. The Agency Indians had run from their camp and were hiding in the Umatilla River bottom north of the Agency buildings.

"I'm hit!" shouted Corporal William Roberts of I Company, Twenty-First Infantry. An Indian bullet had struck his leg. The wound was bleeding profusely as he squirmed on the ground in agony.

Miles shouted to his battery chiefs, "Batteries D and G, Action-Front. Canister-Load!" From the caissons the gunners removed the hollow tin cylinders filled with one hundred and fifty lead balls. Returning quickly to the guns, the metal canisters were rammed down the barrels and onto the powder charges. Miles raised his arm upward. "Ready!" He brought his arm down abruptly. "Fire!" he shouted as he brought his field glasses to his eyes.

The Indians on the field were busy shooting at the Agency when the cannons fired again. They saw the white smoke and orange fire belch from the eight muzzles in front of them, then heard the boom. Instantly there was a deafening "CRAACK!" and flash over their heads as lead balls tore downward into them, shredding men and horses. A pink bloody mist hung amongst the struggling victims for an instant. Oits and War Jack screamed at the soldiers, jabbing their rifles towards them. They had never seen such awesome destruction before. The whites were "Devils!"

Once the Umatillas had seen this display of firepower, they had refused to join the Hostiles against the Army. Oits and the rest of the Hostiles were on their own now. The warriors led by Oits and War Jack stayed their distance from the troops during the rest of the day, only occasionally closing within firing range to exchange a few shots. The artillery would open fire, sending a volley into the Indians' positions, striking trees and showering shattered tree limbs and splinters down upon the warriors. The warriors still continued a harassing fire on the Agency. It was a very hot day for everyone. Several miles to the east in Pendleton, a few brave citizens had climbed the north hill above the small town and watched the smoke from the artillery and heard the low rumbling booms as they peered through their field glasses.

Late in the afternoon, Miles approached Captain Bendire where the captain stood beside the formed men of his Company K, First Cavalry. The mounts were anxious to get into the fight as they fidgeted and stomped the ground beneath them. "Captain, how would you like to push those people back into the mountains where they came from?" asked Miles, smiling. Bendire returned the smile and ordered "Assembly" sounded. Soon sixty-six mounted troopers stood at attention before the black muzzles of the now silent artillery batteries. Behind the company, nervous civilian volunteers readied themselves in various states of preparation. Bendire turned his head slightly to the side at the same time, shouting "Company, draw-revolver!" Blue Army revolvers came out of black leather holster barrels, pointed skyward. The captain turned to his trumpeter. "Forward!" he ordered, waving his arm. The high brassy bugle notes filled the air as the line of cavalrymen moved out at a walk. "Trot!" The line instantly picked up speed.

The volunteers trailed behind in the dust, hacking and coughing as they tried to control their horses. The trumpet frightened the animals. Once the company was half way across the field, the Indians opened fire. "Charge!" screamed Bendire and the line jumped forward as if struck by a lightening bolt. Like a locomotive, it rumbled across the field towards the firing Indians. Corporal Charles Brown felt the impact of a bullet as it struck his arm, plowing through it and spraying blood into his eyes. He lost his revolver but continued on in line with the charging company. The warriors again seemed to lose cohesion and leadership during a crisis. They began to mount their horses in small groups and galloped away to the southwest. After giving the Indians chase for several miles, Bendire gave up the pursuit, deciding to spare his horses and men.

Back at the Agency, the wounded were being cared for and the rifled cannons were being cleaned and pampered by their gun crews under the watchful eyes of Artillery Sergeants and corporals. In the distance, an old veteran first sergeant slowly puffed on his pipe as he watched the inbound Cavalry Company's dust approaching in the far distance. Something told him deep down within himself that he should remember the scene before him so that in his twilight years he might draw it out again and remember. The Indian wars were closing. Bendire's dust came nearer, approaching the Agency. Everything was going to be all right now. The fears of death and dying were gone for the moment. Slowly, the Agency Indians returned to their tents, some finding ragged bullet holes torn through them. They too knew that there would be no more trouble from the Hostile Dreamers. The Dreamers amongst the Umatillas were sullen and quiet. In his stained white field tent, Captain Bendire sat at his field table, making entries in the notebook on the table before him. The first line read "07-13-78. Camped at Umatilla Agency before dawn. Attacked by hostile Indians after daybreak. Charged and scattered Hostiles at 6:00 P.M."

"My brothers, I think we ought to go and kill him. (Umapine) We have never done them (Umatillas) any harm, and have always been kind to them when they came on our reservation. We have given them presents."

Leggins, Northern Paiute.

"Friends, we have come to talk to you. Now tell us what our subchief Egan, has done to you that you should kill him, and have him cooked in the way you did. Was he good to eat?... For four years you have come on the Malheur Reservation, and told Egan and Oytes to make war against the whites. You have called them fools for staying on the Reservation to starve.... You are nothing but cowards; nothing but barking coyotes; you are neither persons nor men... Now we cease to be friends, and after the soldiers quit fighting with the Bannocks and with Oytes' men, we will make war with you for the wrong you have done us. [Professed speech to Umatilla Dreamer Prophets,]

Natchez Winnimucca, Northern Paiute.

"Buck Indians do not come to town of late. A few squaws make their appearance, however. Ben. Beagle and S.L. Morse started a buck from town last Sunday in a hurry, on account of his insolence. Ben. knocked him down and Morse applied a hot rock to his back and told him to get, and he got."

East Oregonian, Saturday, Aug. 3, 1878.

Editorial:
"The Indians and the whites can not live together here in peace. One or the other must give way, and we are not of the opinion that it will be the whites."

East Oregonian, Saturday, Aug. 17, 1878.

Chapter 15

Fruits of Assassination – The Road Home

The night air was warm and still in the Indian camp situated near the summit of the Blue Mountains. There were no large bonfires or drumming in the village. The cries of mourning women broke the night's stillness. There were many dead. Oits sat in War Jack's lodge, talking with him. The meeting was held secretly, without Egan or his men's knowledge. Each man had his own bodyguards standing in the shadows behind him. The smell of sweating bodies and smoke reeked throughout the lodge. The stench of unwashed wounds hung in the air. Oits spoke first. "The Numa are not happy with the way things are happening. Perhaps Egan was right when he told us to move on and not stop to fight with the whites." His eyes no longer blazed with Dreamer fever. A bloody scratch showed on his cheek.

"Egan is not right! Egan is a coward fool!" shouted War Jack, startling everyone, including Oits, whose eyes were betraying the first signs of fear.

"Egan will not stop your travels," a voice interrupted from the shadows. Umapine stepped into the dim firelight. Three bright red stripes of war paint were drawn across his face. White teeth contrasted with his dark features. War Jack and Oits threw Umapine a cautious look. Umapine understood the meaning of the look. Egan might have friends among the bodyguards around them. Umapine gave both chiefs a sly, reassuring glance and stepped back into the shadows.

The two chiefs looked at each other with a strange sense of relief. Egan's Paiute warriors would be sorely needed in the days to come. And, after all, if Egan's death could be placed at the feet of the Umatillas, then surely Egan's followers would remain with War Jack and Oits for protection and leadership. The act would have to be done skillfully and completely. There must be no witnesses to tell what was done. It was a bold and bloody plan.

War Jack smiled at Oits, who returned a nervous half-smile. He feared Egan. He also feared Egan's warriors, who would kill him slowly if they knew of the assassination plot to kill him. The two chiefs quickly changed the subject and discussed their next move. It was decided to send out scouts to find the location of the Army troops around them. When the time was right, they would move east under the cover of darkness. The full moon, however, was against their traveling that night.

Across the encampment in a small lodge sat Honey. He watched his wife, Hattie, with tired, loving eyes as she rocked their small son to sleep. The child was weak from malnutrition, as they all were. He slept quietly in his mother's arms. "My father wishes to leave us and surrender to the Soldier Chief Howard. Umapine has promised to guide him and my mother through the lines safely so that he may return with the Army and save us," said Honey softly.

"I do not trust Umapine. He is bad. Egan should not leave us with Oits," Hattie said, looking into Honey's dark eyes. Her black shiny braids glistened in the firelight. The firelight danced upon her high cheekbones, accenting her large narrow eyes as she slowly rocked her little one. Honey knew that she was weak from hunger and that her belly hurt like everyone else's.

Honey shook his head sadly. "I don't trust Umapine either, my wife, but my father wishes us to remain here with the Numa to protect them from Oits and to give them hope until the soldier chiefs come and take them to safely. He wishes me to lead them should anything happen to him or my mother. He tells me that it is our only hope." He continued to shake his head in bewilderment as he carefully wiped the action of his rifle with a soiled piece of rag.

Charley sat in Egan's wikiup, which was near Honey's at the outer edge of the large encampment. They had seen the glares of anger from the other Paiute and Bannock warriors during the battle of the Umatilla Agency today. Egan had purposefully stationed his warriors at the far east end of Oits and War Jacks' fighting positions. They had been safer there, as they had been at the Battle at Birch Creek four days ago.

The Old Woman was busy slicing dog meat for the cooking pot. It was the last one. The dried venison and elk meat had been eaten long ago. There weren't as many dogs barking in the camp these days, Evening Star had cautiously taken her two daughters to visit with Charley's wife, Honey Bear, her sister-in-law.

"Egan?" A voice whispered outside the lodge's entrance. Hands went to weapons quicker than a snake could strike. The Old Woman scampered into the shadows at the rear of the wikiup like a mouse to its hole.

"Who is there?" called Egan quietly as he smoothly cocked the hammer back on his Colt revolver.

"Umapine. With information," Umapine hissed.

"Come," said Egan from within the lodge. The door flap opened and Umapine entered, closing the door flap behind him and sitting where Egan directed. Umapine looked at Charley and then at Egan. Egan looked stronger to him as he sized him up. He had healed well. Egan slowly eased the hammer down on the cocked revolver and laid it in his lap as he stared at Umapine. Umapine glanced at the weapon indifferently. As much as Egan disliked Umapine he tried to hide it as he spoke. "My people are hungry and sick. Many suffer from wounds from the fighting. Some now have the white man's coughing sickness and we have no medicine to help them. When you take me to General Howard, the Soldier Chief, I will ask him to save the rest of my people from the evil hearts of Oits and the other bad men in this group." He rested for a minute, then continued, "It saddens me to leave them." Charley nodded slowly in agreement.

"It will be done then," said Umapine with a nod as he stood up. He left the lodge, leaving its three occupants sitting in silence. From the shadows in the rear of the wikiup a low hum came from the Old Woman, filling the lodge's atmosphere with a strange aura of dread.

That evening Egan and Honey took a walk outside the encampment, away from the others. Charley and three bodyguards followed them at a safe distance. Egan stopped to look at the miles of flat land in the gathering darkness below them. Dark scratches were still visible in the closing light, showing where the white man had plowed and tilled the soil for growing wheat. The dark scratches appeared as small spots on the coat of a new fawn, surrounded by the untilled lighter colors of untouched prairie and sagebrush.

"My heart cries at the thought of leaving you, my son," Egan said softly, more softly than Honey had ever heard him speak before. Honey felt a strange sense of resignation in his father's voice. It worried him.

"I have made a great mistake by taking this road and I will forever feel sadness for having taken it," Egan continued. "As we have talked before, your mother and I must leave you soon, as the time has come to surrender to the Soldier Chief Howard. I must trust Umapine to take me to them. I have no other way to go. The bad Indians or white men would kill us on sight if we went alone."

He drew in a breath and turned once again, looking downward at the now invisible landscape far below them, cloaked in the dark blue shades of nightfall. "You must now lead the Numa. Where you take them is now up to you until I return." Egan turned, facing Honey, his face nearly invisible in the gathering darkness. Honey felt his knees tremble and his teeth begin to chatter from an overwhelming feeling of grief. He fought to control it.

"Father, I have always learned from you and love you for teaching me the ways of life and war," Honey responded softly to the dark figure before him. "While I cannot bear the thought of you being killed, you have taught me well the meaning of life and death for the animals we kill for food and the people we kill to survive. I will do my best to lead the Numa until your return. The only thing I ask is for you and my mother to return safely to our people and to take us home." Honey's voice trembled. The dark shape before him gently took his arm and the two walked back to where the warriors stood silently in the darkness.

Late that night, five miles to the north deep in the valley of the Umatilla River, a council was held. The full moon bathed the river bottom in light silvery hues. The teepee of Chief Homily, a Dreamer Prophet and teacher, was filled with Umatilla, Walla Walla, and Cayuse warriors. To one degree or another, all were followers of the Dreamer faith. Homily was a Walla Walla and a jealous competitor of Smohalla, the great Dreamer-Prophet who lived on the upper Columbia River to the north. He stood facing the leaders in the cramped tent. "Egan the Paiute has failed his followers and led them away from the true Dreamer faith. He has displayed cowardice in battle against the soldier dogs who have invaded our land," Homily said to the men watching him intently. Grunts of agreement hummed amongst them. "He has killed his own people in the past and now must pay for his treachery with death."

Egan had been captured from the Umatillas as a child forty-five years earlier by the Shoshoni and then traded to the Paiute, where he had risen to become a successful war chief among them. Umapine's quivering voice rose in volume as he stood. "Death is too good for one who has tasted the blood of my own family! I will cut out his heart and eat it!" shouted Umapine, shaking his rifle at Homily. Shouts of agreement rent the interior of the tent. Umapine's eyes blazed thirsty for the blood of Egan. The vendetta of blood would soon be settled. Guttural sounds of agreement filled the lodge.

Homily raised his hand, quieting the warriors. "We must not speak of our plan to anyone. The Army would punish us. It must be kept quiet and there must be no one left alive to talk of it later." A murmur of agreement filled the tent. "Good. It is settled. We will go to the meeting place in two days and wait for the non-believer." Outside the teepee drumming

280

had started. Men and women were beginning to dance slowly in the circle. Soon, they would speak with the dead. The moon had passed overhead and lay low in the western sky, shrouding the Umatilla River and the camp at Thornhollow in darkness.

The next few days at the large Indian encampment in the Blue Mountains were spent playing cat and mouse, scouting for the location of the Army, which seemed to be everywhere and nowhere at the same time. A small group of supply wagons had been attacked by Indian scouts, the troopers murdered. Buildings were burned at the telegraph station at Cayuse Station. Egan waited for the appointed time to make his escape from the camp.

"It is time," whispered Charley outside the entrance of Egan's wikiup. It was dusk. The full moon was beginning to climb its way into the approaching darkness with the close of July 14, 1878. Charley opened the wikiup door flap and helped Egan stand to full height outside the lodge. He held his rifle at the ready. It had been cleaned and loaded very carefully. At Charley's side stood a Cayuse Indian whom Egan didn't recognize.

"Hurry," said Charley. "Honey Bear and my children wait with the horses." Egan nodded and helped Evening Star through the entrance, followed by the two girls, who were assisting the Old Woman with her things. They carried a few small belongings. Blanket rolls were tied to their backs. Their eyes darted back and forth, showing fear and anxiety, but they trusted their husband and father and were determined to follow him through anything. The group of seven slowly wound their way through the village, passing teepees and wikiups containing families eating what evening meals they could provide. Warriors carrying rifles eyed the group, then quickly turned their attention to other matters.

A strange feeling overcame Egan as he walked through the village. Why didn't Oits' warriors question them as they passed through the large camp? They kept walking. Soon they had passed through the camp safely and had been led into the trees at the east end of the camp. Through the twilight filtering through the trees, Egan saw Charley's wife, Evening Star's sister, and her four teenaged children anxiously waiting for them. They were holding their horses as well as Egan's buckskin and the small Cayuse belonging to Evening Star. Charley's children were holding the girls' horses. Everyone exchanged nervous glances as the Cayuse guide instructed them to mount their horses and follow him down the canyon leading to the foothills. After riding quietly for a mile, the Cayuse guide raised his arm. Everyone stopped. Soon a sharp whistle sounded from the copse of trees to their front. The Cayuse leaned forward on his horse and whistled back toward the dark trees. The guide nudged his horse forward toward the trees.

Egan's survival instincts began to haunt him. His stomach began to churn. The caravan slowly and quietly wound its way down the canyon towards a copse of pine trees that loomed ahead in the growing darkness. The moon began to lighten the countryside.

As they rode closer to the grove of trees, Egan could make out the light of a bonfire throwing out flickering yellow light from within. He could make out men standing around the fire. The Cayuse guide stopped and told the refugees to dismount before entering the trees, but told Egan that he would be allowed to remain mounted. The women and children, followed by Charley, obeyed the Cayuse guide's instructions and dismounted. Egan felt his large buckskin warhorse tense beneath him. He'd sensed danger. So did Egan as he gripped the revolver hidden beneath his red blanket. His rifle rested inside its scabbard, strapped to his white man's saddle. He suddenly wished he had it in his hands rather than the revolver.

As the group entered the open area near the bonfire, its light highlighted each person's features as he approached. Egan was the last one into the circle. It was only then that he saw that the surrounding men were not soldiers but Cayuse and Umatilla warriors, armed to the teeth and wearing warpaint. Egan now realized this was a trap, but it was too late. Five Crows grabbed the buckskin's bridle. As he did so Egan drew his revolver, trying to aim it at Five Crows. The buckskin jerked and pulled back, preventing Egan from getting a clear shot. A Cayuse to Egan's right was trying to grasp his right foot and tie his feet together. The buckskin reared its hooves, slicing the air. Egan's revolver accidentally went off, firing harmlessly into the air.

Immediately the warriors began firing at the shocked and stunned Paiutes. Forty-three rifles fired simultaneously. The flash from rifle muzzles lit the scene like a lightning bolt, striking the women and children as they fell in heaps or attempted to run to their parents. Multiple bullets struck Charley; his lifeblood sprayed and spouted from his wounds. His finger jerked spasmodically, firing a shot harmlessly into the air. His wife, Honey Bear, limped toward him, having been shot in the hip. Her body spun as bullets struck her, throwing her to the earth, dying. The brief screams of the women and children were suddenly cut short and turned to moans as bullets plowed through and shredded their bodies.

Egan heard Evening Star's scream as a bullet struck her in the forehead. He watched as her head jerked backward from the impact of the bullet. She half-turned, facing him with a blank expression, one arm raised toward him, flopping doll-like, then falling to the earth, her unseeing eyes looking skyward. Both daughters lay just feet away from their mother, their young lifeblood pumping into the dry pine needles, their bodies jerking in the last throes of death. They were immediately jumped upon and hacked and clubbed to death.

Homily raised his rifle and pointed it at Egan, pulling the trigger. His rifle roared. The bullet struck Egan in the chest, knocking him backward on his horse as he struggled to draw his revolver upon the struggling horse. Amazingly, he remained mounted, spouting blood as he reeled upon the red blanket covering the back of his beloved warhorse. Five Crows stopped struggling with the horse's bridle. Furiously he drew his revolver, pointing it into Egan's face with both hands, and fired. The bullet plowed into Egan's head, flying out the back. Umapine's Winchester roared, its bullet striking Egan in the chest. The chief's lifeless body fell to the ground with a sickening thud. A shout erupted from the warriors as they finished killing and mutilating the dead. Charley's body was rolled over, his lifeless arm flopping out to the side as the warriors scalped and slashed his body. His wife, Honey Bear, lay motionless beside him, her face partially hacked away. Their four children lay in small ragged clumps on the forest floor.

Three miles to the north at Meacham Station where the Cavalry Battalion was headquartered, Sarah sat straight up in her blankets from a deep sleep. "Egan!" she screamed, her face glistened with sweat. Mattie jumped towards her, trying to comfort her, wrapping her small arms around the sobbing woman.

The next morning as the sun began climbing high into the pale blue sky, two Cayuse Indians rode into Meacham Station carrying two bloody scalps tied to a pine bough. Also hanging from the pole was a brightly beaded knife scabbard. "Egan!" grunted one of them as he shoved it towards Surgeon FitzGerald, who stood on the front porch of the hotel buttoning his blouse.

"Show us," responded FitzGerald, as Rube Robbins approached them.

A patrol was quickly assembled and followed the two Indians downward into the foothills. After a short ride the patrol entered the grove of trees in the deep canyon. Scattered around the grassy clearing lay the bloody remains of the dead Paiutes, stiffened in various positions of death. All had been scalped and mutilated. FitzGerald and Robbins dismounted and walked through the carnage. Coyotes had feasted on the bodies over night.

"Egan here!" grunted one of the Cayuses, pointing to a corpse lying in the tall grass. The face was unrecognizable. His naked breast showed where a fire had been built upon it, charring the body's upper torso.

As Robbins approached, he slowly removed his hat. He paused for a moment and spoke to FitzGerald. "That's him, Captain. See the bandages and the slung left arm? I gave him them wounds at Silver Creek. Yessir!" He pointed a soiled finger at the corpse. "That's Egan all right and over there's ol Charley," blurted Robbins.

FitzGerald returned to his horse, shaking his head, and withdrew a small medical kit and returned to Egan's body. He carefully opened the kit, exposing shining scalpels secured in separate pockets. He withdrew a large scalpel and a bone saw and began cutting through the flesh of Egan's neck. Robbins walked away, disgusted by the grisly scene surrounding him. Charley was identified and Honey Bear's body was dragged from where it lay upon one of her husband's feet. His head was also removed. Wrapped in a towel, it was given to one of the Cayuse to carry. The Indian took it proudly. The Army Museum in Washington would study them.

As the detail mounted and prepared to leave the scene, a weak, ragged high-pitched keening sound came from the edge of the clearing. Everyone looked startled. The Old Woman lay beside a dead buckskin horse. She was matted in dried blood from bullet and knife wounds. She had wrapped Egan's bullet-torn red blanket over her head as a shroud. She was too weak to move and was dying. FitzGerald was beginning to dismount when Robbins grabbed his arm. "No, Captain, let her die in peace. She don't have more than an hour at the most. Leave her be." FitzGerald nodded and spurred his mount forward with the rest of the patrol. The patrol soon disappeared in its own dust and was gone.

Far below, in the grove of lodge pole pines, the faint keening stopped and all was silent. As the sun climbed higher in the sky over the small grove of pines, the song of a meadowlark again drifted over the foothills of the Blue Mountains.

Far away on the road of Gosipa, a family was at last reunited amongst the stars of the Milky Way. They would never part again.

THE END

"Often in the stillness of the night, when all nature seems asleep about me, there comes a gentle rapping at the door of my heart. I open it; and a voice inquires, 'Pokagon, what of your people? What will their future be?' My answer is: Mortal man has not the power to draw aside the veil of unborn time to tell the future of his race. That gift belongs of the Divine alone. But it is given to him to closely judge the future by the present, and the past."

Simon Pokagon, Potawatomie.

Dedicated to "Chief Egan"

His People…

High upon that mountain he stood
Overlooking the enemy
Deep within his mind he knew
His people…
He had to lead the fight
For survival
He had to give so that his people
Could live
The people were as one
The Paiutes he loved as his own
His people he led freely
Over the land he cherished
Mother Earth
Where life is everlasting
Only the Paiute people that have followed
Could believe the dream he had for
His people…
To Honor and to Love
With Sincere Respect
His people will live on…

2001

Nancy L. Egan (Qua-see-ah)

Epilogue

The Bannock–Paiute Indian War didn't end here. The Indians' pilgrimage continued southeastward, through the Blue Mountains of eastern Oregon. Disillusioned survivors were leaving the group quickly, attempting to sneak back to their tribes unseen by the Army which was pursuing them. Some made it, others didn't. Finding themselves lost, separated from their own people, they sought refuge in canyons and ravines as they huddled in fear and hunger. The Army and its new-found allies, Umatilla and Cayuse Indians, repeatedly turned on them and now fought on its own terms, striking them relentlessly. The survivors crossed the Snake River in August and headed into eastern Idaho Territory, where it had all begun. Most surviving Bannocks quietly slipped onto their reservation at Fort Hall, while others drifted southward into Duck Valley. But at least one last deadly encounter was to transpire.

On September 12, 1878, the first gray light of dawn pushed back the darkness of light on the twenty sleeping lodges of the surviving fugitives. They had been pursued relentlessly by the persistent Cavalry, and had fought their way through an ambush sprung by bounty hunting Crow Indian scouts on September 5. They lost: twenty-eight were killed.

Although hungry and exhausted, the frantic Dreamers were getting closer to Canada and the Sioux medicine man, Sitting Bull. They would soon be up and riding from this camp at Dry Fork, a Snake River tributary in Wyoming. With the approaching daylight, yawning sentries began to stir and fight off sleep. They weren't as alert as they usually were, due to fatigue and lack of sleep. They didn't notice the stir of their emaciated horses whose noses were pointing towards the timber which encircled the camp. From within the darkness of the timber, Colonel Nelson A. Miles, commander of the Department of the Yellowstone, sat upon his horse, watching the still sleeping camp. He had quietly surrounded the small encampment with his Cavalry and Artillery during the night. His troops were mounted and ready.

The muzzles of the small Hotchkiss Guns were adjusted and aimed at the camp. Their deadly canister rounds would be aimed waist high.

The sounds of a crying baby drifted from one of the lodges. Small fires began to glow from within the shelters. Outside, it was light enough to aim and shoot. No dogs barked, all having been eaten or killed long ago.

A bugle call split the morning stillness, but strangely, no Cavalry charge followed.

Inside lodges, red hands instinctively grabbed Winchesters and other weapons. Quickly, men and women sprang out of the their lodges, prepared to fight to the death.

"Whoa!" a shout came from the timber. The Bannock stood their ground, heads snapping left and right, trying to locate their unseen enemy.

"Drop your weapons and you won't be harmed. The Army has you surrounded!" shouted a Crow Scout in broken Bannock from the treeline.

The Bannocks glanced at one another, chests heaving. Most of the warriors quickly eyed their women; the thin frail women resembled bony skeletons beneath their clothing. Their sunken eyes betrayed their thoughts. They were through. They began to pick up what belongings they could carry and stared silently at their men.

The warriors also knew they were through. They laid their weapons onto the ground at their feet. Some wept.

Mounted Cavalrymen emerged from all sides of the timber and stopped. Suddenly a Hotchkiss Gun barked, sending a round through the camp, exploding as it struck a lodgepole, spraying lead balls in all directions. Warriors screamed their death songs as they snatched up weapons from the grass and began firing into the troopers.

It was too late. Other Hotchkiss Guns opened up, and troopers' carbines cracked, joining the crescendo of whistling death driving its way into the now burning lodges. A bugle sounded again, ordering cease-fire. The only sounds coming from the smoldering remains of the camp were low cries and groaning. The entire camp was down. It had taken only seconds.

Mounted troopers cautiously approached the camp, carbines at the ready. They hadn't expected the scene before them. The warriors, women, and children not killed outright were sitting or lying wide eyed in shock. All shivered convulsively and most were bleeding. No one cried. Bright red streaks in the tall grass contrasted with dried-yellow grass, slick with blood. Entrails lay glistening in the morning sunlight.

Thus ended the three and one-half month war between the U. S. Government and the Bannock-Paiute Indian Dreamers. Survivors were taken to Forts Vancouver, Washakie, Keogh, Hall, Omaha Barracks, and to Camp Brown.

A few fugitives managed to escape; others simply disappeared forever.

Ancestor Photos

Herbert Egan (Qua-see-ah), grandson of War Chief Egan, was as an infant carried by his mother (Hattie) and father (Honey) on the 1878 War trail. He is the father of Hubert Egan, who is shown on the back cover. He died in 1960 at the age of 82. Photograph courtesy Patricia Egan and Nancy L. Egan (Qua-see-ah). (Nancy Egan was given permission by her family to take the name of her great-great grandfather.)

Corporal Philip H. Murphy's grave marker at Mountain View Cemetery, Walla Walla, Washington. All "Congressional Medal of Honor" winners are authorized a white stone with gold inlaid symbol and lettering. This is Murphy's final resting place; he was author Greg Hodgen's great-great grandfather.

Murphy was an Irish immigrant from Kilkenny County, who brought his wife, Bridget, and three small children with him to America. He enlisted in the Eighth Cavalry on April 20, 1867, at Detroit, Michigan, and was assigned to Company F, Camp Logan, Oregon. Most of the Eighth Regiment was transferred to the Arizona Territory in 1868, where he was promoted to the rank of corporal. At the Battle of Seneca Mountain, fighting Apache Indians, he was awarded the "Congressional Medal of Honor."

The Corporal re-enlisted in Company E, First Cavalry, and was transferred to Fort Walla Walla, Washington Territory. He fought in the Nez Perce Indian War at the Battle of Looking Glass in 1877. In the Bannock-Paiute Indian War in Oregon in 1878, he fought in the Battle of Birch Creek, and in the retreating Indian rear guard action on the North Fork of the John Day River. Photograph courtesy Greg Hodgen.

Jerimah Boon (Jerry) DeSpain was a successful Pendleton businessman who had built the DeSpain Building, still standing on S.E. Court Street in Pendleton. He owned large sheep herds, and farmed an area north of Pendleton that became known as DeSpain Gulch. He moved his family, as others had done, to Fort Walla Walla where protection was thought to be better. (He is a relative of Larry Purchase). Photography courtesy "An Illustrated History of Umatilla and Morrow Counties, State of Oregon," by William Parsons, p.437.

WITNESSES TO THE 1878 BANNOCK/PAIUTE INDIAN WAR

U.S. GOVERNMENT

RUTHERFORD B. HAYES. Nineteenth President of the United States. Term of Office: March 4, 1877 to March 4, 1881.

WILLIAM TECUMSEH SHERMAN. Named Commanding General of the Army by President U.S. Grant in 1869 and served in that capacity until his retirement in 1883. Born February 8, 1820, in Lancaster, Ohio, and died in New York City on February 14, 1891.

IRVIN McDOWELL. Major General, U.S. Army, Commanding Military Division of the Pacific, Precedio, San Francisco, California, 1876 to 1882.

OLIVER O. HOWARD. Brigadier General, U.S. Army, Commanding Department of the Columbia, Fort Vancouver, Washington Territory, 1874 to 1880. Awarded the Congressional Medal of Honor during the Civil War. Suffered the loss of his right arm during the battle of Fair Oaks, Virginia. Founder of the Lincoln Memorial and Howard University. Served as Superintendent, West Point Military Academy. Promoted to Major General in 1886. Retired on November 8, 1894. Born on November 8, 1830. Died at 7:20 P.M. on October 26, 1909. Buried at Lakeview Cemetery, Burlington, Vermont. Wife: Elizabeth "Lizzie" Waite.

REUBEN F. BERNARD. Captain, Commanding Compamy G, First Cavalry Regiment, U.S. Army, Fort Boise, Idaho Territory. Enlisted as a private in Company D, First U.S. Dragoons, serving in the Mexican and Civil Wars. He was commissioned on September 15, 1862. His first wife, Alice, died on January 20, 1891, of a miscarriage at Jefferson Barracks, Missouri. Bernard had one surviving son, who was a career Army officer. He was promoted to Lieutenant Colonel on July 22, 1892, and retired from active service on October 14, 1896, with forty-one years of service. Born on October 14, 1832, and died on November 17, 1903, of acute influenza.

JENKINS (JOHN) A. FitzGERALD. Surgeon, Captain, First Cavalry Regiment, U.S. Army, Fort Lapwai, Idaho Territory. Graduate of Jefferson Medical College, Philadelphia, Pennsylvania. He served as Bernard's field surgeon during the 1878 Indian War. Died on August 11, 1879, from lung complications contracted during the Nez Perce Campaign of 1877. Buried at Columbia, Pennsylvania, Wife: Emily McCorkle.

THOMAS McGREGOR. Captain, Commanding Company A, First Cavalry Regiment, U.S. Army, Fort Boise, Idaho Territory. Served with the First Cavalry Regiment during the Civil War. Promoted to

Lieutenant Colonel on November 26, 1894. Retired from active service on June 26, 1901. Born in Scotland. Wife: Jennie.

EVAN MILES. Captain, Commanding Company E, Twenty–first Infantry, U.S. Army. Promoted to Colonel on May 4, 1897. Retired from active service on July 19, 1899.

WILLIAM V. RINEHART. Agent, Malheur Reservation, Department of the Interior, 1878. Major, Oregon Volunteers.

NARCISSE.A. CORNOYER. Agent, Umatilla Reservation, Department of the Interior, 1878.

SCOUTS

ORLANDO 'RUBE' ROBBINS. Chief scout, born in Phillips, Franklin County, Maine, on August 30, 1836. Married Corilla J. Tallman Brassfield in Boise, Ada County, Idaho, on December 9, 1882. Died in Boise, Idaho, on May 1, 1908. An active leader of Idaho volunteers during the Nez Perce War of 1877, and the Bannock-Paiute War of 1878, serving under General O. O. Howard in both wars as a civilian Army scout. He also served as a town marshal.

WILLIAM MYERS. A volunteer scout, born in 1830, New York. In the early 1870's, Myers made his living as a miller and teamster at Ora Dell, Oregon, near the present city of La Grande. There he met his future wife, Cornelia Richardson. Myers was the proprietor of the Miners' Hotel in Atlanta, Idaho. Enlisted as a volunteer scout during the Bannock-Paiute Indian War on June 3, 1878, in Boise City, Idaho. Captured and killed in action by hostile Indians at the Battle of Silver Creek, Oregon, on June 23, 1878. His remains were buried near the battlefield along with those of soldiers killed in action. The U.S. Government paid his wife Cornelia $87.50. Through the efforts of Rube Robbins, the Treasurer of Idaho Territory reimbursed her with a horse, a blanket, a rifle, and $30.00 in gold, for the items lost by her husband on the battlefield. She was not reimbursed however, for the fine silver heavy-cased watch, valued at $60.00, lost by her husband William on the battlefield.

AMERICAN INDIANS

EGAN, (E-hee-gant / Ezich`que-gah). (Blanket Wearer). Born a Cayuse and raised as a Paiute. Chief of three bands of Northern Paiute Wadatokas, "Seed Eaters," Malheur Agency, Oregon. Taken as a child by Shoshoni slave raiders and sold to the Paiute Tribe, who raised him as one of their own. He tried rather successfully to comply with the U.S. Government's unrealistic agency policies and restrictions upon his bands while working with the Malheur Indian Agent Samuel Parrish. Unfortunately, when Agent W.V. Rinehart replaced Parrish, Egan's relationship with the Department of the Interior and the

Malheur Reservation became strained. Out of desperation and under peer pressure, Egan acquainted himself with Oits, a Paiute Dreamer-Prophet, and agreed to accompany him on the deadly outbreak in 1878. When he witnessed the wanton killing and slaughter committed by other Bannock and Paiute warriors during their exodus, he finally made an attempt to conspire secretly with the U.S. Army through channels assumed to be trustworthy Umatilla Indians, who were in fact Dreamers. He sought a peaceful, bloodless surrender of the bands that he led. He was ultimately betrayed by the Dreamers, resulting in the death of his wife, Evening Star, and their two daughters, as well as his own, on July 14, 1878, two miles from the town of Meacham, Oregon.

His skull and arm bones, along with those of his brother-in-law, Charley, were removed by Surgeon FitzGerald at the scene of the assassination, as was official War Department policy at the time, and sent to the U.S. Army Medical Museum, in Washington, D.C. The remains were released recently by the U.S. Government and were returned to Egan's beloved home by his descendent, Nancy L. Egan. The bones were interred in the Burns Paiute Reservation Cemetery, where they now lay in peace. Egan was born in 1833.

EVENING STAR (Ashohu). Wife of Egan, sister to Chief Shenka, Malheur Agency, Oregon. Remained with her husband during the war and died at her husband's side, along with their two daughters, on July 14, 1878. Born in 1825.

HONEY EGAN (Ezich'que). Northern Paiute, Son of Egan and Evening Star, Malheur Agency, Oregon, and Duck Valley Agency, Idaho. Remained with Egan's three bands in the Blue Mountains while Egan attempted to escape to the US Army to negotiate terms. When Umatilla Dreamers assassinated Egan and his mother and sisters, Honey fled with his wife and baby to the Duck Valley Reservation in southwest Idaho. The Army never pursued him or his family. Born in 1849.

HATTIE EGAN. Wife of Honey Egan, Malheur Agency, Oregon. She and her husband escaped from the U.S. Army and fled to live on the Duck Valley Agency, Idaho. Born in 1854.

HERBERT EGAN (Qya-see-ah). Son of Honey and Hattie Egan, Chief Egan's grandson, Cayuse/Northern Paiute, Malheur Agency, Oregon, and Duck Valley Agency, Idaho. (General Howard identified Egan as a Umatilla, resulting in confusion down through the years.) Carried by his mother and father on the war trail as an infant. Born in 1878, and died September 4, 1960.

SARAH WINNEMUCCA (Toc-Me-To-Ne / Shell Woman). Northern Paiute, contract interpreter, Malheur Agency, Oregon. Sarah's life and story is too voluminous to address here. She spent her lifetime attempting to gain fair treatment and influence with the U.S. Government in its dealings with the Northern Paiute people. Aided and assisted General Howard in his campaign in dealings with the Indians.

MATTIE WINNEMUCCA. Daughter of Chief Shenka, adopted daughter of Chief Egan, Northern Paiute, Malheur Agency, Oregon. Mattie was an interpreter for the U.S. Army and General Howard during the 1878 campaign. Mattie was Sarah Winnemucca's sister-in-law, being married to Sarah's brother Lee Winnemucca. Mattie died as a result of a head injury from a horse fall sustained at Camp Harney, Oregon, in the winter of 1878, and is buried at Fort Simcoe, Washington.

SMOHALLA. Extremely influential Wanapam Dreamer prophet and spiritual leader of Indians living in the Pacific Northwest. Preached the Dreamer doctrine. Actively involved in the Nez Perce outbreak in 1877, prodding young Chief Joseph to unsuccessfully take his band of Nez Perce from the United States into Saskatchewan, Canada, there to join Sioux medicine man, Sitting Bull, and his renegades. He tried the same thing the following year with the Bannock-Paiute.

OITS (Left Hand / Johnson). Northern Paiute, Dreamer Prophet, acolyte of the Wanapam Dreamer Prophet Smoholla. Political enemy of Chief Egan within the Paiute bands. Conspirator in the assassination plot to kill Chief Egan. Died on March 16, 1915, at the Warm Springs Reservation, where he had served as a Indian policeman. Wife: Sallie, Malheur Agency, Oregon.

UMAPINE. Cayuse, Umatilla Agency, Oregon. A feared warrior among local tribes as well as whites. Known for his quick temper and ferocity.

HOMILY. Umatilla, a Dreamer Prophet, Umatilla Agency, Oregon. Although he did not get along with Smohalla, he organized and led a group totaling over forty followers located near Thornhollow, Oregon. He was suspected of being actively involved in the assassination of Chief Egan and his family.

FIVE CROWS. Chief, Cayuse, Umatilla Agency, Oregon. Reported by Shantee, "Egan of the Paiutes," to have held War Chief Egan's horse just before the latter was shot.

STATE OFFICIALS

MASON BRAYMAN. Governor, Idaho Territory.
Republican.
Term of Office: 1876 to 1878.

STEPHEN FOWLER CHADWICK. Governor, State of Oregon.
Democrat.
Term of Office: 1877 to 1878.

ELISHA P. FERRY. Governor, Washington Territory.
Republican.
Term of Office: 1872 to 1880.

MUSTER ROLL OF UMATILLA COUNTY MOUNTED VOLUNTEERS

Listing People Killed and Wounded, Horses, and Property Lost at the Battle of Willow Spring

July 6, 1878

Captain John L. Sperry, Company Commander
(He was also the Umatilla County Sheriff)

NAME	STATUS	REMARKS	LOST VALUE
1. Sperry, John L., Captain		Horse killed, saddle and bridle lost.	$185.00
2. Kirk. M., 1st Lieutenant		Horse killed, saddle and bridle lost.	$80.00
3. Blakely, William M., 2nd Lieutenant			
4. Lamar, William E., Orderly Sergeant	Killed (2 Shots)	Horse killed, saddle and bridle lost.	$75.00
5. Ferguson, T. S., 1st Duty Sergeant		Horse killed, saddle and bridle lost.	$116.00
6. Coleman, J. C., 2nd Duty Sergeant		Horse killed, saddle and bridle lost.	$180.00
7. Ellis, J. William, 3rd Duty Sergeant		Horse, saddle, and bridle lost.	$131.00
8. Eastland, R., 4th Duty Sergeant		Horse killed, saddle and bridle lost.	$150.00
9. Baker, Andy, Private			
10. Bishop, George, Private		Saddle and bridle lost.	$35.00
11. Blanchard, Louis, Private			
12. Crisfield, Arthur, Private	Wounded (Ankle)	Horse, saddle, and bridle lost.	$175.00
13. Daugherty, B. E., Private			
14. Donaldson, W. L., Private		Horse killed, saddle and bridle lost.	$100.00
15. Frazer, Jacob, Private	Wounded (Calf of leg)		
16. Furgeson, F. D., Private			
17. Gerking, M. P., Private		Saddle and bridle lost.	$25.00
18. Gerking, S. I., Private		Horse killed, saddle and bridle lost.	$120.00
19. Graves, George, Private		Horse, saddle, and bridle lost.	$135.00
20. Grubb, W. P., Private		Saddle, bridle, and blankets lost.	$25.00
21. Hale, Harrison, Private	Killed (3 Shots)	Horse, saddle, and bridle lost.	$80.00
22. Hannah, Frank, Private	Wounded (7 Wounds*)	Horse killed, saddle and bridle lost.	$70.00
23. Harrison, Walter, Private			
24. Henderson, Charles R., Private	Wounded (Below knee)	Horse killed, saddle and bridle lost.	$120.00
25. Howell, H. H., Private	Wounded (Shoulder)	Horse, saddle, and bridle lost.	$75.00
26. Kellogg, A. R., Private			
27. Landson, Sylvester L., Private	Wounded (Thigh)	Horse killed, saddle and bridle lost.	$150.00

Name	Wounded	Amount	Loss
28. Manning, B. L., Private		$100.00	Horse killed, saddle and bridle lost.
29. McKay, T. C., Private		$45.00	Saddle, bridle, blankets, and canteen lost.
30. Metzger, W. M., Private		$90.00	Horse, saddle, and bridle lost.
31. Ogle, Benjamin F., Private		$110.00	Horse, saddle, and bridle lost.
32. Ogle, Joseph, Private		$130.00	Horse killed, saddle and bridle lost.
33. Ogle, Thomas, Private		$100.00	Horse, saddle, and bridle lost.
34. Oglesby, Dr. William W., Private		$140.00	Horse, saddle, and bridle lost.
35. Perkins, James B., Private		$110.00	Horse, saddle, and bridle lost.
36. Reed, W. R., Private		$100.00	Horse, saddle, and bridle lost.
37. Rockfellow, H., Private			
38. Rothchild, Samuel, Private	Wounded (Below knee)	$50.00	Horse, saddle, and bridle lost. Horse later found.
39. Ryan, P. J., Private		$150.00	Horse killed, saddle and bridle lost.
40. Salisbury, Harold A., Private		$165.00	Saddle, bridle, rifle, watch, money lost.
41. Salisbury, John W., Private	Wounded (Thigh, foot)	$175.00	Horse killed, saddle and bridle lost.
42. Scott, A., Private		$200.00	Horse killed, saddle and bridle lost.
43. Smith, J. L., Private		$45.00	Saddle, bridle, and blankets lost.
44. Smith, S. W., Private		$120.00	Horse, saddle, and bridle lost.
45. Stone, J. M., Private		$100.00	Horse, saddle, and bridle lost..
46. Sullivan, Andrew, Private			
47. Titsworth George W., Private	Wounded (Rt. chest)	$70.00	Horse, saddle, and bridle lost.
48. Townsend, Clarence C., Private		$80.00	Horse, saddle, and bridle lost.
49. Warren, R. F., Private		$100.00	Horse killed, saddle and bridle lost.
50. Wilson, James H., Private			
51. Woodward, C. P., Private		$100.00	Horse killed, saddle and bridle lost.

Sergeant William Lamar – Buried at Pendleton Pioneer Cemetery, possibly re-interred at Olney Cemetery, Pendleton Oregon.
Private Harrison Hale – Buried at a small cemetery east of Heppner, Oregon.

References:
1. East Oregonian Newspaper, Pendleton, Oregon, July 4, 1978, pgs. 9 and 10. Story by Virgil Rupp.
2. East Oregonian Newspaper, Pendleton, Oregon, July 13, 1878, p. 2. James H. Turner, Business Editor.
3. Parsons, Col. William, "An Illustrated History of Umatilla and Morrow Counties," pgs. 477 to 488, titled "War with the Snakes, Bannocks and Pahutes," (sic).
4. Muster Roll, Oregon State Archives, Salem Oregon, Box 89A-12-126, folder 50 (Courtesy Warren Aney). (Note: This reference shows the name Andy Baker, references 1,2, and 3 above show an Al Action, instead.) (The 52 volunteers referred to in the text assume that Baker and Action are two people.)

*Arm, backside, leg: dangerous

BIBLIOGRAPHY

BOOKS

Aney, Warren (Sergeant First Class). Eastern Oregon's Own--A Military History. LaGrand, Oregon: HQ and Troop, 3rd Squadron, 116th Armored Cavalry, Oregon Army National Guard, 1984. 70 pgs.

Arnold, R. Ross. Indian Wars of Idaho. Caldwell, Idaho: The Canton Printers, Ltd., 1932. (Chapter 4, pgs. 169 to 217.)

Bailey, Paul. Ghost Dance Messiah. Tucson, Arizona: Western Lore Press, 1986. 206 pgs.

Bailey, Paul. Wovoka, the Indian Messiah. Tucson, Arizona: Western Lore Press, 1957. 223 pgs.

Bancroft, Hubert Howe. History of Washington, Idaho, and Montana, 1845-1889. San Francisco, California: The History Company Publishers, 1890. (Pgs. 472, 517 to 526.)

Beck, Warren A. and Haase, Ynez D. Historical Atlas of the American West. Norman, Oklahoma: University of Oklahoma Press, 1989. 200 pgs.

Boring, Mel. Wovoka, The Story of an American Indian. Minneapolis, Minnesota: Dillon Press, Inc., 1981. 69 pgs.

Brady, Cyrus Townsend. North West Fights and Fighters. Williamstown, Massachusetts: Corner House Publishers, 1974. 373 pgs.

Brimlow, George Francis. The Bannock Indian War of 1878. Caldwell, Idaho: The Caxton Printers, Ltd., 1938. 241 pgs.

Brimlow, George Francis. Cavalryman Out of the West, Life of General William Carey Brown. Caldwell, Idaho: The Caxton Printers, Ltd., 1944. 442 pgs.

Brimlow, George Francis. Harney County, Oregon, and Its Range Land. Portland, Oregon: Binford and Mort, 1951. 316 pgs.

Canfield, Gae Whitney. Three American Indian Women, Pocahontas, Sacajawea, Sarah Winnemucca of the Northern Paiutes. New York, New York: MJF Books. Reprinted Norman, Oklahoma: University of Oklahoma Press, 1983. 300 pgs.

Carpenter, John A. Sword and Olive Branch, Oliver Otis Howard. Pittsburgh, Pennsylvania: University of Pittsburgh Press, 1964. 379 pgs.

Corless, Hank. The Weiser Indians, Shoshoni Peacemakers. Salt Lake City, Utah: University of Utah Press, 1990. (Chapter 6, The Bannock War of 1878, pgs. 87 to 113.)

Dorsey, R. Stephen. American Military Belts and Related Equipment. Union City, Tennessee: Pioneer Press, reprint 1984. 139 pgs.

Faust, Patricia L. Historical Times, Illustrated Encyclopedia of the Civil War. New York, New York: Harper and Row, 1986. 850 pgs.

FitzGerald, Emily McCorkle. An Army Doctor's Wife on the Frontier. Lincoln, Nebraska, and London, England: University of Nebraska Press, 1986. (Part V - The Front Lines, 1878, pgs. 335 to 352.)

French, Giles. Cattle Country of Peter French. Portland, Oregon: Binford and Mort, 1965. (Pgs. 66 to 72.)

Fuller, George W. A History of the Pacific Northwest. New York, New York: A.A. Knopf Publisher, 1931. (Pgs. 276 to 277.)

Gilbert, Frank T. Historic Sketches of Walla Walla, Whitman, Columbia, and Garfield Counties, Washington Territory; Umatilla County, Oregon. Portland, Oregon: A.G. Walling Printing and Lithographing House, 1882. 316 pgs.

Glassley, Ray H. Pacific Northwest Indian Wars. Portland, Oregon: Binford and Mort, 1953. (Chapter 9, The Bannock War, pgs. 225 to 238.)

Graham, Ron; Kopec, John A.; and Moore, C. Kenneth. A Study of the Colt Single Action Army Revolver. Dallas, Texas: Taylor Publishing Company, 1985. (Pgs. 361, 367, 368.)

Gregg, Jacob Ray. Pioneer Days in Malheur County. Los Angeles, California: privately printed by Lorrin L. Morrison Printing and Publishing, 1950. (Chapter 12, The Bannock-Piute (sic) Indian War of 1878, pgs. 131 to 148.)

Hanley, Mike and Ellis, Lucia. Owyhee Trails, The West's Forgotten Corner. Caldwell, Idaho: The Caxton Printers, Ltd., 1973. (Pgs. 124 to 147.)

Harer, Holly Jo. Camas Prairie County - A History of Ukiah-Albee. Pendleton, Oregon: Pendleton Press, 1986. (Pgs. 6, 7.)

Hart, Herbert M. Old Forts of the Northwest. Seattle, Washington: Superior Publishing Company, 1965. (Photos of Nelson A. Miles and Oliver O. Howard, pgs. 11, 17, 18.)

Heitman, Francis B. Historical Register and Dictionary of the United States Army, from its Organization. September 29, 1789, to March 2, 1903. Washington Government Printing Office, 1903. Reprint 1965, Urbana, Illinois: University of Illinois Press. (Vol. 1, 1,069 pgs. and Vol. 2, 636 pgs.)

Hopkins, Sarah Winnemucca. Life Among the Piutes (sic): Their Wrongs and Claims. Reno, Nevada: University of Nevada Press, 1883, Reprint 1994. 268 pgs. (Chapter 7, The Bannock War, pgs. 37 to 202.)

Howard, O.O. (Major General). Autobiography of Oliver Otis Howard, Major General, United States Army. New York, New York: Baker and Taylor Company, 1907. (2 vols., 610 pgs. and 620 pgs.)

Howard, O.O. (Major General). Famous Indian Chiefs I Have Known. New York, New York: The Century Company, 1908. Reprint 1989, Lincoln, Nebraska, and London, England: University of Nebraska Press. 364 pgs. (Pgs. 199 to 277, 322 to 352.)

Howard, O.O. (Major General). My Life and Experiences Among Our Hostile Indians. Hartford, Connecticut: A.D. Worthington and Company. Library of Congress, Washington, D.C., by act of Congress, 1907. 570 pgs. (Pgs. 365 to 407.)

Hunter, George. Reminiscences of an Old Timer. San Francisco, California: H.S. Crocker and Co., 1887. 454 pgs.

Hussey, Larry. <u>Fort Walla Walla, Then and Now</u>. Walla Walla, Washington: privately published, 1994. (Pgs. 58 to 62.)

Jocelyn, Stephen Perry.   <u>Mostly Alkali</u>. Caldwell, Idaho: The Caxton Printers, Ltd., 1953. (Chapter XVII, 1877-1879, pgs. 264 to 285.)

King, Charles. <u>Campaigning with Crook and Stories of Army Life</u>. New Canaan, Connecticut: Readex Microprint Corp., 1996. 295 pgs.

Knight, Oliver. <u>Following the Indian Wars, the Story of the Newspaper Correspondents Among the Indian Campaigners</u>. Norman, Oklahoma, and London, England: University of Oklahoma Press, 1960. 348 pgs.

Knight, Oliver. <u>Life and Manners in the Frontier Army</u>. Norman, Oklahoma: University of Oklahoma Press, 1978. 280 pgs.

Lockley, Fred. <u>Conversations with Bullwhackers, Muleskinners, Pioneers, Prospectors, '49ers, Indian Fighters, Trappers, Ex-Barkeepers, Authors, Preachers, Poets and Near Poets</u>. Eugene, Oregon: Rainy Day Press, 1981. 357 pgs.

Macnab, Gordon. <u>A Century of News and People in the East Oregonian 1875-1975</u>. Pendleton, Oregon: East Oregonian Publishing Co., 1975. (Chapter 5, pgs. 36 to 51, 132 to 235.)

Madsen, Brigham D. <u>The Bannock of Idaho</u>. Caldwell, Idaho: The Caxton Printers, Ltd., 1958. (Chapter 8, The Bannock War of 1878, pgs. 202 to 230.)

Madsen, Brigham D. <u>The Northern Shoshoni</u>. Caldwell, Idaho: The Caxton Printers, Ltd., 1980. (Chapter V, Camas Prairie War, pgs. 75 to 89.)

Mark, Frederick A. <u>Great Western Indian Fights, by Members of the Potomac Corral of the Westerners</u>. New York, New York: MJF Books, 1960. (Chapter 22, the Bannock Indian War of 1878, pgs. 270 to 280.)

May, Keith F. and May, Christina Rae. <u>A Field Guide to Historic Pendleton</u>. Pendleton, Oregon: Drigh Sighed Publications, 1997. 206 pgs.

McArthur, Lewis A. <u>Oregon Geographic Names</u>. Portland, Oregon: Oregon Historical Society Press, 6th Edition, 1992. 957 pgs.

Mooney, James. <u>The Ghost Dance</u>. North Dichton, Massachusetts: J. G. Press, Inc., published approximately 1896. Reprint 1996. 498 pgs.

Morgan, Thomas. <u>My Story of the Last Indian War in the Northwest; The Bannock, Piute (sic), Yakima, and Sheep Eater Tribes, 1878-1879</u>. (city and state unknown): privately published, 1954. 29 pgs.

Morrison, Dorothy Nafus. <u>Chief Sarah</u>. Portland, Oregon: Oregon Historical Society Press, 1990. 170 pgs.

Munnick, Harriet D. and Munnick, Adrian R. <u>Catholic Church Records of the Pacific Northwest, Missions of St. Ann and St. Rose of the Cayuse 1847-1888, Walla Walla and Frenchtown 1859-1872, Frenchtown 1872-1888</u>. Portland, Oregon: Binford and Mort, 1989. Various paging.

Nielsen, Lawrence E. <u>In The Ruts of the Wagon Wheels, Pioneer Roads in Eastern Oregon</u>. Bend, Oregon: Maverick Publications, 1987. 129 pgs.

Oliver, Herman. <u>Gold and Cattle Country</u>. Portland, Oregon: Binford and Mort, 1961. Reprint 1962. 312 pgs.

Parker, Aaron F. <u>Forgotten Tragedies of Indian Warfare in Idaho</u>. Grangeville, Idaho: Idaho County Free Press, 1925. 11 pgs.

Parsons, William (Colonel). <u>An Illustrated History of Baker, Grant, Malheur, and Harney Counties</u>. (city and state unknown): Western Historical Publishing Co., 1902. (Pgs. 743 to 754.)

Parsons, William (Colonel) and Shiach, William S. <u>An Illustrated History of Umatilla and Morrow Counties, State of Oregon</u>. (city and state unknown): W.H. Lever, Publisher, 1902. 581 pgs. (Pgs. 211 to 220, and 477 to 488.)

Pioneer Ladies Club, and Umatilla County Historical Society. <u>Reminiscences of Oregon Pioneers</u>. Pendleton, Oregon: East Oregonian Publishing Co., 1937. Reprint 1993. (The Indian War of 1878, Samuel Rothchild, pgs. 125 to 131.)

Quartermaster of the U.S. Army. <u>U.S. Army Uniforms and Equipment. Originally published under the title: Specifications for Clothing, Camp, and Garrison Equipage, and Clothing and Equipage Materials</u>. Philadelphia, Pennsylvania: Published by direction of the U.S. Quartermaster General of the Army at the

Philadelphia Depot of the Quartermaster's Department, 1889. Lincoln, Nebraska: University of Nebraska Press. Reprint 1986. 375 pgs.

Rodenbough, Theo. F. (Brevet Brigadier General) and Haskin, William L. (Major, First Army). The Army of the United States. Historical Sketches of Staff and Line, with Portraits of Generals-in-Chief. New York, New York: Argonaut Press, Ltd., 1896. Reprint 1966. 748 pgs.

Ruby, Robert H. and Brown, John A. The Cayuse Indians, Imperial Tribesmen of Old Oregon. Norman Oklahoma: University of Oklahoma Press. 1972, 1975, Reprint 1987. 345 pgs. (Pgs. 282 to 296.)

Ruby, Robert H. and Brown, John A. Dreamer-Prophets of the Columbia Plateau, Smoholla and Skolaskin. Norman, Oklahoma, and London, England: University of Oklahoma Press, 1989. 257 pgs.

Ruby, Robert H. and Brown, John A. A Guide to the Indian Tribes of the Pacific Northwest. Norman, Oklahoma, and London, England: University of Oklahoma Press, 1986. 289 pgs.

Ruby, Robert H. and Brown, John A. Indian Slavery in the Pacific Northwest. Spokane, Washington: Arthur H. Clark and Company, 1993. 36 pgs.

Ruby, Robert H. and Brown, John A. Indians of the Pacific Northwest. Norman, Oklahoma, and London, England: University of Oklahoma Press, 1981. Reprint 1982, paperback, 1988. 294 pgs.

Russell, Don. One Hundred and Three Fights and Scrimmages, The Story of General Reuben F. Bernard. Washington, D.C.: U.S. Cavalry Association, 1936. (Chapter 8, pgs. 114 to 133.)

Searcey, Mildred. Way Back When. Pendleton Oregon: East Oregonian Publishing Company, 1972. (Pgs. 96 to 101.)

Skovlin, Jon. Fifty Years of Research Progress: A Historical Document on the Starky Experimental Forest and Range, Pacific Northwest General Technical Report - 266. Portland, Oregon: U.S. Department of Agriculture, Forest Service, Pacific Northwest Research Station, May 1991. 58 pgs.

Skovlin, Jon and Donna. <u>Hank Vaughn</u>. Cove, Oregon: Reflections Publishing Co., 1996. 219 pgs.

Stephen, Randy. <u>The Horse Soldier 1776 - 1943</u>. Norman, Oklahoma: University of Oklahoma, date unknown. (Vol. 2, 1851 to 1880 - The Frontier Wars, Mexican Wars, Civil War, Indian Wars.) 215 pgs.

Stewart, Betty Booth., <u>Meacham - A Wide Spot on the Oregon Trail, Where the Meadowlark Still Sings</u>. Tigard, Oregon: Crossroad Books 1996. 192 pgs.

Timmen, Fritz. <u>Blow for the Landing</u>. Caldwell, Idaho: The Caxton Printers, Ltd., 1973. (Pgs. 148 to 150.) (Gunboat "Spokane" photos and descriptions.)

Turnbull, George S. <u>Governors of Oregon</u>. Portland, Oregon: Metropolitan Press, 1959. (Pgs. 40 to 41.)

Umatilla County Historical Society. <u>Umatilla County: A Backward Glance</u>. Pendleton, Oregon: East Oregonian Newspaper Master Printers, 1980. 270 pgs.

Umbarger, Doralee. <u>Early History of Pilot Rock</u>. Pilot Rock, Oregon: Pilot Rock High School, April 21, 1969. (P. 3.) (Stage coach route through Willow Spring, and other details.)

Utley, Robert M. <u>Frontier Regulars</u>. New York, New York: Macmillan Publishing Company, Inc., 1973. Lincoln, Nebraska, and London, England: University of Nebraska Press, 1984. 462 pgs.

Van Arsdol, Ted. <u>Northwest Bastion, The U.S. Army Barracks at Vancouver, 1849 - 1916.</u> Vancouver, Washington: Heritage Trust of Clark County, 1991. (Pgs. 42 to 43.)

Weatherford, Mark V. <u>Bannock-Piute (sic) War, The Campaign and Battles</u>. Corvallis, Oregon: Lenhert Printing Co., May 1957. 93 pgs.

Weiber, Don. <u>Custer, Cases and Cartridges; The Weiber Collection Analyzed</u>. Billings, Montana: private publishing, 1989. 328 pgs.

White, Richard. <u>It's Your Misfortune, and None of My Own. A History of the American West</u>. Norman, Oklahoma: University of Oklahoma Press, 1991. 644 pgs.

Wood, Erskine Jr. <u>Life of Charles Erskine Scott Wood</u>. Vancouver, Washington: Rose Wind Press, 1978. Reprint 1991. (Pgs. 21-24.)

U.S. ARMY REGULATIONS

(Manuals) in effect and to be complied with at the time of the 1878 War.

Cavalry

Cooke, Philip St. Geo. (Colonel). <u>Cavalry Tactics of Regulation for Instruction, Formations, and Movement of the Cavalry of the Army and Volunteers of the United States</u>. Vol. I and II. Washington, D.C.: Government Printing Office, 1861; Vol. I, 217 pgs. and Vol. II, 108 pgs.

Artillery

Lyman, Wyllys (Brevet Major). <u>Artillery Tactics, United States Army, A Collection of Tactical Studies. Assimilation to the Tactics of Infantry and Company</u>. (city, state, publisher unknown), 1874. 582 pgs.

Infantry

Upton, Emery (Brevet Major General). <u>Upton's Infantry Tactics, Double and Single Rank</u>. New York, New York: D. Appleton and Company, 1873. 392 pgs.

NEWSPAPER ARTICLES

A. **"Portland Oregonian, Morning"** Portland, Oregon Territory (became Sunday Oregonian in 1904).

1. June 8, 1878, Vol. XVIII, A daily, center column, main article on the Indian War appeared on the front page from Saturday, June 8, 1878, for 37 consecutive issues, six days a week, until Tuesday, July 23, 1878. Microfilm, Multnomah County Library, Portland Oregon.

2. Jan. 13, 1879, "Indians Hanged," p. 3.

3. Jan. 18, 1879, "The Death Penalty," p. 1.

4. Dec. 11, 1904, "How Whiskey Worked Ruin of Indian Chieftain, Peo, of the Umatillas, Once Powerful, Proud and Trusted, Now a Worthless Vagabond," by Bert Huffman, p. 53.

5. April 14, 1929, "Vivid Tale of Bannock War Told in Alarm for Pension," by Henry E. Heppner, Sec. 2, p. 1.

6. June 25, 1929, "Bernard's Cavalry in Fight," by J. W. Redington, p. 6.

7. December 4, 1950, "First Citizens of the Northwest," p. 12.

8. May 2, 1999, "The Return of the Chief, A Paiute Leader is Carried Home to Oregon for His Final Journey, 121 Years After He Is Slain." Front page Sunday Oregonian feature article, pgs. A1 and A14.

B. **"Portland Journal"** Portland, Oregon (became Oregon Journal in 1932).

1. May 25, 1930, Sec. 4, p. 6.

2. June 30, 1931, "Impressions and Observations of the Journal Man," by Fred Lockley, p. 10.

3. April 3, 1932, "After That-Peace," magazine section, p. 1.

4. May 5, 1959, "River Steamer Ends Indian Scrap," column 6, p. 4-B.

5. June 14, 1959, "Survivor, Describes Horror of '78' Bannock Indian War," (A story of Chris C. Anderson) by Larry McCarten, p. 25.

C. **<u>"East Oregonian"</u>** Pendleton, Oregon Territory.

1. July 13, 1878, "1st Willow Spring Fight Report, and Birch Creek Fight Report."

2. July 27, 1878, "Fictitious Umatilla Fight/Turners Retreat."

3. Aug. 3, 1878, "The Army Worm." (Referring to General Howard.)

4. Aug. 17, 1878, "Mr. & Mrs. Perkins Murdered, Jewell Memorial."

5. Aug. 24, 1878, "Battle of Willow Springs," part 1.

6. Aug. 31, 1878, "Battle of Willow Springs" part 2, and "Grand Council at Umatilla Reservation."

7. Sept. 7, 1878, "Stock, Sweet, Pascapam Erroneously Charged."

8. Sept. 14, 1878, "Major Throckmorton Won't Round Up Indians For Sperry."

9. Sept. 28, 1878, "Trial of Indians — Erroneously Charged."

10. Oct. 5, 1878, "Indian Jim Killed, Justified?"

11. Oct. 12, 1878, "General Howard Has Left the Country." (An advertisement.)

12. Oct. 26, 1878, "J. C. Lamar Brought to Pendleton (Oct. 20)."

13. Nov. 2, 1878, "Gen. Howard Says Arrest the Whites."

14. Nov. 16, 1878, "Indian Trial, Quit-A-Tumps and White Owl."

15. Dec. 7, 1878, "Sentenced to Death."

16. Dec. 14, 1878, "Prisoners of War."

17. Dec. 21, 1878, "Abandon the Umatilla Reservation."

18. Feb. 1, 1879, "Indian News."

19. Sept. 16, 1926, "Colonel Raley Story and Others."

20. Sept. 17, 1926, "Deadman's Hill" article.

21. Sept. 17, 1926, "Last Battle with Piutes (sic) and Malheur Indians is Pictured; Epic Interest," Pendleton Round-Up Souvenir Edition.

22. Sept. 18, 1926, "Nancy DeSpain" article.

23. Sept. 16, 1932, "T. D. Ferguson of Pendleton and Mart Gerking of Ritter Are Only Survivors, Willow Spring Battle."

24. Sept. 17, 1937, "Indian Fighter Rests in Park."

25. July 6, 1938, "60th Anniversary of Famous Indian Fight."

26. Sept. 16, 1938, "Famous Indian Battle Occurred 60 Years Ago."

27. April 16, 1948, "Battle Painting Given Library."

28. April 24, 1948, "Engagement at Willow Springs Fought by Pendleton Volunteers."

29. April 24, 1948, "Famous Battle Between Indians and Whites Painted by Pioneer." (Includes newspaper photo of painting by Mrs. B. F. Swaggart.)

30. Oct. 22, 1949, "Indian Scare of 1878 Recalled by Johnson Memoirs."

31. April 1, 1950, "The Vivid Poem 'Butter Creek Panic of 1878' penned by Veteran of Battle of Willow Springs, Arthur Crissfield."

32. April 1950, "Sam Rothchild, Volunteer Scout, Shot in Leg."

33. July 21, 1953, "Flight to Weston Before Rampaging Indians Retold."

34. Nov. 11, 1959, "Bannock War Threatened Settlement Here - July 4, 1878 - Pendleton Almost Fell to Indians."

35. June 2, 1978, "Along the Oregon Trail . . . Olney P. McCoy, Killed by Indians."

36. July 4, 1978, "The Bannock-Piute (sic) War of 1878," pgs. 9, 10 by Virgil Rupp.

D. **"Blue Mountain Eagle"** John Day, Oregon.

1. April 11, 1952, "Chief Peo Warned Friends of Indian War Threat."

2. Nov. 5, 1959, "Early Pioneer Took Part in Gory Indian Wars Which Occurred in Grant County."

3. May 14, 1964, "Old Timer Says."

4. May 28, 1964, "Old-Timer Says, Cont." by Howard Black. Folder 1, Item 2 Indexed JJ81.

5. Feb. 9, 1967, "In Grant County 1878; Letter Reveals Indian Uprising Crises."

F. **"The Desert Evening News"** Salt Lake City, Utah.

June 13, 14, 21, 1878. (Vol. XI, No. 171, 172, and 178.)

G. **"The Idaho Enterprise"** Oxford, Oneida County, Idaho Territory.

1. September 11, 1879. (Vol. I, No. 15.)

2. January 15, 1880. (Vol. I, No. 33.)

H. **"The Sunday Spokesman – Review"** Spokane, Washington.

1. "The Story of Whirlwind The Medicine Man." (No date.)

I. **"Owyhee Avalanche"** Silver City, Idaho Territory.

1. June 15, 1878, "Stage Driver McCutchan Killed."

2. June 22, 1878, "McCutchan Body Found Below Owyhee Ferry."

3. August 3, 1878, "Stage Driver William S. Hemmingway Killed."

4. August 10, 1878, "Hemmingway Killed at Mondays Ferry."

J. **"Boise City Statesman"** Boise City, Idaho Territory.

1. 1877 to 1878. (Vol. XIII, No. 1, 23, 30, 39, 41, 42, 43, 44, 46.)

2. June 27, 1878. Statesman Extra; "Particulars (sic) of Col. Bernard's Battle With the Indians."

K. **"Walla Walla Bulletin"** Walla Walla, Washington.

1. April 26, 1936, "Mendenhall Recalls Outbreak of Bannock and Piute (sic) Indians."

L. **"Sho-Pai News"** Duck Valley Indian Reservation, Owyhee, Nevada.

1. April 1999, "The Return of the Chief," Vol. 6, No. 58, pgs. 1, 4. (The story of the return of Chief Egan's Skull to his homeland.)

OTHER PERIODICALS

Benson, Claudia J. Deadman's Hill. Oregon Motorist, August 1932.

Benson, Claudia J. Injuns, A Pioneer's Story of the Willow Springs Battle. Oregon Motorist, July 1930.

Brimlow, George F. <u>Two Cavalrymen's Diaries of the Bannock War, 1878. Part I. Lieutenant William Carey Brown, Co. L, 1st U.S. Cavalry; Part II. Private Frederick Mayer, Co. L, 1st U.S. Cavalry</u>. Portland, Oregon: Oregon Historical Quarterly, September 1957, pgs. 221 to 258.

Calef, John H. <u>Department of Practical and Military Instruction, Artillery Exercises Class A, Description and Service of Machine Guns</u>. Fort Monroe, Virginia: U.S. Artillery School Publishers, 1886; 2nd printing 1969; 3rd compiled and edited by Jacobsen, Jacques Noel Jr., Union City, Tennessee: Pioneer Press, 1989. Pamphlet of 57 pgs.

Clark, George M. <u>Scalp Dance, The Edgerly Papers on the Battle of the Little Big Horn, Compilation of Documents</u>. Oswego, New York: Heritage Press, 1985. Pamphlet of 96 pgs.

Cox, Kurt Hamilton and Longellier, John P. Longknives. <u>The U.S. Cavalry and Other Mounted Forces</u>. Mechanicsburg, Pennsylvania (sic): Stackpole Books, 1996. Pamphlet of 80 pgs.

<u>Frank Leslie's Illustrated Newspaper</u>. July 20, 1878, p. 344; July 27, 1878, pgs. 351 to 353, 360, 361; August 3, 1878, p. 366.

<u>Harpers Weekly, Illustrated Newspaper</u>. July 6, 1878, pgs. 536, 537; August 17, 1878 cover story, p. 65, Vol. XXII. No. 1129.

<u>Indian Agent's Letter - Book: I The Piute (sic)-Bannock Raid of July 1878</u>. Portland, Oregon: Oregon Historical Quarterly, March 1928, Vol. XXXIX, pgs. 8 to 15.

Marvin J.D. <u>Instruction for Use and Care of Naval Gatling Guns</u>. (No publisher): 1875. Pamphlet of 43 pgs.

Metschan, Phil. Sr. <u>Canyon City "Fort-up" 1878</u>. Portland, Oregon: Oregon Historical Quarterly, March 1969, Vol. LXX, No. 1, pgs 56 to 59.

<u>Pioneer Trails</u>. Pendleton, Oregon: Umatilla County Historical Society Quarterly:

A.   Anderson, Helen Ogle. <u>Sarah and Ben, Two Pioneer Spirits. Homesteading at Willow Springs</u>. Fall 1993, Vol.17, No. 2, pgs. 13 to 16.
B.   Aney, Warren. <u>The Wild Horse Rangers</u>. Spring 1996, Vol. 20, No. 1, pgs. 3 to 11.

C. Cornell, John G. <u>The Battle of Camas Prairie</u>. Spring 1995, Vol. 19, No. 1, pgs. 8 to 15.

D. Crow-Grover, Dr. Dorys. <u>Sap-at-Kloni, Hish-tu-poo-lia-hoph</u>. Summer 1995, Vol. 19, No. 2, p. 18.

E. Grafe, Steven. <u>Lee Moorehouse, Umatilla Indian Agent, Part II</u>. Summer 1998, Vol. 22, No. 2, pgs. 12 to 18.

F. Grover, Dorys Crow. <u>Name Reflects Tragedy Deadman Pass</u>. Fall 1998, Vol. 22, No. 3, pgs. 12 to 16.

Santee, J.F. <u>Egan of the Paiutes</u>. Seattle, Washington; The Washington Historical Quarterly, January 1935, Vol. 26, No. 1.

Schaefer, A.C. <u>The Death of Chief Buffalo Horn</u>. Frontier Times (a magazine), Oct.-Nov. 1968. Vol. 42, No. 6, pgs 25, 34.

Watson, Chandler B. <u>Recollections of The Bannock War</u>. Portland, Oregon: Oregon Historical Quarterly, September 1967, Pgs. 317 to 328.

Wood, C.E.S. <u>Private Journal, 1878.</u> Portland, Oregon: Oregon Historical Quarterly, March 1969, Vol. LXX, No. 1, Pgs. 5 to 38.

MANUSCRIPTS

Birks, Roberta Margaret. <u>Early Times in the Roundup Country – 1892</u>. Portland, Oregon: Oregon Historical Society, published manuscript 1984, pgs. 32 to 47.

Corless, John. <u>Daily Diary of Civilian Chief of Transportation for Army Supplies, June 23, 1878 to November 6, 1878</u>. 15 pgs. typed. Mss. 1178, Oregon Historical Society, Portland, Oregon.

Crisfield, Arthur. <u>The Butter Creek Panic</u>. Poem 6 pgs. handwritten on July 20, 1878. Mss. 784, Oregon Historical Society, Portland Oregon. (Note: typed version was published in the East Oregonian on April 1, 1950.)

Ellidge, D.W. <u>Narrative on 1878 War</u>. 6 pgs. handwritten in July, 1931. Mss. 1178, Oregon Historical Society, Portland, Oregon.

Gray, William P. <u>Patrolling the Upper Columbia River During the Indian War of 1878</u>. Mss. 220, Oregon Historical Society, Portland, Oregon.

Kegler, F.H. <u>Historical Facts of Harney County</u>. 10 pgs. handwritten. Mss. 120, Oregon Historical Society, Portland, Oregon.

Moorhouse, LaVelle. <u>The Bannock War in Eastern Oregon</u>. 6 pgs. typed. Mss. 2300, Oregon Historical Society, Portland Oregon.

Raley, James H. <u>Bannock and Piute (sic) War of 1878</u>. 16 pgs. typed. Mss. 970.5, R13, Umatilla County Library, Pendleton, Oregon.

Redington, Eleanor Frances Meacham. <u>Redbird of Meacham on the Old Oregon Trail, Lee's Encampment</u>. Chapter XI, pgs. 122 to 132, typed. Mss. 2562, Oregon Historical Society, Portland, Oregon.

Redington, John. W. <u>Description of Buffalo Horn</u>. 3 pgs. typed. AX93/ box 6/ folder 2, manuscript in Special Collections, University of Oregon Knight Library, Eugene, Oregon.

Rinehart, W.V. <u>With The Oregon Volunteers, 1862 to 1866</u>. 24 pgs. typed. Mss. 471, Oregon Historical Society, Portland, Oregon.

Rothchild, Samuel. <u>Account of the Fight at Willow Springs on July 6, 1878</u>. 10 pgs. handwritten on October 9. 1897. Mss. 1514, Oregon Historical Society, Portland Oregon.

Sharon, Julian Lindley. <u>Pendleton – Umatilla County and The Oregon Country.</u> Pgs. 17 to 32, 136 pgs. 1940. Umatilla County Library Manuscript, Pendleton, Oregon.

Slater, J.D. <u>Letter to Mr. Fred Lockley, concerning those killed at Dead Man's Hill</u>. 2 pgs. typed on June 1, 1931. Mss. 1178, Oregon Historical Society, Portland Oregon.

Tucker, Gerald J. <u>History of the Northern Blue Mountains</u>. Pgs 79 to 81, 170 pgs. Umatilla National Forest, Headquarters Library, Pendleton Oregon.

Wood, Charles Erskine Scott (Second Lieutenant). <u>Note Book, entries from June 7 to July 6, 1878</u>. 2 pgs. typed. Mss. 800b, Oregon Historical Society, Portland, Oregon.

MICROFILM

National Archives and Records Administration, Washington, D.C. <u>Record Group 094.</u>
<u>Adjutant General's Office U.S. Army Muster Rolls, April 30 through August 30,</u>
<u>1878</u>, 35 mm Camera Negative. 72 negatives, Troops A, D, F, G, H, I, K, L, 1st
U.S. Cavalry. (Note: E Company Records were lost.) Company F, 2nd U.S.
Infantry; Companies B, D, E, G, H, I, 21st U.S. Infantry; Batteries D, G, 4th U.S.
Artillery. (Note. This information source includes the names of all military
participants in the war, by unit and rank, as recorded in the monthly returns, or
reports.)

National Archives and Records Administration, Washington, D.C. <u>Military Official File,</u>
<u>Adjutant General's Office, Record Group 094. Bernard, Reuben F.,</u> 35mm Camera
Negative, R&P 761.926, 350 negatives.

National Archives and Records Administration, Washington, D.C. <u>1878 Annual Report</u>
<u>for the Department of the Columbia,</u> Microfilm Roll 543, Letters Received by the
Office of the Adjutant General (Main Series), 1878 to 1880. Microfilm Copy 666.
(Includes surgeon's killed and wounded report with details of named soldiers'
injuries plus projectiles that struck them.)

National Archives and Records Administration, Washington, D.C. <u>Office of the Adjutant</u>
<u>General, 1871 to 1880,</u> (Main Series), Rolls 377, 138, and 379. November 1877 to
September 1878 Letters. Microfilm Copy 666.

National Archives and Records Administration, Washington, D.C. <u>Returns from Military</u>
<u>Posts 1800 to 1916,</u> Roll 1344, Fort Walla Walla, Washington Territory, August
1873 to December 1885. Microfilm Copy 617.

National Archives and Records Administration, Washington, D.C. <u>Returns from Military</u>
<u>Posts 1800 to 1916,</u> Roll 594 Fort Lapwai, Idaho, January 1874 to August 1884.
Microfilm Copy 617.

National Archives and Records Administration, Washington, D.C. <u>Returns form Regular</u>
<u>Army Cavalry Regiments 1833 to 1916,</u> Roll 6, 1st Cavalry 1867 to 1876.
Microfilm Copy 744.

National Archives and Records Administration, Washington, D.C. <u>Returns from Regular Army Cavalry Regiments 1833 to 1916</u>, Roll 7, 1st Calvary 1877 to 1886. Microfilm Copy 744.

University of California, Berkley, California. <u>Oregon Weekly Tribune</u>. 1874 to 1877, Microfilm Negative, Call Number NMP 6147.

University of Oregon, Knight Library, Eugene, Oregon. <u>The East Oregonian</u> (Weekly), Pendleton, Oregon Territory, January 6, 1877 to March 12, 1881, Microfilm Reel 1.

AERIAL PHOTOGRAPHS

U.S. Department of Agriculture, Aerial Photography Field Office, Salt Lake City, Utah, <u>Aerial Photograph, Willow Spring, Oregon</u>; Roll 7016, Exposure 72 EC.

U.S. Department of Agriculture, Aerial Photography Field Office, Salt Lake City, Utah, <u>Aerial Photograph, West Birch Creek, Oregon</u>; Roll 7035, Exposures 66R and 67R.

U.S. Department of Agriculture, Aerial Photography Field Office, Salt Lake City, Utah, <u>Aerial Photograph, Umatilla Indian Agency</u>; Roll 7014, Exposure 6 L.

OTHER (Theses, and Guides, Etc.)

<u>American Indians, A Select Catalog of National Archives Microfilm Publications</u>. p. 79.

Department of Interior, Office of Indian Affairs. <u>Annual Report of Commissioner of Indian Affairs to the Secretary of the Interior for the Year 1878</u>. Washington, D.C. GPO 1878, U.S. Serial Set No. 1850, 45th Congress-3rd Session, House Executive Documents, No. 1 Part. 5, Interior Vol. 1, Nov. 1, 1878, (pgs. 446 to 455) and Vol. 9, (pgs. 545 to 638).

Individual Agency Annual Reports are as Follows:

Indian Agency	Location	By	Page
1. Fort Hall	Idaho Territory	W.H. Danielson	545
2. Lemhi	Idaho Territory	John A. Wright	547
3. Nez Perce	Idaho Territory	Jno. B. Montieth	548
4. Pyramid Lake	Nevada Territory	A. J. Barnes	598
5. W. Shoshoni	Nevada Territory	Levi A. Green	600
6. Klamath	Oregon	J. H. Roork	609
7. Malheur	Oregon	W. V. Rinehart	611
8. Umatilla	Oregon	N. A. Cornoyer	618
9. Warm Springs	Oregon	John Smith	620
10. Yakima	Washington Territory	James H. Wilber	635

Ducey, Brant E.. John Watermelon Redington — Hell on Hogthieves and Hypocrites. Eugene, Oregon: University of Oregon, Published Master's Thesis, June 1963. 205 pgs.

Guide to Genealogical Research, in the National Archives, National Archives and Records Administration Publication, 1985. 304 pgs.

Guide to Records in the National Archives — Pacific Northwest Region, Seattle Washington. National Archives and Records Administration Reference Information Paper 85, 1994 edition, (pgs. 15 to 17).

Historical Facts Pertaining to the Pioneers of Harney County, Oregon, 1871 to 1878. (10 pages handwritten.)

Military Service Records, National Archives and Records Administration Publication. A select catalog of National Archives Microfilm Publications, 1985. 330 pgs.

Muster Roll of Indian Scouts 1880. Oregon Historical Society, Portland Oregon.

Nesmith, James W. Poster dated July 4, 1878, soliciting volunteer militia troops to fight in Eastern Oregon, from the Chemeketa Hotel, Salem, Oregon.

Ogle, Geo. A. Standard Atlas Of Umatilla County, Oregon, (includes a plat book), 1914. p. 46.

Regional Government Documents Depository, Indian Agent Report to the Commissioner of Indians.

Smithwick, Mike. <u>Distant Suns</u>, A computer program, Version 2.0g, developed between 1991 and 1994. Published by Virtual Reality Laboratories, Inc., San Luis Obispo. California 93401. (Note: Used to determine that on the night of June 14, 1878, there was a full moon.)

Thompson, C.R. (Captain). Camp McDermit, Nevada, June 25, 1878, Letter to W.V. Rinehart, Indian Agent, Malheur Agency. Subject: Asking for pay for Jerry Long, interpreter: Received September 12, 1878; National Archives, Pacific Northwest Region, 6125 Sandpoint Way, N.E., Seattle, Washington 98115; Record Group No. 75, BIA-Malheur Agency, Letter Received 1878 (Preliminary Inventory 163, Entry 1113).

Umatilla County Deed Records, Book E, p. 815; Book I, pgs. 475 to 476.

U.S. Department of Interior, Bureau of Indian Affairs, Office of Vital Statistics, Warm Springs Indian Agency, Affidavit: Approval of Heirship, Estate of Oits (Johnson), Agency Roll Number 739, May 26, 1915. 7 pages.

U.S. Department of Interior Bureau of Indian Affairs, National Archives — Pacific Northwest Region, Seattle, Washington: Record Group 75, Mulheur Agency Census 1877, (PI 163, entry 1113). 4 pages.

U.S. Department of Interior Bureau of Indian Affairs, National Archives — Pacific Northwest Region, Seattle, Washington: Record Group 75, Mulheur Agency Letters Received 1878, (PI 163, entry 1113). 4 pages.

Wiland, Mary. <u>Examining the Causes of the Bannock Indian War of 1878</u>. Boulder, Colorado: University of Colorado, Unpublished Honors Thesis, April 1, 1996. 160 pgs.

Note: (sic) = A misspelled word in the original document. Here it is not a mistake and should be read as it stands.
Brevet = An honorary commission promoting a military officer without increasing pay or authority.

About the Historical Novel

The book is the result of several years of research on the Bannock-Paiute Indian War of 1878. Specific pains were taken to use the actual names of participants. Dates, times, and locations are based on the research of events that actually happened, and were found in books, old and new newspapers, U.S. Army official records, and historical society publications. The weather and moon phases mentioned were all meticulously researched.

In the case of Chief Egan, care was taken to depict the details of the deaths of members of his family, his wounds, and what he might have been thinking throughout the ordeal. Only after studying what had been written about him before and during the war by several reliable authors, did work on the novel progress. Several of the writers consulted during the research for this book, such as Brigadier General Howard, and Sarah Winnemucca, knew Chief Egan personally.

About Greg Hodgen

Greg Hodgen lives in Portland, Oregon, with his wife, Doris. They have three grown children and four grandchildren. Greg was born and raised in Pendleton, Oregon. He has made a lifelong pursuit of the study of the Civil War, the Indian Wars, and in particular, the Cavalry and Native Americans who fought in them. The author's interest was heightened during his impressionable years by his father, Tuck Hodgen. His active involvement began when his father was Property Director of the Pendleton Round-Up's "Happy Canyon" pageant in the 1950's, and early 1960's.

Greg is employed in public service. He served in the U.S. Army from 1962 to 1964. He is a life member of the Custer Battlefield Historical and Museum Association and is an associate member of the Little Bighorn Associates.

Greg is a fifth generation descendent of Philip Murphy, who served as a Cavalryman (saddler) in Company E, First U.S. Cavalry, and who fought in the Battle of Birch Creek in 1878, which is depicted in this historical novel. Trooper Murphy had actively served the year before (1877) with General Howard during Chief Joseph's famous Nez Perce attempted retreat to Canada. In 1867, he had served as a Corporal in Company F, Eighth U.S. Cavalry, Arizona Territory, against Tonto Apaches, where he was awarded, for heroic action, the "Congresional Medal of Honor."

About Larry Purchase

Larry K. Purchase lives in Vancouver, Washington State, with his wife, Wenonah. They have two married children and three grandchildren. He was born and raised in Pendleton, Oregon, and is a descendent of participants in the Bannock-Paiute Indian War of 1878. He is descended from Jeremiah DeSpain of Ukiah, Oregon, who was a nephew of Jeremiah (Jerry) DeSpain of Pendleton, Oregon, businessmen whose families witnessed the conflict.

He graduated from Oregon State University in 1965 with a B.S. degree in Range Management, and attended the U.S. Army Signal Corps Officer Candidate School in 1967. Larry, who saw action with the Second Battalion, Twenty-eighth Infantry, First Infantry Division in Viet Nam in 1967 and 1968, retired as a Lieutenant Colonel in 1995 from the U.S. Army Reserves in Portland, Oregon. He has been employed by the Bonneville Power Administration for the last twenty-nine years.

About the Future

The authors have full intention of eventually publishing a complete detailed history of the 1878 conflict. It would include information on another half dozen skirmishes, deaths of other important participants, pre- and post-war events, and discussion on why the war occurred. If you have or know of additional information handed down in your family, and wish for it to be acknowledged, please notify the authors. Of course, all comments, omissions, corrections, and general debate are welcome.

If you have genealogy interests and want to know if any of your relatives participated as a soldier in the 1878 War, we may be able to help you. On microfilm, we have Company and Regimental Monthly Returns on all Cavalry, Infantry, and Artillery Units, listing all soldiers by name.

About Private Property

If you choose to visit the battlefield sites (they are all on private land), please be courteous and respectful to the land and its owners. Always ask for permission before entering and close all gates that you open. Do not dig or attempt to recover artifacts, as it is against State and Federal Law. Without permission from the landowner, you are also subject to trespass laws.